10699546

Let the World Listen Right

Let the World Listen Right

The Mississippi Delta Hip-Hop Story

Ali Colleen Neff

Foreword by William Ferris

UNIVERSITY PRESS OF MISSISSIPPI
JACKSON

www.upress.state.ms.us

The University Press of Mississippi is a member of
the Association of American University Presses.

Manufactured in the United States of America

First printing 2009
∞
Library of Congress Cataloging-in-Publication Data

Neff, Ali Colleen.
Let the world listen right : the Mississippi Delta hip-hop story / Ali Colleen Neff ; foreword by William Ferris.
p. cm. — (American made music series)
Includes bibliographical references and index.
ISBN 978-1-60473-229-0 (cloth : alk. paper) 1. Rap (Music)—Mississippi—Delta (Region)—History and criticism. I. Title.
ML3531.N43 2009
781.6409762'4—dc22 2009008536

British Library Cataloging-in-Publication Data available

This piece is dedicated to Rebecca Hood-Adams, who loves the Mississippi Delta infinitely.
This work has been buoyed by our laughter.

The Highway 49 roadside south of Clarksdale, Mississippi. Photograph by the author.

Many underclass black people who do not know conventional aesthetic theoretical language are thinking critically about aesthetics. The richness of their thoughts is rarely documented in books. . . . We must not deny the way aesthetics serves as the foundation for emerging visions. It is, for some of us, critical space that inspires and encourages artistic behavior.
—bell hooks[1]

Contents

Foreword

No American region is better known and more intensely studied for its history and culture than the Mississippi Delta. Generations of writers, scholars, photographers, and filmmakers have traveled Delta roads and captured its worlds in memorable ways. William Faulkner, Eudora Welty, Tennessee Williams, and Richard Wright wrote powerfully about the Delta. Folklorists and music critics from Alan Lomax, John Lomax, and John Work to David Evans, Adam Gussow, Robert Palmer, and Elijah Wald have written important books on Delta blues.

Ali Colleen Neff's *Let the World Listen Right: The Mississippi Delta Hip-Hop Story* is both part of this tradition and distinctly different from it. Not since Hortense Powdermaker's classic 1939 work on Indianola, *After Freedom: A Cultural Study in the Deep South*, has a major study of the Mississippi Delta been published by a woman. As a young white woman, Neff's perspective is distinctly different from those of the men who explored Delta worlds before her. Her work deals with the region's contemporary musical worlds and with both the men and the women who compose and perform hip-hop music in the Clarksdale community. In developing her study, Neff pays tribute and integrates into her own work research done in the Mississippi Delta throughout the twentieth century.

After working as a freelance music journalist in San Francisco, Neff and photographer Tim Gordon moved to Clarksdale in search of authentic roots music. The Mississippi Delta and its symbolic association with the Crossroads drew them, as it had earlier collectors who were attracted by the region's music. Her trip and the experiences that followed forever changed her life. Neff was clearly on a mission, and this book documents her journey and how it transformed her life.

Clarksdale is arguably the most important musical city in the Mississippi Delta. It is the home of celebrated artists like Sam Cooke, John Lee Hooker, Ike Turner, and Muddy Waters, as well as traditional blues performers like Wash Herron, Big Jack Johnson, Pine Top Johnson, Jasper Love, and Maudie Shirley. While Neff pays homage to these artists and to the writers who have studied them, her primary focus is on Clarksdale's role in the hip-hop nation and the region's "Dirty South" sound.

Shortly after arriving in Clarksdale, Neff met Jerome "TopNotch" Williams, a young hip-hop composer and performer. TopNotch became Neff's mentor and introduced her to Clarksdale hip-hop worlds through his family and the families of others with whom he performs.

Neff's narrative voice flows deftly between that of scholar and that of diarist as she describes the musicians with whom she works. She confesses at one point, "I'm an outsider here; I've been an outsider in the Delta all year."

Sipping tall beers on hot summer nights in Delta clubs, Neff enters the flow of life in Clarksdale and in surrounding communities like Merigold, Friar's Point, Bobo, and Indianola. She describes how the black community prepares for a weekend of music, dance, and food enjoyed at clubs in these towns.

> Renowned hairstylist Ronnie Vaughn at International Hair Design works thirteen-hour days as the weekend approaches, meticulously styling elaborate 'dos for the Delta's most fashionable ladies. These are wild styles that take entire afternoons to press, dye, and curl into unique, flourishing shapes. Meanwhile, customers line up at the Super Soul Shop downtown, a traditional Lebanese-owned store stocked with bright zoot suits and shiny vests.

Colorful dress and hair styles transform and celebrate Clarksdale in ways that are reinforced by the lyrics of hip-hop music. In their songs composers like TopNotch rename the city "Clarks Vegaz," and Neff suggests that "If Clarksdale is a broken old plantation held together with slave-driven nails . . . Clarks Vegaz is a beautiful, Afrocentric world, transformed by the word."

Delta hip-hop music is grounded in traditional storytelling, hymns, prayers, blues, proverbs, and lyrics that the performer draws on. Like colorful pieces sewn together in a quilt, these traditional Delta musical forms are woven into a new musical form by hip-hop composers. Neighborhood competitions with the dozens are an important training ground for the back and forth lyrical battle of hip-hop performances.

In the tradition of Clarksdale's Ike Turner and the Kings of Rhythm who recorded "Rocket 88" at Sun Records in 1951 and launched the rock and roll era, TopNotch and his friends are making music history with their hip-hop recordings. The parallels are interesting to consider. While traveling to Sun Records, Turner's amplifier fell from the roof of his car, and its damaged speaker later gave the recording a distinctive sound. In similar fashion, TopNotch records hip-hop songs in his friend K-Deezy's bedroom using a microphone taped to a closet door with a filter made of panty hose.

Neff explores the worlds of women in Clarksdale and reminds us that they have played a significant role in every form of Delta music—from gospel music in church to blues in clubs. She describes how female rapper Kimyata Dear develops a woman's perspective in lyrics that she performs.

Delta women also take on the role of "second moms," as they nurture and encourage young people. TopNotch's second mom, Miss Martha Raybon, explains that she has "an open-door policy for any child."

To probe newly minted sounds of hip-hop in the blues-drenched Mississippi Delta is an act of courage by Ali Neff. She shows that hip-hop, a music associated in the popular mind with East and West Coast urban centers like New York and Los Angeles, also has deep roots in Delta worlds like Clarksdale.

Equally daring, she draws on a broad array of scholarship from John Dollard, John Work, and the Lomaxes to Greil Marcus, Robin D. G. Kelley, and Mark Anthony Neal. And she acknowledges the deep, enduring relationship between young and older musicians of the Delta—as well as successive generations of scholars who have studied their music.

Neff recalls meeting a tourist in a Clarksdale blues club who asked her what she was doing in the area. When Neff replied that she was studying hip-hop, the tourist assured her, "You won't find any hip-hop here." And his wife added, "That's right. Not one iota. This is a blues town."

The Mississippi Delta is and has always been a place of musical change, and its latest gift to the world is blues inspired hip-hop. Thankfully Ali Neff has parted the veil so that we can appreciate Delta music in a new and exciting way.

William Ferris
University of North Carolina at Chapel Hill

Acknowledgments

First and foremost, I thank Jerome "TopNotch the Villain" Williams, who has put as much work into this document as I have, and whose beautiful words have both shaped my understanding of the Mississippi Delta and taught me how to live with style.

I also thank my many consultants and friends in the Delta, including Terry "Big T" Williams and Bobbi Collins, Miss Martha Raybon, the people of First Oak Grove Missionary Baptist Church, Pleasant Grove Missionary Baptist Church, St. James Temple Church of God in Christ, Red, Wesley Jefferson, Puttin' Hatchett, DJ Dr. Pepper, Po' Monkey, Larry Grimes, and Jeweline Williams. The members of DA F.A.M. provided me great inspiration in the past three years, and created much of the poetry of this book: Keithan Dear, Timothy Williams, and Anthony DeWayne Buggs. Kimyata Dear has been an amazing friend and a generous consultant, and she has shown me that it is always possible to rise.

Friends in the Delta who opened doors and provided much-needed support include Luther Brown and Henry Outlaw of the Delta Center for Culture and Learning, Tricia Walker and the faculty and staff of Delta State University, Robert Birdsong, Jim Field, Bill Talbot, Semmes Luckett, Marilyn Fontenot, Christopher Coleman, Bill Abel, James and Kathy Butler, Roger Stolle, Jen Stolle, John Ruskey and family, Patti Johnson, Frank Ratliff, Lula and Michael Mabry, George and Myrtle Messenger, and Troy Catchings. Bobby Tarzi and the Tarzi family provided excellent biscuits and even better gossip. Maie Smith of the Delta Blues Museum has been my blues mentor and a wonderful friend. Craig Gill, my editor, has contributed immense time and patience in bringing this project to fruition.

Much support has been provided by the faculties of UNC–Chapel Hill and Duke University, including Robert Cantwell, Marcie Cohen-Ferris, Dan Patterson, Larry Grossberg, Renee Alexander, Eric King Watts, Wahneema Lobiano, Tom Rankin, and Della Pollock. Many ideas that inform this book were taken from lectures and class discussions with Trudier Harris. Jim Peacock and Mark Anthony Neal provided patient and creative support. My best work is a product of their generosity, guidance, and intellectual creativity. I extend a special thanks to my mentor Bill Ferris, upon whose incredible work, visionary imagination, and undying patience this manuscript has been built.

The Center for the Study of the American South, Folkstreams.net, and UNC's ScreenArts program, especially Barb Call and Ayse Erginer of CSAS, provided support for this piece in important ways. Andrew Kropa's photographs illustrate the contemporary Delta throughout this piece. Katherine Doss, Sarah Honer, John Keaka, Tiki Jim, Eddie Huffman, Sarah Poteete, Stace Treat, Joey Young, Brian Graves, Pat and Jay Gordon, Kate and Aden Biehl, Shannon O'Neill, Rosa Castaneda, Tony Young, The Crews Inn's Alton Balance, Mr. Arthur Spencer, Awa Sarr, and my SCALI cohort and my classmates in the UNC Folklore Curriculum and Communication Studies Program supported this work through their friendship and collaboration. My students at UNC and Duke, particularly the "crunkologists," have contributed their creativity, energy, and collaboration. Thanks to my father, Allen Neff, and my brother, John Neff, for believing in me.

Tim Gordon made this research possible and provided many of the photos within. I might never have seen my first juke joint without his partnership. I thank him most for letting me go ahead and do my thing.

Let the World Listen Right

The vestiges of the classic Clarksdale crossroads. Old Highways 61 and 49 are now the New World district's Martin Luther King and East Tallahatchie Streets. Photograph by the author.

Introduction

Emergence at the Crossroads

East Tallahatchie Street and Martin Luther King Boulevard converge quietly among the crumbling ruins of the New World district of Clarksdale, Mississippi. They trace the faint spines of ancient Native American trade routes that first brought civilization to the land, intertwine with the Mississippi and Sunflower Rivers, and rest upon burial mounds that keep these ancient paths dry from yearly floods: these routes, once labeled Highways 61 and 49, quietly mark the crossroads of American music. The famed Blues Highways were filled with traveling, working, creating, and living blues people, and their sounds and styles continue to resonate far beyond this patch of loamy soil. World-famous folklore claims that Delta bluesman Robert Johnson sealed his fate at this very location, selling his soul to the devil for a set of guitar licks in the 1920s.

This lost black downtown has been dwindling since the dawn of the automated cotton picker that—along with the crop-hungry boll weevil, Jim Crow, and the development of labor-hungry northern industry—sparked the Great Migration north in the first half of the twentieth century. Nearby lie the footprints and skeletons of some of the world's earliest blues venues: the Savoy, the New Roxy, and the Dipsie Doodle collapse into the soft muddy soil. Yellow construction tape marks buildings ravaged by the elements; stripes of orange paint delineate those scheduled for demolition. Old hand-painted signs for haircuts and sno-cones fade from storefronts as the defunct chitlin circuit haunts of local players Ike Turner, John Lee Hooker, and Muddy Waters crumble. Apartment houses that once provided temporary shelter for legions of train and bus riders are pushed up against the narrow streets in long rows, reduced to foundations; a few tenacious shops and venues persist from the early days, decorated with bare light bulbs and chipped, hand-painted signs. The old juke joints are nearly all gone, but Clarksdale's blues community remains, generations after the hopes that fueled the mass movement to the Promised Land were wrecked on the streets of Chicago. The bulk of the city's black population—about three-quarters of its twenty thousand or so residents—is

Abe's Barbeque, a Lebanese-owned culinary landmark at Clarksdale's contemporary version of the blues crossroads. Photograph by Andrew Kropa.

annexed into a series of rental houses arranged into loose, poor neighborhoods south of the train tracks. These tracks, which once carried hopeful sharecropping families to the North, are defunct and overgrown. Today, the historic roads are outstripped by channels of fast grey pavement that claim the Blues Highways' names—61 and 49—while bypassing the neighborhoods that built their legacy. These two-lane highways are lined with the occasional Wal-Mart, Western Sizzlin, and bright ad for a nearby second-rate casino. Although the location of the famed 61/49 crossroads has shifted a half-dozen times since Robert Johnson's heyday, local tourism interests have chosen to label a contemporary junction of Highway 161 (the town's commercial strip) and Yazoo Avenue (an interim version of 49) with three jigsawed blue guitars, facing anywhere, lofted above a cursive sign: "The Crossroads."

Nearby barbeque joints and abandoned motels sit back from the roadway; corporate gas stations, a pawnshop, and a check-cashing office mark its boundaries. Here, in its neon desperation to create substance from nothing, Clarksdale resembles any American ghetto. But these constructed and controlled crossroads mark the heart of flourishing blues tourism. They serve as a beacon for the scores of blues travelers who drive Highway 61 from Memphis down to New Orleans, imagining contact with the blues conjuration. At midnight one might find a Japanese or Norwegian tourist clutching a guitar at this imagined landmark, glibly trampling the shrubs surrounding the proud sign in his desire

The New Roxy Theatre on the New World district's Issaquena Street, a movie theatre and venue at which musician Ike Turner once worked. Photograph by the author.

for the world's most substantial souvenir; he is waiting for the black trickster to approach, tune his instrument, and imbue him with blues virtuosity. Countless rock and blues revivalists have named groups, albums, and songs after landmarks at or near this spot, and their aim is true: they revere the blues and its practitioners. Their well-intended dollars have the potential to economically invigorate, if not transform, the region as they frequent juke joints, photograph gravestones, and erect museums. Some write books.

Today, catfish farms and vast beige casinos patch over the corners of many old Delta plantations. Wal-Mart is the new company store for the regional underclass, offering its revolving group of employees six dollars an hour and a place to spend it. But behind the concrete eggshell of economic modernity, the substance of sharecropping society remains: Delta infant mortality rates are among the highest in the nation; illiteracy, illness, and malnutrition are common; unemployment is phenomenally rampant. The economy is growing steadily more precarious as small businesses and factories abandon the Delta for cheaper foreign labor. Meanwhile, young people face stifling economic odds: piecemeal formal educations, a weak (and often inaccessible) social infrastructure, and a desperate job market. The few who manage to find a decent job are paid rock-bottom wages, a symptom of economic failure and labor surplus. A century and a half after Emancipation, the circumstances of day-to-day survival remain difficult for most black residents of the Mississippi Delta.

Representations of Clarksdale's blues legacies decorate area businesses and public spaces. Photograph by Andrew Kropa.

Millennial U.S. Census data show that 45 percent of Coahoma County children live in poverty. Official unemployment figures hover around 14 percent after cotton-ginning season ends. Scores of families live in boarded-up shotgun shacks without electricity or running water.[1] The Brickyard, a neighborhood delineated by piles of abandoned industrial debris, and Riverton, a former sharecroppers' encampment, are overpopulated with tenant families who cannot afford adequate housing and food. The town looks and feels like a war zone, desiccated by swamp rot and poverty, but it is also punctuated with quiet lots of whitewashed country churches, glowing with cellophane-pasted windows and hand-painted signs.

And then there is the blues. A handful of classic juke joints remain, clustered around the crossroads in the vestiges of the New World district. The most visible are spottily patronized by out-of-town tourists seeking the "authentic" blues experience, a souvenir from a place they heard might be the last juke joint standing. These weekend explorers clumsily jam with their shiny harmonicas and hunt the old, poor bluesman with whom they can snap uncomfortable photos.

The blues was not always withering with age. During its heyday in the early twentieth century, the blues was crafted by young black people as a soundtrack for dance, a music of sadness, a poetry of protest, an expression of love and sexuality and, most importantly, an assertion of black strength and power. It is precisely that dynamic power—the flash of its shifting and brilliant core—that has driven the blues into new eras, sounds, and styles. Today, from the corners of the New World district, a new Mississippi Delta blues is rising, one created by and for young people. On Saturday night, old Chevys with big rims bump beats from their trunks as young people gather on street corners, in clubs, and

The New World district has decayed considerably since its heyday. Photograph by the author.

behind the barbeque stand to socialize. Here, members of the current generation of Delta music makers meet and rap. They improvise rhymes in greeting, in introduction, and in competition, referencing popular songs from the radio and sayings from around the way. Some work into a verbal duel that lasts until one participant fails to come up with a sufficiently witty rhyme in good time. The most accomplished rappers perform longer pieces that deal with their history, neighborhoods, current company, and the possibilities of the night at hand. They are experts at keeping the rhythm.

To the uninitiated, Delta hip-hop reflects, on its surface, the strains of popular hip-hop filtered through the waves of commercial radio or BET videos. But to those who live its language, who twist and push its styles into a realm of greater possibility by reconfiguring the popular and the traditional, hip-hop offers an unlimited expressive form with complex layers of creativity and meaning. For the young people of the contemporary Delta, freestyle hip-hop artists enjoy the prominent social role once reserved for blues musicians. These artists do not break with tradition; they live by it, bringing blues styles and techniques into conversation with the moment at hand.

Musical talk has been the medium of expression in the Delta from the time enslaved and conscripted black people were forced to drain and clear its vast farmland. Freestyle rap, the contemporary iteration of this powerful expressive blend, draws deeply from these work songs, spirituals, folk proverbs, and blues. The tradition is dynamic: styles shift, rhythms update themselves, and lyrics speak to contemporary circumstances, but tradition, history and the infinite style of diasporic creativity are grounded in every beat. And although the verbal texts of the blues are themselves highly stylized, they are only one dimension of a larger, performative blues aesthetic that extends from the tone color of a slide guitar to the clothing and dance styles of its participating audience. Blues style is deceptively simple in form, especially when its text is flattened into its elements: twelve bars, three chords, and a repeated chorus. A deeper understanding of the musical life of the Mississippi Delta requires extended immersion, participation, and collaboration, through which the aesthetic fullness of the music can be recognized within the meaningful context of community.

Delta rap performance is also inextricably bound to the global hip-hop movement. Urban rap styles from RocaWear to Neptunes-produced hip-hop hits travel effortlessly over the waves of commercial radio and television. This cultural exchange ties the urban and agrarian ghettos in a thick aesthetic call-and-response. During the great northern migration of black southerners in the World War II era, thousands of families left the Delta for Chicago's South and West Sides, Detroit, East St. Louis, and Southern California's Long Beach. Young people from these communities return to the Delta to spend summers with grandparents and cousins, other families collectively move back and forth from these areas as economic circumstances demand. Inner-city hip-hop draws from the agrarian traditions of musical rhyme—toasting, the dozens, the blues—that were developed in the generations before the Great Migration. Through radio and television airwaves as well as the networks of live performance, urban rap remains deep in conversation with the contemporary southern corner of the African American diaspora.

Nommo, according to scholar Molefi Kete Asante, is the "life-giving power of the word" upon which Afrodiasporic culture is structured.[2] Essential to this power is the element of transformation, through which slavery, the central historical fact of African American existence, is negotiated. By mastering *nommo*, a practitioner harnesses and directs this transformative power for the sake of his or her community, countering the effects of institutionalized racism. "What is clear is that the Black leaders who articulated and articulate the grievances felt by the masses have always understood the power of the word in the Black community,"[3] Asante states. The master of words, schooled in the art of *nommo*, holds an elevated position of leadership in black community life. For black residents of the Mississippi Delta, such transformation is essential to surviving the stifling conditions of everyday life. Missing paychecks are made, by community potluck, into plates of catfish, discarded junk is resurrected in the form of vivid folk art, and the institutionalized lack of "America's Ethiopia"[4] is converted, by the power of the word, into a vibrant universe of black cultural practice.

The master of words has always held a central role in the black Delta community, and the strong voices the region has produced over the years continue to resonate globally. Sam Cooke, Muddy Waters, Memphis Minnie, Pops Staples, Fannie Lou Hamer, Reverend C. L. Franklin, and Robert Johnson all came from the Mississippi Delta. Each of these voices has reached from the region's low flood plains to a global resonance. But the overwhelming international success of black orators and musical artists from the Delta was fostered in the local contexts of family and community. In the Mississippi Delta, the skills of oral and musical improvisation are highly valued and are carefully cultivated through everyday practices of creative challenge and hard work. The country preacher and the blues shouter are omnipresent in the Delta, as are the gospel singer and child playing rhyming games. Radio and club DJs rap over blues records, teens trade dozens, and cousins recite poetry at family reunions. Smooth contemporary southern soul singers inflect their modern sound with double entendres drawn from classic Delta blues. Young Delta rap artists combine the formal elements of popular hip-hop with their own regional cultural legacy to command the transformative power of the word. Like the singers and orators of previous generations, artists wield the rhythmic verse in order to create emergent conceptualizations, relationships, understandings, and representations.

Jerome "TopNotch the Villain" Williams, my collaborator and guide for this ethnography of the Delta hip-hop community, is recognized throughout the region as a gifted hip-hop practitioner. As the head of an increasingly popular rap group called DA F.A.M. (For All Mississippi), a youth mentor and cultural activist, he has cultivated in himself, and duly achieved, the kind of leadership that matters to young people in the region today. His diligent work in creating, chronicling, and advocating through rhyme has earned him a privileged place in the community life of Clarksdale and its surroundings. TopNotch is also a master interlocutor who finds purpose in sharing his experience and that of his community with those far beyond the Delta. Like the bluesman, country preacher, orator, and gospel singer before him, TopNotch has earned a position of leadership and respect within his community by proving his talent with *nommo*. To young Clarksdalians who grew up with both the classic blues and the boom-box sounds of L.L. Cool J, the local hip-hop artist holds the ultimate, emergent expressive power. As citizens of a self-styled community they call Clarks Vegaz, these young people stand in two realms: the hip-hop nation and the contemporary American "Dirty South."

Southern hip-hop's star has been steadily rising on the national pop music scene since the late 1980s, when Miami's 2 Live Crew and Houston's Geto Boys brought the concept of the "Dirty South" to an uninitiated MTV audience. Today, Southern hip-hop tops the international charts. The crunk movement, which drew from agrarian gangsta and pimp tropes to create a new Southern vernacular of "hard," drew a particularly potent brand of Southern hip-hop into the spotlight in the first years of the twenty-first century. In crunk's wake, new iterations of the Southern sound continue to expand the possibilities of what hip-hop can be. But from its first days on the popular stage, Southern hip-hop has been subjected to the distortions of partial representation and stereotype. The commercial hip-hop that filters through the airwaves, produced by major-label executives to appeal to dominant tastes, represents only the tip of African American musical creativity. The glib lyrics of popular Southern hip-hop, processed down to the three-minute pop hook, are judged more harshly than other popular forms despite the complex aural aesthetic that surrounds the text. And for every vapid major-label crunk creation, a thousand MCs spit realities and dreams on the sidewalks of their 'hoods.

TopNotch the Villain allowed us access to his community and creative process in order to, in his words, "let the world listen right" to what young people in the Mississippi Delta are saying through their music. Through his willingness to share his story, we will come to understand that hip-hop in the Mississippi Delta is defined by the interaction of Black Atlantic aesthetic practice, local cultural tradition, and global networks. I have worked for five years in close collaboration with artists and community members in the Mississippi Delta to document and interpret the ways in which these forces influence the forms and functions of regional expressive culture.

In this light a more complicated picture emerges. The story of this community does not begin or end with the waning sound of the acoustic Delta bluesman—nor does the power of the blues community's resistance to oppressive socioeconomic institutions and its ability to form alternative social structures of its own. Most importantly, these rural artists are engaged in a global call and response with the greater Black Atlantic diaspora, a network of cultural practitioners who draw from and, in turn, replenish the shared well of global creativity.

Because researchers have spent over a century chronicling the Delta blues, an ethnographic study of the contemporary musical life of the Mississippi Delta allows the elements of musical change and continuity to come to light. The process of engaging, documenting, and analyzing culture is the basis of ethnographic practice: the exercise of "writing culture."[5] Representations of the culture of the Delta have been written into being by a range of people and interests, including WPA photographers, rock musicians, documentarians, A&R reps, and urban journalists. But they are most importantly made and remade by members of the Delta community, whose creative work is interwoven with important declarations of "who you are and where you're from." Literary works

Bluesman Terry "Big T" Williams's juke joint in the New World district. Photograph by the author.

about the Delta blues—the ethnographic form preferred by academics and journalists—often begin with an account of the brave blues traveler looking southward wistfully, boarding his vehicle, and sailing past Memphis deep into the earthy, moist Delta. These gendered narratives are patterned on Joseph Conrad's carnal description of the European descent into the African *Heart of Darkness*: the anthropologist/journalist/explorer enters into this strange land and dips down into the earthly cultural well, omniscient, from his gliding vessel. He catalogues his encounters, strange and quaint.

My ride was not so easy. I approached the music of the Mississippi Delta from the outside. I could hear the sounds emanating from cracked bedroom windows, chapel doors, rattling trunks. By the time the cotton bolls dried on the stem the following summer, I would be wrapped in the richly textured juke joints and living rooms of the Mississippi Delta. In thirteen months' residence in the Delta I learned the language of the blues through a series of teachings and trials: from the hard pews of a little white church house, on the front porch of a close friend, in the back seat of a police car. These are painful and guilty lessons, and ones not easily forgotten. In the years since, I have returned often to the Delta as an observer, collaborator, community member, writer, reveler, student, and friend. I had to understand these roles were not my right. To realize the Mississippi Delta is to encounter the blues on its own terms, to stand at the crossroads of the living and the dead, the known and the emergent. TopNotch and his community have allowed (and often collaborated with) me to document their creative world, the rich context in which contemporary expressive culture in the Delta developed.

It is important not to oversimplify the relationship between the blues and hip-hop. This is not a linear progression in which hip-hop subsumes the blues. Rather, the stylistic innovations of yesterday and today remain in constant conversation, both in the local context and within global cultural networks. Delta hip-hop artists are not simply avatars of the blues tradition. Their skills are not the products of genetics or osmosis. These rappers are master oral/musical practitioners, skilled and schooled in the power of the word. The communities of the Mississippi Delta place an emphasis on this kind of artistry both in privileged spaces of performance—the church, the club—and in everyday interactions. The foregrounding of sophisticated modes of artistic expression fulfills a host of important functions in the Delta. Many of these community needs arise from the indelible regional socioeconomic legacy. The consummate inhumanity of the Delta cotton plantation, and the surveillance that preserved its hierarchy, fostered a need on the part of black residents to create hidden transcripts, cautionary tales, and signified resistance. But the music is more than reactive; it is also a creative mode of expression that has been cultivated by the musicians, rappers, preachers, singers, mothers, schoolmates, leaders and workers of the Mississippi Delta. Hidden transcripts serve not only to obscure communication from unwanted listeners; they also provide the artist with new dimensions of expression, elaborate modes of meaning. Celebration, the collaboration that comes from performer-audience relationship, community-building, and the challenge of individual mastery are also important functions of music-making in the Mississippi Delta. For many participants, transcendence is the ultimate goal.

Issues of difference have sharply arisen throughout the course of this research. Race, in particular, has threatened to slash borders through my relationships in the Delta. In a place James Cobb dubbed "The Most Southern Place on Earth,"[6] where the plantation social structure has traditionally drawn a sharp distinction between black and white, it becomes easy to perceive identity in monochrome, a world of opposites. Like the Crossroads, however, it is the intersections that matter. The line between speaking and music-making blurs in a culture where speech is as rhythmic and melodic as music. Tradition and innovation join in the constant creation of emergent cultural meaning. The sacred and the secular intertwine in their mutual reach for emergence. Dualistic racial identities, constructed in opposition here to reckon with plantation inhumanity, constantly shift and combine in the symbolic worlds of cultural practitioners. In the possibilities of practice, categories fall away and the creative experience begins to take shape. More than anything, I share with my consultants a deep love for music. In the spaces where music is made, I found

A sign on the front of Po Monkey's longstanding rural juke joint in Merigold, Mississippi. Photograph by Andrew Kropa.

(to use the words of Paul Gilroy) cultural routes, not musical roots. This is the story of music that reaches beyond difference, rhythms that pound out new networks of meaning, sounds engaged in an aesthetic and intellectual global call and response.

In an atmosphere of intense international curiosity surrounding "The Land Where Blues Began,"[7] popular representation of the Delta holds the power to affect the course of tourism development. This representation is often contested by residents of the Mississippi Delta themselves. This study explores the possibility that the blues community preserves culture on its own terms; that instead of fading away, the blues defies the strains of time by updating and strengthening itself, remaining relevant to the community's contemporary needs. The people of the Mississippi Delta not only recognize the value of their music; they center their lives on it. The dynamic nature of Black Atlantic music defies genre labels and historical definitions, which in turn frustrates a dominant market that relies on the branding of an "authentic" product. The market will not sell what it cannot define. If the blues cannot be labeled, then it cannot be packaged, priced or controlled. By design, black music slips the yokes of commodification and domination. Cultural practice in the Mississippi Delta resists, at its deepest levels, efforts to dictate the boundaries of its creativity according to the rhetoric of blues authenticity. It offers an alternative, community-centered script that begs surface interpretation by the mainstream while remaining under the control of its practitioners, deeply embedded in the context of community life.

Ethnographic work in the Mississippi Delta requires vulnerability, humility, and a good measure of self-effacing laughter. My many generous consultants—the DJs, preachers, singers, poets and rappers of the Mississippi Delta—celebrated, guided, and (often) corrected this work throughout its development. The process of interpreting the rich artistic practices of the Delta requires collaboration. When we surround a depiction of the complex work of Delta music makers with their own dense descriptions of their everyday lives and practices, when we stop simply looking at or listening to others long enough to give emotional witness to the creative practices of the Mississippi Delta, and when we remain accountable for the ethnographic missteps that line our path, the longstanding stereotypes of blues pathos, piteousness, and provincialism unravel. Preservation is important; we strengthen our cultural understandings by remembering and celebrating the work of past masters. At the same time, the efforts of contemporary inheritors of the blues tradition deserve recognition and support. In listening to the blues, gospel, hip-hop, and other regional musics we are challenged to understand the language of the Mississippi Delta, to train our ears to a deeper rhythm. In doing so, I had to reckon with the boundaries of my own understandings. The fullness of the story of Delta music can be told only in partnership with practitioners of the living blues. Through their words, rhythm, and rhyme a world of meaning emerges.

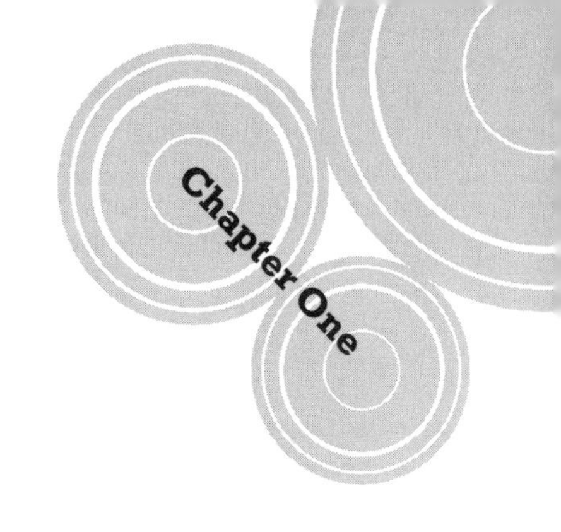

"This Game Is for Life!"

Black rap music is primarily the musical expression of the paradoxical cry of desperation and celebration. . . . Without a utopian dimension—without transcendence from or opposition to evil—there can be no struggle, no hope, no meaning.
—Cornel West[1]

Red's Juke Joint, one of many sprinkled throughout the abandoned downtowns of the Mississippi Delta, sits on the boundary of Clarksdale's historically black New World district. Beneath its foundation are the edges of ancient Tunica burial mounds. These Native American ceremonial ridges, packed architecturally with loamy soil and ancestral bodies, doubled as powerful levees for the once-mighty Sunflower River, which runs behind Red's establishment through a barrier of dense thickets of tall grass and cane break. From the front door of the bare plywood building, the looming stone sculpture of a sorrowful angel can be seen by the lamplight of Grange Cemetery, where the graves of the white town founders are decorated with Confederate flags yearly.[2]

"I've got the river behind me and the graveyard in front of me," shouts Red from his stool outside the club on a slow Sunday night, a wry smile on his face. "That there is my guardian angel. This game is for *life*!" His eyes are hidden behind a pair of deep red shades despite the blackness of the night.

At Red's, the beers are huge and cold and insulated with thick swaths of brown paper towels. The management prefers to use colored light bulbs, mostly red, that peek out from bends in the walls to give the room a surreal, warm glow. Glossy posters of sexy girls in hot pants are thumbtacked throughout the room, nearly covering the dubious holes leaking light through the bathroom walls. At the back of the room, just left of the cove that holds the old pool table, a two-foot-tall mirrored plaque decorates the wall. It reads, BUDWEISER, KING OF BEERS and features a silk-screened photo of an African king, complete with war paint and a spear, gazing down at the club's patrons in a powerful antiphony to the crumbling white angel outside. This was one of a cynical series of advertisements the beer company made for black clubs during the Black Power movement of the 1970s; I have seen them frequently both in the juke

Red's Lounge at Martin Luther King and Sunflower in Clarksdale. Photograph by the author.

joints of the Delta and in the little bars in my old neighborhoods in Brooklyn and Oakland. Red does not seem concerned about the politics of the object.

"Don't mess with me," he often says, pointing toward the plaque, clowning: "or my uncle Shaka Zulu up there will get you. I kill for *fun*!" He chuckles as his eyes peek above his shades. I shake his hand and enter. In the years since my arrival in the Delta, I have witnessed Red's establishment shift reputations within white tourist circles; once considered a dangerous dive appropriate for only the bravest of blues travelers, Red's is now considered the seat of Delta blues authenticity by the current group of tourists and tourism-friendly white locals alike, who enjoy the club's down-home atmosphere. When the roof nearly collapsed in the wake of the 2005 hurricane season, local tourism interests and visiting blues travelers quickly jumped to the rescue, shelling out donations in exchange for a T-shirt reading: THE GAME IS FOR LIFE!

But what appears timeworn and quaint to authenticity-hungry outsiders in fact contains richness far beyond that of the interiors of corporate rock 'n' blues joints of Middle American renovated downtowns. Those are festooned with famous guitars in acetate cases, framed record albums nailed to the wall, flavored martini specials. Red's is a jewel box of Delta style; the use of color, surface, and texture combine to create an intensely social and rich aesthetic experience. Red's may have been composed from worn materials, but in its use of the familiar the juke joint retains a wealth of local meaning, history, and

Red of Red's Lounge. Photograph by the author.

style. Disco mirrors lining the near wall; a pool table, dramatic lighting, and a booming sound system pieced together from salvaged amplifiers contribute to an assemblage that, although tinged with wear from the destructive climate, functions perfectly as a stimulating and well-equipped space for group creativity. Red, a shrewd businessman with a son in a science Ph.D. program at Mississippi State, consciously cultivates a double image for his spot: both outsiders' juke joint and locals' club. The club's repurposed materials signal authenticity to tourists, who are often not attuned to the meaning ingrained in the hand-remade, custom space.

Few weekend blues tourists remain in town on Sunday nights, and Red's becomes filled with locals. Neighborhood friends move forward from the corners to occupy the entire space. Clarksdale bluesmen Big Jack Johnson, Wesley "Mississippi Junebug" Jefferson, and Arthenice "Gasman" Jones tumble through on these off nights, exchanging places behind the microphone as local schoolkids sit in on rhythm. Big Jack "The Oilman" Johnson, the revered bluesman whose secondary legacy was driving the town's biggest fuel truck, has agreed to play a short, early set tonight. Around 8 p.m. the crowd swells to fifteen and Big Jack begins to tune his guitar. This juke-joint gig offers him a chance to play for his hometown friends in between the closely scheduled blues festival gigs that are his bread and butter. It also allows him to experiment and improvise in ways that the festival arena does not. Big Jack Johnson is Clarksdale's blues

Blues singer and guitarist Wesley "Mississippi Junebug" Jefferson at Red's Lounge. Photograph by the author.

royalty, and he knows that at Red's he will be able to see the faces of his familiar audience and hear their voices respond to a lick with a collective whelp.

As Johnson finishes his set with a revved-up medley of traditional songs ("Will the Circle Be Unbroken," "Amazing Grace"), Clarksdale bluesman Terry "Big T" Williams takes the reins and begins to play a deep blues riff. T and Junebug alternate turns at the microphone throughout the night, rounding out a loose group of local musicians. A number of Jefferson's family members are in attendance, and many of them pick up an instrument or sing a song as the players rotate throughout the evening. The set list is improvised as one member of the group begins a song and the others jump in. The songs range from the deep, dirty blues to heart-wrenching soul songs that vary just the tiniest bit from the local gospel sound: smokier, and rounded with guitar work rather than a chorus. A set might include a Delta blues classic like Muddy Waters's "I Be's Troubled," a dirgy "make-up" song with a hodgepodge of old-time and improvised lyrics, and a contemporary R&B southern soul teaser like Theodis Ealey's "Stand Up in It": "She said Theodis, men think they know what women want / But the truth about the whole thing is boy they really don't. / . . . But you ain't done a doggone thing until you stand up in it."[3]

Wesley Jefferson is the best shade-tree mechanic in this part of the Delta; with a pinch of the fingers under the hood and a sniff of their contents, he can diagnose an engine problem in seconds. He impeccably fixed up our '69

Ford Econoline van for a dime. He is married to Miss Sara Carr, daughter of legendary Jelly Roll Kings drummer Sam Carr, and is the father of a number of talented children, all of whom are musical, and one of whom is serving in the war in Iraq. Wesley's version of the blues is gritty but nuanced, with his wah-wah voice and stomping cadence. He is also willing to let another player step into the spotlight while he takes a beer break.

Big T tells me he is excited to play bass with Big Jack, whom he considers an elder and a mentor. The influence of Big Jack's legendary guitar technique on Big T's style is apparent, and although Big T tends to shine in the spotlight, T is happy to spend the first half of his night behind the Oilman. Lee Williams, a nineteen-year-old graduate of the Delta Blues Education program, sits in on drums, which he plays with the combination of swing and precision that characterizes the Delta blues.[4] An anonymous white blues tourist in an iridescent blue shirt steps in and holds his own on rhythm guitar behind the group. He donated a pocketful of cash to the musicians for the privilege. Local blues singers Razor Blade and Mr. Tater play a song from time to time as well.

Red's has no stage; its performance space is a leftover swath of casino carpet, about twelve by ten feet, laid out to take up half of the room's floor space. A huge tin tip tub, a stack of old guitar amps and P.A. equipment, and bare floor space for dancers and revelers line the periphery of the performance space. The edges of the room are filled with little round tables and chairs for larger groups of early-arriving locals and valued regulars. Stragglers situate themselves at the bar, where an assortment of Red's friends and a few squirrelly foreign, hipster, or blues traveling tourists crowd in. The music envelops us all. There is a certain lack of boundary between audience and performer in the Delta that gives the music its electricity; in this room, whooping and dancing with the rest, my hand tight around a Bud tallboy, I feel like I am as much a part of the music as anything.

Bullshitting with Red is a favorite pastime for his regulars. He has spent a lifetime developing his "talk," a skill that he cultivates in others by challenging them to wild verbal duels. This process involves Red jibing his trainee loudly, usually with a series of clever insults (clothing, intelligence, facial structure, or—in my case—race) meant to be answered with coolness and wit. Over the course of my three years of working and living in the Delta, I have enjoyed an increasingly difficult series of such challenges, and although Red often leaves me speechless, we are able to engage each other in this kind of conversation for a few minutes at a time. He has told me before that he likes me because, in his words, I "know how to talk," but I have noticed that he will often let me get away with stumbling over a response—or staring at him blankly as my mind searches unsuccessfully for one. In this situation he turns his head and laughs

Toast-teller Antonio Coburn of Red's Lounge. Photograph by the author.

kindly, ending the session without making me too uncomfortable. Or he will turn his attention to a less vulnerable target: "You white people sure are actin' funny these days," he will say as he gestures toward a pale, long-haired drunk meandering his way back from the liquor store on a little girl's pink bike. "Now, I can't argue with that," I respond.

Antonio Coburn, Red's bartender, is a robust young man with a smiling round face. He knows Delta toasts a century older than his thirty or so years. Fresh from his maintenance job with the county in a striped blue shirt, Antonio can be cajoled into tailoring a classic folk rhyme—either about the signifying monkey (the notorious jungle master of words) or Shine and Dolemite. He says he learned these rhymes both from mentors in the community and from Blaxploitation films. After a little begging and a promise that I will not be offended, Antonio gives in and begins "The Signifyin' Monkey." A group of onlookers pull their barstools up to his little table in the corner of the room as he continues his explicit version of the old rhyme about a shit-talking monkey and his victim, the powerful old lion. His performance is exceptional, rolling rhythmically with the repeated refrain, "This made the lion mad." Eventually the patrons begin to repeat these words with him, and he continues after each chorus to describe the lion's unwitting reaction to the monkey's antics. There are no clocks, but the performance seems to last around twenty minutes. The audience is attentive and titillated. Antonio's response is to launch into a rendition of a second toast, entitled "Shine and the Titanic," with matching aplomb. Or he will tell friends to pick up their drinks and offer a quick one:

This is for a frog
Who sat on a log
Waiting on a rich man's daughter.
For the tears he shed,
His ass turned red,
So BLOOP! he fell in the water.

A night at Red's does not begin and end with the blues players' set. The entire aesthetic experience matters: taste, talk, music, temperature, color, light, interaction. Movement, collectivity, and improvisation are highly valued. Style is king. Red chooses elements carefully and incorporates them into the entirety of the club's aesthetic. Some nights, a bluesman from the hill country northeast of the Delta—T Model Ford or Robert Belfour—plays for a crowd of five. During the musician's frequent breaks, Red entertains his customers with his characteristic boisterous talk. Patrons stand and dance solo to favorite Southern soul classics playing over the sound system, flirting with a desired partner. A young couple plays a game of pool or chats on the corner couch. Frequently, especially on off nights, a lady from the audience—a bluesman's daughter or a respected matron—gets up to sing a song with the band. The players hang on her first vocal riff to determine what chords to play and then launch in to meet her at the chorus. She ends her song and sits back in her chair as her friends pat her back and pour her another drink. Or the band begins a familiar riff without any particular singer at hand, daring anyone in the audience to assume the role of emcee. Sometimes Wesley Jefferson Junior, the bluesman's son, rises from the audience and, after singing a stanza or two, begins to speak in rhyme, addressing a loved one in improvised verse. As the audience cheers him on, he proves his wit through his freestyle oratory: impassioned, skilled, and created in the thick moment of performance.

Delta Blues on the Coolin' Board

To Wesley Jefferson, Terry "Big T" Williams, and the community members who breathe energy into the creative atmosphere of the Mississippi Delta, the blues is alive and well. All the while, blues record labels, fan clubs, and documentaries claim to be responsible for "keeping the blues alive." This dichotomy has characterized the interaction of the blues with the popular imagination. Invigorated by the flash of creativity and haunted by hellhounds, the Delta blues, like the crossroads at which it was conjured, calls upon themes of life and death. In much sub-Saharan African belief, the crossroads represents a horizontal line between the living and the spiritual realms and a vertical path between those two worlds. According to art historian Robert Farris Thompson, "This means that one must cultivate the art of recognizing significant communications, knowing what is truth and what is falsehood, or else the lessons of the crossroads—the point at which doors open or close, where persons have to make decisions that will forever affect their lives—will be lost."[5]

Many Afrodiasporic narratives tell of the traveler who approaches this powerful intersection and encounters the spirit of a trickster figure, often resembling the Yoruba deity Eshu-Elegba, who challenges the wanderer to account for all possible perspectives before choosing his or her route. This encounter can be a maturing or a deadly experience, and its lessons echo through popular legends surrounding Delta bluesmen Robert Johnson, Tommy Johnson, Peetie Wheatstraw, and others. At the crossroads, it is said, these musicians traded their souls for the ability to play guitar:

> Take your guitar and you go down to where a road crosses that way, where a crossroad is. Get there, be sure to get there just a little 'fore twelve o'clock that night so you know you'll be there. You have your guitar and be playing a piece sitting there by yourself. You have to go by yourself and be sitting there playing a piece. A big black man will walk up there and take your guitar, and he'll tune it. And he'll play a piece and hand it back to you. That's the way I learned how to play anything I want.[6]

These words of bluesman Tommy Johnson illustrate the symbolic power of the crossroads as a magical and creative space where fate is sealed. Crossroads narratives have been central to popular interests in blues music, and their supernatural tones echo through scores of rock songs, album titles, and films. Whether or not Johnson actually sold his soul to the devil in this liminal, or transitional, space, it is clear that he used the crossroads to symbolize his decision to make secular rather than sacred music. The idea that Johnson may have placed himself in this sensational story to increase his cachet as a working blues musician has been raised within and outside the blues community.[7] A trade with the devil—actual or symbolic—certainly provided a lyrical wellspring for Robert Johnson, a prewar[8] bluesman who patterned his style and his reputation on that of Tommy Johnson: "You may bury my body, ooh, down by the highway side / So my old evil spirit can catch a Greyhound bus and ride."[9]

Robert Johnson's legacy has been the beacon for blues revivalists who find a rally cry in his supernatural lyricism. His words mark his intimate understanding of death on one hand and a strong belief in transcendence on the other. He laments his mortality while also suggesting an escape route: a ride north on Highway 61, across the imagined line between stasis and freedom. The trickster devil of the Delta, more a stylistic symbol than an object of ritual, was a figure who conjured opportunity and power; decisions of life and death in this region are a matter of God's judgment.

To young members of the black Delta community, the crossroads continues to hold symbolic power. When, over a drink on a slow night at a Clarksdale blues club, I announced to a group of thirty-something Clarksdalians that I was researching hip-hop in the Delta, they began to suggest points of local interest. One of the men insisted that he wanted to make his own documentary about the crossroads. I asked him what the crossroads means to him, and he began to list local figures who achieved artistic success: "John Lee Hooker, Ike Turner, Muddy Waters, Big Jack Johnson, O. B. Buchanna . . ."

I ask him where he heard that Buchanna, a young southern soul singer from Clarksdale, had sold his soul.

"How could he not have sold his soul? I heard he was offered five figures for his first album straight out the gate!"

"Which crossroads do you mean?" I asked. "The famous old crossroads in the New World district, or the commercial strips out by the Church's Chicken?"

"The ones out by the viaduct!" He said, referring to the latter, a landscaped, shiny landmark recently constructed by the Chamber of Commerce for the sake of tourists' photo albums.

For these young men, the crossroads, whatever its location, provides both a symbol for sudden creative success and a conviction in the power of place. Contemporary Clarksdale folklore places Puttin' Hatchett (also known as Obbie Lee Barnes and Fast Black), a prodigious seventy-seven-year-old three-card monte player and dice magician, at the crossroads during a critical period in his youth. Kids in town who have never heard of Robert Johnson are familiar with Hatchett's purported encounter. "I'm a baaad man," he will tell anyone. His talent is real: he has been banned from the card tables at local casinos for his overwhelming winning streaks. But he has insisted to me many times that although he remembers carving dice from a black cat bone in the New World district at the age of thirteen, and despite his story about waiting for the devil at the midnight crossroads, his soul is in no danger.

> "Back in 1941, my granddaddy came into the cotton field, wantin' me to pick cotton. Gave me a flour-sack. I didn't want to work, I didn't want to steal, I didn't want to rob. I took these dice here and started playin' dice. I saw a man doin' three-card monte. So I got me a deck of cards, and I switched to the cards.

And I've been doin' it all my life. I got about eight Cadillacs. . . .

"I wanted to find somethin' else to do in life, and that's what I did sho' nuff, the crossroads. . . .

"The night I went down there, they got my picture, and I fell down on my knees and everything, and I told the Devil that I'm comin' to him now. So I've been with the Devil now about seventy-somethin' years."

"And what," I asked, "Did the Devil say to you?"

"He told me to go ahead and do my thing."

Puttin' cracks a smile for a second here, and then again assumes his cardsharp face. I ask him what happened next.

"I left in 1957 goin' to Florida. I left Clarksdale, and it took me three weeks to get there. When I got there, [I had] eight thousand and somethin' [dollars]. So that's why I went to the crossroads."

"And now, do you think your soul is going to be damned from going to the crossroads?"

"I don't know about my soul is still up there. I ain't gonna care about my soul no way until I'm dead and gone. I'm enjoying myself while I'm livin'. . . . When the Lord tells you it's time to go, you gotta leave here. The Lord give me five cents, I'm gonna use my five cents 'til I die."

Puttin' holds two dice between his thumb and forefinger.

"You got good eyesight?" he says.

"Yeah," I say. I have been playing my part in Puttin's routine for years.

"How many you see up there, baby?"

"Um, twelve," I say, seeing his double-sixes, which quickly, magically, transform into a five and four with a flick of his wrist.[10]

To Puttin', a deal with the Devil does not represent eternal damnation. Rather, a visit to the crossroads—or the gleeful narration of such a supernatural visit—is a rite of passage for anyone who wants to excel at his or her craft. The functional complexity of crossroads folklore cannot be overlooked. Historically, the crossroads Robert Johnson referred to in his songs would likely have been located further south in the Delta, near Rosedale or Dockery Plantation, where Johnson began his career, but it is unlikely that even he was concerned with their physical geography. To residents of Clarksdale it is not the latitude and longitude of the crossroads themselves that matters, but the continued importance of the crossroads as a signifier of power and creativity.

Themes of death resonate throughout the cultural practices of the Mississippi Delta. The verses of prewar bluesmen reveal intimate familiarity with the subject. The "coolin' board," an unhinged front door used to lay out recently deceased members of the household, makes a common appearance in blues

Obbie Lee "Puttin' Hatchett" Barnes at Ground Zero Blues Club. Photograph by the author.

lyrics, as does the "cold, cold buryin' ground," the "lonesome graveyard," and "the shallow grave." Clarksdale bluesman Son House, a contemporary and mentor to Robert Johnson, illustrates this gothic take on mortality in "Death Letter Blues."

I got a letter this morning, how do you reckon it read?
"Oh, hurry, hurry, gal, you love is dead"
I got a letter this morning, how do you reckon it read?
"Oh, hurry, hurry, the gal you love is dead"

I grabbed my suitcase, I took off up the road
I got there, she was laying on the cooling board.
I grabbed my suitcase, I took on up the road
I got there, she was laying on the cooling board.[11]

House's thundering basso, ripped from the church pulpit and summoned from the deepest reaches of his lungs, reflected in its aesthetic not only the pangs of poverty but also the resolution of resistance and strength. House's voice seems to stand in stark antiphony to Robert Johnson's vocal pangs. House was a contemporary of Johnson's, and the sheer force of his voice shakes the stereotypes of pathos projected on the work of the early bluesmen. House's style was undead, earth-shaking, and signified a man with no boss. The rich, rough-edged tones of his voice are representative of the powerful vocal techniques still preferred by male and female singers in the Delta today. The unsteady mobile recording units and highly surveilled sessions that were necessary to prewar folkloristic songcatching may have served to distort the power of the early Delta blues sound, including Johnson and his contemporaries.

The starvation and sickness that were part and parcel of Delta poverty were often addressed in song, as were the environmental ravages of flooding, disease, and disaster. Against the backdrop of debt peonage that bound black residents of the Delta to lifetimes of deprivation, sorrow was no stranger. The very real experience of oppression informed the death tropes played out in blues lyrics, from plantation abuse and exhaustion to the treacherous environmental conditions of the sharecropping system. A visiting team of doctors in the 1960s found "homes without running water, without electricity, without screens, in which children drink contaminated water and live with germ-bearing mosquitoes and flies everywhere around."[12] Few Delta residents could afford to eat more than once a day, and their diets were limited to empty, nutritionless food.[13] Starvation was the norm. Blues lyrics dealt with these issues head-on, including these lyrics about the murderous Delta flood of 1927: "Oh, Lord, oh Lordy, women and grown men down, / Ohhh, women and children sinkin' down. [Spoken: Lord have mercy] / I couldn't see nobody home and wasn't no one to be found."[14] The meeting of the Mississippi and Yazoo rivers that gives the Delta its character was both the source of constant flood and disaster and a site for Pentecostal Baptismal cleansing: the medium of death and of salvation.

As W. C. Handy, the famous African American bandleader who documented and brought the blues into national popularity, waited in Tutwiler for his train to Clarksdale in 1903, he encountered the Delta blues for the first time: "the weirdest music I ever heard," played by a "lean, loose-jointed negro" who sung about his hope to escape poverty by catching a northbound ride at a Delta railroad crossing.[15] The Delta blues was subject to caricature even in its first popular representation. Handy went on to brand the blues both on the bandstand and as a sheet music composer, sparking national interest in the genre. Alan Lomax, whose 1941 and 1942 Library of Congress forays into the Mississippi Delta provided the basis for his seminal book, *Land Where the Blues Began*, describes the role of death in the region in lurid terms:

> Country people are not afraid to look death in the face. He is familiar in their lives, especially in the violent jungle of the Delta. They have seen him in the houses drowned by the great river and in the towns splintered in tornadoes; they have seen him in the faces of the young men shot down in the gambling hall or in the guise of an old fellow who came home to die after a hard day's plowing, his body on the cooling board still bent from years stooping over the cotton rows.[16]

Lomax's work was based in a legacy of anthropological interest in the culture and folklore of black communities in the South. After sociologists including Howard Odum and Guy B. Johnson published their early work on African American folk songs at the turn of the century, folklorists Lawrence Gellert and John and (later, his son) Alan Lomax continued to collect and compile southern

The Tutwiler water tower, near which popular African American bandleader and composer W. C. Handy first heard the Delta blues while waiting for a train. Photograph by Timothy Gordon.

African American folklore in the prewar years. The latter group, involved with the workers' movement of the 1930s and 1940s, infused their work with a progressive, anticapitalist agenda. Gellert found that African American folk song contained tools for political resistance and discovered the element of protest in a mode of cultural expression previously regarded as docile and simple. John and Alan Lomax helped to popularize the work of folk artists such as Huddie "Lead Belly" Ledbetter, whose songs contained jibes against the cruel masters and oppressive circumstances of the American South. To increase Lead Belly's countercultural cachet, the Lomaxes encouraged the singer to wear prison garb and sing work songs well after his release from prison.

For Alan Lomax, who continued his family's folklorist work with a special focus on the cultural practices of Southern African Americans, the politics of representation were bound by a progressive social agenda. He took a cue from anthropologist John Dollard, who in league with Hortense Powdermaker completed an intensive ethnographic study of the Delta town of Indianola, Mississippi, in the 1930s. Dollard, concerned with the need for federal poverty relief in the Delta, depicted circumstances for African American residents of the region in terms of socioeconomic caste. Faced with the dire circumstances of life behind the "Cotton Curtain," blues people sublimated their frustration and anger in the form of cruel rhyming games and self-effacing blues lyrics.[17] Lomax, informed by these studies, did his best to document and preserve the music and culture of the blues people of the Mississippi Delta, whose struggles provided a potent example of the inequality he sought to eliminate. Fascinated with the story of Robert Johnson's trade with the devil at the crossroads, Lomax joined a group of Fisk University researchers in a search for the cursed bluesman. Instead, he found that Johnson had been poisoned to death in a land Lomax would later tout as the birthplace of the blues.

Like his father's promotion of Lead Belly, Lomax's representations of the Delta blues helped draw public attention to the cultural work of the black southern underclass. The result was the popularization and appreciation of this music on the national stage: the Delta blues became internationally known through John Hammond's Spirituals to Swing folk festivals, Smithsonian Folkways records, and popular articles, and held special appeal for the young, white middle-class Americans who sought an alternative script to mainstream postwar life.

The concept of the blues' birth began to intrigue fans beyond the Delta, along with a growing concern with the genre's demise. The Delta blues, often depicted as a product of the suffering caused by the pathological effects of institutionalized racism, would surely end up on the coolin' board. "Keeping the blues alive" became a mantra for blues organizations and fans, who rallied around the genre as a symbol of working-class opposition. The themes of life and death that had so deeply influenced the Delta blues became ingrained in the popular consciousness, and the sensational legacy of Robert Johnson's violent and untimely demise grew to define popular notions of the Delta blues. Identified with the haunting "otherness" represented by these supernatural narratives, the Delta blues became associated with poverty and death itself instead of the act of musical transcendence symbolized by the crossroads.

The collection methods of early folklorists in the region added further constraints to the study of the Delta blues. White ethnographers were largely prohibited from entering black community spaces both by wary Delta African Americans and by local law enforcement. During the civil rights era, the police were charged with heavily discouraging interaction between blacks and white potential agitators. Blues songs were largely collected on front porches or visitors' hotel rooms, and featured a single player, often without any accompaniment. One can imagine the trepidation with which a young black musician presented his craft—and poetry—to unfamiliar outsiders under the plantation boss's surveillance. Thus decontextualized from the spirit of community-centered performance, early recordings of Delta blues players represent a partial perspective on a multifaceted musical form. In the popular imagination, these tinny recordings conjured visions of lonely old bluesmen withering in the Delta cotton fields, rather than master performers who epitomized wit and style.

Perhaps the most substantial distortion of the blues spirit can be found among some fans and critics who tout the notion of the "real, down-home, country" blues depicted in popular film and music. Many of these definitions are based on a romantic notion of blues authenticity that, as a by-product, designates the blues as a reactive form, borne of a black agrarian poverty that is necessary to the music's creation. Charles Kiel calls the tendency to apply these notions of authenticity to the living blues the "moldy fig mentality."[18] A song by the Blues Brothers, two white comedians who made a career of assuming blues identities, sums up the sentiment: "I throw away my money, I move back to that shack / . . . When times are bad, the less I had, the better I played the blues / I buy myself some turkey and wine, and howl it at the moon / 'cause I can't play the blues in an air-conditioned room."[19] Here, the lone black bluesman with his guitar, shoeless in a cotton field or affected with a disease, loses his blues when equipped with a full stomach. The figure of the blues musician, here inhabited by a wealthy white comedian, begs to be returned to his state of poverty so that he can continue to create. A list of "authentic" blues traits was circulated online via websites and inboxes in 2005, featuring a checklist for blues authenticity. I received the list through fellow folklorists twice via mass e-mail, and a basic Web search turns this list up on dozens of blues fan Websites.

HOW TO SING THE BLUES

If you are new to Blues music, or like it but never really understood the why and wherefores, here are some very fundamental rules:
1. Most Blues begin with: "Woke up this morning . . ." . . .
4. The Blues is not about choice. You stuck in a ditch, you stuck in a ditch . . . ain't no way out . . .
12. No one will believe it's the Blues if you wear a suit, 'less you happen to be an old person, and you slept in it.
13. Do you have the right to sing the Blues?
Yes, if:
a. you're older than dirt
b. you're blind
c. you shot a man in Memphis
d. you can't be satisfied
No, if:
a. you have all your teeth
b. you were once blind but now can see
c. the man in Memphis lived
d. you have a 401K or trust fund . . .
16. If death occurs in a cheap motel or a shotgun shack, it's a Blues death. Stabbed in the back by a jealous lover is another Blues way to die.
So are the electric chair, substance abuse, and dying lonely on a broke down cot. You can't have a Blues death if you die during a tennis match or while getting liposuction . . .

20. Blues Name Starter Kit

a. name of physical infirmity (Blind, Cripple, Lame, etc.)

b. first name (see above) plus name of fruit (Lemon, Lime, Kiwi, etc.)

c. last name of President (Jefferson, Johnson, Fillmore, etc.)

For example: Blind Lime Jefferson, Pegleg Lemon Johnson or Cripple Kiwi Fillmore, etc. (Well, maybe not "Kiwi.")

21. I don't care how tragic your life is: if you own a computer, you cannot sing the blues, period.[20]

As middle-class interest in the Delta blues grew throughout the latter half of the twentieth century, the attempts of white ethnographers to fully depict suffering in the Deep South became conflated with the cultural politics of cool. This "everything but the burden"[21] mentality allowed whites to credentialize themselves in blues cool while simultaneously reinforcing the economic status quo. The stereotype of the Delta blues as a dying form fulfills a number of functions for dominant American culture. Middle-class postwar youth found a rallying cry in the blues' opposition to bourgeois norms. The popular American record industry, based on the model of minstrelsy, found a ready market for sensational depictions of the bluesman. The blues could be easily packaged, and bought and sold on the popular market. If the blues was finite, able to be captured in the grooves of a record, then the music—and the cultural capital of blues cool—could be owned. American popular culture found another safe vessel for its socioeconomic reckoning, sometimes tragic, sometimes supernatural, but never fully human.

The contemporary blues community of the Mississippi Delta is well aware of the marketability of popular blues stereotypes. I have known a blues musician or two in Clarksdale to concoct firsthand stories about jealous poisoning, devil sightings at the crossroads, or fantastic bloodbaths at the juke joint. One singer, whose musicianship dates back no further than the 1990s, points toward any of a number of nearby houses and insists to a British camera crew, "I lived in this house here with John Lee Hooker. I used to be in his band!" They are familiar with the stories these blues travelers want to hear; these tropes are elicited time and time again for TV documentaries, blues fanzine articles, and travel blogs. Some artists expect cash or publicity in exchange for their efforts in maintaining the fiction of authenticity for the sake of the tourists' experience. The same stories are repeated for blues researchers and tourists alike, especially those concerning the rigors of the cotton fields and the intrigues of the devil.

Roger Abrahams, whose research in Afrodiasporic performative speech broke critical folkloristic ground, found that studies of African American culture by researchers based in the dominant culture often reinforce hegemonic stereotypes of pathology and lyrical death-centeredness. "Studies of Afro-American cultures and societies continue to be haunted by the shape-shifting, pursuing spirit of stereotypy. The deprivation and pathological arguments are the latest incarnations of this spirit, both relying on mainstream Western values and practices as norms."[22] These norms emphasize form over process, repetition over improvisation, and verbal text over musical performance. They take literally the blues singer's tragic laments while overlooking the life-affirming nature of his creative practice.

Albert Murray, a journalist and scholar, sought to break blues stereotypes in his 1976 book, *Stomping the Blues*. He points out that the entry on blues music in the *Standard Dictionary of Folklore, Mythology and Legend* describes the poetry of the blues as "'tender, ironic, bitter, humorous, or typical expressions of deprived people . . .'"[23] He also discusses formal definitions of the blues as a twelve-bar format with a twice-repeated stanza and then a third, rhymed punch line. These definitions of the blues were representative of the dominant culture's invested depiction of the blues. Murray displaced these notions with eloquence.

> Not that blues music is without fundamental as well as immediate political significance and applicability. But the nature of its political dimension is not always as obvious as promoters of folk-music-as-social-commentary seem to believe. The political implication is inherent in the attitude toward experience that generates the blues-music counterstatement in the first place. It is the disposition to persevere (based on a tragic, or better still, an epic sense of life) that blues music at its best not only embodies but also stylizes, extends, elaborates and refines into art.[24]

To Murray, who spent a lifetime participating in the living blues arena in his own black Alabama community and in clubs and juke joints across the country, the blues was life-affirming, dynamic and Afrocentric in both content and form.

> Nor has anybody ever been able to get rid of the blues forever either. You can only drive them away and keep them at bay for the time being. Because they are always there, as if always waiting and watching. Retirement is out of the question. . . . all you have to do is keep them in their proper place, which is deep in the dozens, is to pat your feet and snap your fingers.[25]

John W. Roberts suggests that the academic concern with verbal texts has miscast black culture in a model of simple, linear development that ignores "the Afrocentric process or the ways in which Africans in America transformed their cultural forms and created a dynamic folk tradition in America."[26] Researchers often brush away the meaning grounded in rhythmic and musical aesthetics, ideas generated in the movements and expressions of the performer, hidden transcripts buried in signified meaning, and the contexts of community celebration and transcendence. In the case of the Delta blues, this means oversimplified interpretations of blues lyrics. On the written page, a cotton-field lament or a murder narrative taps in to a deep pathos. But in the club on a Saturday night, these songs become life-affirming, energetic, and dynamic.[27]

Chris Thomas King, the blues musician and rapper from Louisiana who played bluesman Tommy Johnson in *O Brother, Where Art Thou?* finds that the contemporary music industry fails to recognize the dynamic nature of the blues. He started his own record label that celebrates the blues in its full, Afrocentric modernity:

> I've created my label to try to make it easier for some artists to get heard, because there's a whole new sound out there that's happening. The bands I have signed, 21 C-B-Boyz and Nublues, have made excellent albums, but these records wouldn't have been released by some of the other blues labels since they don't fit into some cliché these label people have in their heads. These people are still trying to say Etta James and Buddy Guy are contemporary blues. Compared to what? We're not cover artists. We're trying to be our own generation.[28]

King practices in his work an expansive and dynamic definition of the blues, one both dressed in a new Saturday night suit and designed to preserve its elusive spirit. Even so, a recent *Down Beat* article lumps King's mission into the same bin as other new blues labels that are less optimistic about contemporary manifestations of the Mississippi blues: "Matthew Johnson, founder of Mississippi's Fat Possum Records, describes the current state of blues in his home state and elsewhere as 'horrible.' 'Blues is dead,' Johnson laments. 'If it does make it, it'll be with house-rockin' blues, and that's not the stuff we ever liked.'"[29] Despite his frustration with the contemporary southern soul styles employed by Mississippi artists, Johnson has helped foster new movements in and attention to the blues as inspired by the gritty sounds of its Hill Country practitioners. His focus is on the blues' handmade qualities, which are rarely a primary aesthetic priority for contemporary Mississippi blues players, who dress in bright silk shirts, shiny cell phone clips, and neon Japanese guitars for their Saturday Night jukin'.

To the community in which it is being created, performed, updated, and renewed, the Delta blues is not climbing into the grave anytime soon. Delta bluesman Terry "Big T" Williams eloquently describes the way music nourishes, and is in turn nourished by, the contemporary blues community. "People say that the blues is dyin' down here. Well, every time they say that, every time it comes out of their mouth, it means the blues is still goin' on. It actually doesn't change. It's still the same. What they do is modify it. They take it to another level."[30] In fact, the Delta blues is sustained and reversioned by members of the blues community, who employ the spirits of tradition and creativity to create sustenance amidst oppression. The living blues, embedded in the context of the community-centered performance, is a tool for transcendence rather than a death rattle of resignation.

A Saturday Night in the Delta

Residents of the Mississippi Delta take Saturday night seriously. Revelers put on their best threads, pick up a favorite bottle from the liquor store, and make a glowing appearance at the club. Clarksdale and its surrounding areas seem to awaken on Saturday night as the sparse regional population gathers at dozens of clubs and juke joints. At least twenty of these nightspots are nestled in or near downtown Clarksdale, and most are closed during the week, see a modicum of business of Fridays, and then staff up for Saturday, the end of the region's traditional six-day plantation workweek. Creaky single-wide trailers in the tiny plantation towns of Bobo and Alligator glow with Christmas lights, barbeque stands billow before tucked-away juke joints on the edges of town, and the downtown streets become lined with vehicles drawn from throughout Coahoma County.

Clarksdale's "grown folks" find a favorite venue in Adel's Delta Blues Room. The club caters mainly to professionals who work in nearby schools, chain restaurants, big-box stores and casinos. It has an urban, dressy feel, enhanced by its location in the heart of Clarksdale's modest business district. The cover charge, collected by a serious middle-aged woman with impossibly glossy hair, is seven dollars, a substantial price for a night out in the Delta. The interior of the room is lined with a series of small and medium-sized tables at which couples and groups of friends sit. The space is just large enough to hold its seventy-five or so patrons, who all seem to know each other. New arrivals run a gamut of greetings as they find their place in the room. DJ Dr. Pepper, a favorite in this part of the Delta, expertly conducts the festivities. The idea is to get patrons on the dance floor through a series of carefully chosen soul, rap, and R&B songs and shout-outs to the crowd over his microphone. The crowd rallies to the dance floor for line dances like the "Electric Slide" and the wildly popular "Cupid Shuffle," in which the entire room moves in tandem until the line "walk it by yourself" calls for dancers to turn any way they please. Dr. Pepper speaks back to the music over his mic, referring to the Keyshia Cole song he is fading out.

Shome-on. Pretty Lady!
Shome-on! Lost evening . . .
Last night baby, and I ain't lyin' . . .
Miss Emma—Miss Emma, now,
I really think you got somethin' on your mind.
Yeah, I'm talkin' to ya, pretty lady.
Yeah, I'm gonna ease your mind
Because I think you got somethin'
[the crowd talks in unison here] on your mind.
You know what I think you got on your mind, darlin'?
Do you know what I think you got on your mind?
Huh?
This is what I think you got on your mind.
Right about now.

Dr. Pepper launches the next song in his set, a sexed-up contemporary R&B version of the black spiritual "Steal Away." The song's meaning has been transposed from a signified call to a hidden prayer meeting to a song about illicit love.

A few blocks away, at the intersection of Delta Avenue and Blues Alley, a dance club called Millennium glows for Saturday night. A barbeque stand smokes outside the club as younger Clarksdalians—those within a decade of the club's twenty-seven-year-old minimum age, filter through the door. The club looks small and quaint from the outside, but management has removed panels to reveal lofted ceilings. The walls of the barroom are painted in Afrocentric reds and greens, and an oversized, framed black-and-white portrait of Bob Marley holds court over the pool table. Through the door at the far end of the barroom is a cavernous back dancehall that belies the size of the lot. It's big enough to hold over twenty card tables with folding chairs, and the dance floor—a clear space at the far end of the room, near the DJ's table—might hold a hundred patrons if the DJ is on his game.

The sophisticated crowd trends toward the early thirties, and the DJs seamlessly mix two decades' worth of underground dance songs and bass classics, mostly via Miami, Detroit, and Atlanta. I am reminded of my favorite dance clubs in the primarily black and Latino neighborhoods of West Oakland, and my group of Delta friends and I feel comfortable amid the friendly crowd. A

DJ Dr. Pepper of the Delta Blues Room at work. Photograph by the author.

ponytailed young man jokingly vogues with his female friends while a duo of zoot-suit dandies, their fingernails freshly buffed, sit impassively behind dark sunglasses at a back table. Style is at a premium tonight; a solid young woman struts through the crowd in a glammed-up vest and top hat while a trio of girlfriends in Apple-Bottom hot pants—a favorite brand in the Delta—and crushed velvet cutout tops hang together at a table. The vibe is tolerant and upbeat.

Hip-hop clubs catering to eighteen-and-up crowds rise and fall every few months in this part of the Delta. Currently the most popular include the Sports Bar and Annie Bell's, out on the sparse end of Business 61. On Fridays and Saturdays the parking lots of defunct dollar stores across the street from these clubs fill up with cars, many of which sport bright paint jobs, big shiny rims, or homemade body customizations. Dirty South hip-hop hits, ranging from the Miami booty bass of the early nineties, Atlanta crunk and trap favorites, Mississippi artist David Banner's banging club anthems, Houston's heavy screwed and chopped artists, and New Orleans' Big Tymers and Lil' Wayne are mixed together on the playlist. Current BET favorites from Nelly to T.I. and T-Pain are favored. Reggae, dance pop, and classic Memphis bass also figure into the mix. Many of the songs include embedded dance instructions, including Lil' Jon's "Snap Your Fingers," UNK's "Two-Step," and Shop Boyz' current hit, "Party Like a Rock Star," which involves rocking back and forth with an air guitar in hand. These clubs get packed every weekend with three hundred or more young people from Clarksdale and its neighboring counties, and their dance floors extend to the bulk, if not the entirety, of the floor space. Papachasa, a local hip-hop management group with connections to up-and-coming rap outfits in Jackson and Memphis, owns Club Champagne, which has both enjoyed recent popularity and suffered from occasional gang violence.

Bluesman "Mr. Tater the Music Maker" and guitarist Kenny Brown at Ground Zero Blues Club. Photograph by the author.

Throughout the New World district, just past the intersection of the old crossroads, neighborhood bars provide a relaxed atmosphere for regulars. Here, locals gather to chat with gregarious bar owners, swap news from wide extended families, tell tall tales about the travails of their workweek, and joke loudly about current events. Conversation is the main attraction for those who are less interested in dancing. Messenger's, a business that has thrived under black ownership for well over a century, offers a series of pool tables and antique dominoes boards. R&B, pop, classic blues, and crunk CDs fill the tireless jukebox as the gamers' cues and tiles clack. Owners George and Myrtle Messenger, popular members of their community, warmly situate their customers with rib tips and cold beers. These are the Delta juke joints in the most classic sense of the term; the mood at these clubs is shaped by the collaborative medium of the jukebox. Alan Lomax is said to have conducted fieldwork at Messenger's during the 1940s and 1980s. Red's Lounge is situated a block away. Wade Walton's Barbershop, the former workspace of Clarksdale's famous "Singing Barber," has been converted into a tiny juke joint called "Big D's Blues Club," for locals who enjoy the southern soul jukebox and their inimitable Monday night wrestling and fish fry party.

Young white locals enjoy nightlife at clubs like the Underground, a pop dancehall that caters mostly to college students visiting home from Ole Miss. But the most popular club in town is Ground Zero Blues Club, a business partnership between actor Morgan Freeman (who grew up in a town just east of the Delta) and a local member of the planter aristocracy. Here, tourism industry heavyweights, members of the planter elite, blues festival transplants, tourists, blues-loving college students, and the occasional extended black family reunion group occupy long tables to scout for local blues musicians and visiting celebrities. Puttin' Hatchett holds court at his personal player's table as tourists test their card skills and snap photos. The stage, lofted above the shoulders of the crowd, features weekly appearances by blues transplants Stan Street and Blue Mikey, as well as a revolving set of contemporary Delta blues musicians, who play smooth versions of crowd favorites during their rationed monthly money gig. Despite the club's strict blues-only booking policy, "Mustang Sally," "The Sky Is Crying," and "Just My Imagination"—songs that fall into the record industry's classic R&B, rock, or soul music rubrics—are standards. The local bluesmen, deftly switching from their improvisatory juke-joint stylings to accommodate the mixed crowd, are likely to throw in a Muddy Waters or John Lee Hooker tune as well. Visitors are encouraged to write their names on the plywood walls with Sharpie; they stake their claim on the Delta with an indelible mark.

Catch a Greyhound Bus and Ride

Even as the specter of death seems to threaten to end the practice and practitioner of the Delta blues in the popular imagination, blues communities continue to create music on their own terms. In the 1960s and 1970s a new wave of ethnographers undertook work on the music of the Mississippi Delta. Researchers including David Evans, Jeff Todd Titon, Paul Oliver, and Samuel Charters, informed by new global discourses surrounding race and power, engaged the blues communities of the Delta in depth.[31] Instead of relying on the observations and assumptions of established scholarship, these scholars used new ethnographic techniques to open up space for the blues artists to represent themselves. This second round of folkloristic collection in the Delta blues also allowed for a look at musical ruptures and continuities over time.

William R. Ferris, a lifelong Mississippi resident, spent many years building relationships with the blues communities of the Mississippi Delta. Working closely with a number of Delta bluesmen, including James "Son" Thomas, "Pine Top" Floyd, and Wade Walton, Ferris was invited into the interior spaces of the Delta: house parties, juke joints, and churches. Here, he witnessed the music of the Delta within the richness of its context. In his book on the topic, *Blues from the Delta*, as well as a series of short films, Ferris privileges the voices

Wade "The Singing Barber" Walton's barbershop, where Ferris conducted ethnography in the 1970s, remains a functional juke joint in Clarksdale today. Photograph by Andrew Kropa.

of the blues community, representing aspects of the living blues that previous researchers had overlooked. Ferris showed that Delta blues singers simultaneously work from memorized lyrics while adding improvisatory lines called *make-ups* that responded to the situation at hand. He documents the rich and vibrant cultural connections between the blues community of the Delta and those of urban areas, especially Chicago. Most importantly, his work highlights the nature of the blues as a tool of community-building and of transcendence, rather than a function of pathos. In this sense, "singing the blues" is the salve for (rather than a symptom of) "having the blues." Blues "talker" Robert Shaw of Memphis illustrates the importance of blues performance in fulfilling these functions:

> Everything here is the blues. It goes back to feelings. How you feel today. You know blues has always been something that you don't have to be black to have the blues. You can have blues, wake up in the morning and something is blue on you—you understand what I'm talking about? Around your bed, and you done got blue, you understand? . . .
>
> Now I'm going to tell you about the life of the blues. Now this is the blues:
>
> *Living ain't easy and times are tough.*
> *Money is scarce, and we all can't get enough.*
> *Now my insurance is lapsed and food is low,*
> *And the landlord is knockin' at my door.*
> *Last night I dreamed I died,*
> *The undertaker came to take me for a ride.*
> *I couldn't afford a casket,*
> *And embalming was so high,*
> *I got up from my sick bed because I was too poor to die.*
> *Now ain't that blue?*[32]

In his stylized blues narrative, Shaw, a hat salesman at Lansky's men's shop on Memphis's famed Beale Street, demonstrates how quick wit can help even the unluckiest of souls rise from the dead. In his adaptation of blues stylings to the unaccompanied "rap," Shaw also shows how easily the blues can shift in form (from sung to spoken) and retain its character, or core aesthetic. By connecting the Delta blues to sermons, rhyming games (and other "blues talk"), gospel music, and deejay styles, Ferris illustrates the shifting nature of the blues genre and breaks stereotypes of the blues as a rigid, dated, and tragic expressive mode.

Ferris's findings dovetailed with those of researchers John W. Work and Samuel Adams, African American researchers from Fisk University who conducted extensive ethnographic work in the music and culture of the Mississippi Delta. These scholars created the Coahoma County Study through which Alan Lomax visited the Delta in 1941 and 1942. According to recent historical discoveries by music researchers Robert Gordon and Bruce Nemerov, the Fisk scholars were pressured to include Lomax (at that time, a Library of Congress songcatcher) in their research plans. As the Fisk scholars spent years in deep engagement with the blues communities of the Delta (including embedding themselves in the community as low-wage cotton pickers), Lomax made do with a couple short excursions. While Lomax's self-described research methods involved brief visits with artists, the Fisk scholars took their time, getting to know members of the community. They catalogued the eclectic mix of records available on local jukeboxes and found that the Delta blues, rather than emerging from a vacuum, were created in conversation with global musical styles. John Work was the first outside researcher to locate a young Muddy Waters on a plantation near Clarksdale, as well as draw important connections between children's games, sacred song, vernacular speech and the Delta blues. The work of the Fisk scholars was purportedly misplaced by the Library of Congress in the 1940s and later recovered in Lomax's personal archive. If their findings regarding the cosmopolitan and open-ended nature of the genre had been released in their time, they might have broken open the notions of authenticity that have nearly parochialized and dated the Delta blues to death.

Intertextual studies of Afrodiasporic expressive modes sparked groundbreaking discourses on the function of aesthetics in cultural meaning-making in the 1970s and 1980s. Robert Farris Thompson represented a dynamic black diasporic culture in terms of a series of aesthetic signifiers including rhythm, coolness, flash, polyphony, and improvisation. This creative character could be easily translated from music to textiles to dance, always lending itself to new interpretations. Lawrence Levine, in his *Black Culture and Black Consciousness*, finds "culture is not a fixed condition but a process: the product of interaction between the past and the present."[33] In this nexus, he concludes, lies the transcendent quality of black verbal art.

> Again and again oral expressive culture reveals a pattern of simultaneous acculturation and revitalization . . . Black verbal art makes clear that a people is, in Ralph Ellison's phrase, "more than the sum of its brutalization." "We had joys back there in St. Louis," Dick Gregory remembered in his account of his poverty-stricken youth, "joys that made us want to live just as surely as the pains taught us how to live."[34]

To study oral/musical practice is to study the confluence of tradition and emergence that characterizes the power of the word. Portia Maultsby, drawing from the work of Thompson and Levine, describes the emergent qualities of black expressive culture in terms of a series of conceptual approaches to music-making. She finds that over time, a diasporic adherence to aesthetic rather than formal features of communication has allowed artists to retain a distinct set of practices while pushing and reconfiguring the boundaries of genre. Expressive styles do not expire in this paradigm; rather, they retain currency by shifting forms.[35]

Cheryl Keyes, a folklorist and ethnomusicologist with strong roots in linguistics, approaches her fieldwork as a participant/observer. She draws her data from myriad sources, including song lyrics and musical notation, oral histories from the popular press, and her own ethnographic accounts of hip-hop shows and in-depth interviews with rap artists. She states explicitly that the discourse on hip-hop should go beyond lyrical analysis to incorporate ethnographic work. Concerned with postmodern analyses of the hip-hop aesthetic, Keyes points out that the genre is "a cultural process over time" and a "dynamic tradition."[36] In her representation, the blues, rather than dying out, brings contemporary musical forms to life through cultural "reversioning—the foregrounding . . . of African-centered concepts in response to cultural takeovers, ruptures and appropriations."[37] Reversioning is a two-way conversation between black American music and expressive culture throughout the diaspora.

Rather than trace African phrases or rhythms through American history, Keyes mines the messiness of its practice, in which musical change is less a linear development than a shifting creative field that brings vast cultural elements into conversation. In the core aesthetic paradigm, the styles manifest in black song translate easily into other creative modes that might include dance, paralinguistic expressions, signifyin' (or double-meaning), melody, rhythmic patterns, foot-tapping, and fashion. She also points out that the early hip-hop of the 1970s Bronx emerged at a time of changes in radio formatting, shifting geopolitics of the Bronx, and the appearance of new technologies—all of which help account for the remixing of traditional musical elements in the form of a new aesthetic movement. This focus on processes of change—on the creation of the new from the materials of tradition—allows for a richer understanding of the dynamic relationship of hip-hop to the blues. The concept of reversioning allows the blues, funk, hip-hop, and gospel to reflect distinct social movements in history while also forming a larger, renewable nexus of black musical creativity. By applying Keyes's conclusions to the situation in the Mississippi Delta, we can begin to unpack the rigid concepts of blues authenticity that lead to the disenfranchisement of young regional artists from the benefits of cultural tourism.

A new cultural tourism emerged throughout the 1990s and 2000s in the Mississippi Delta, where contemporary films including *O Brother, Where Art Thou?* and Martin Scorcese's documentary series *The Blues: A Musical Journey*, as well as a spate of Delta blues cover albums and reissues, revived international interest in the genre. Fundamental to a healthy relationship between the popular realm and the living blues is a willingness of the marketplace to accept the music on its own terms. As the blues continue to unfold, over time and within the context of the communities in which it was created, new meanings and styles are reversioned from the old. A century after its popular dissemination by W. C. Handy and others, in Mississippi the Delta blues remains central to community life. Vibrant, rich, and loaded with the potential for improvisation and transformation, the blues unfolds in private spaces where locals gather. It is dependent on the dynamic of live performance, in which the lines between audience and performer, art and everyday life, and tradition and innovation fall away. The blues is a celebration, replenishing the elements of community and creativity that have sustained the blues people of the Mississippi Delta despite oppressive socioeconomic circumstances. It is not a simply reactive form, a lamentation; rather, the music of the Mississippi Delta is the site for creativity, strength, and transcendence—a positive affirmation of life at the Crossroads.

Residents of the contemporary Delta do not envision their blues as a dark figure alone in a cotton field, but feel them through a common cultural spirit that binds the blues community and sustains its energy as it moves into a new century. In the Mississippi Delta, a site of the nation's most extreme poverty, places like Red's provide space for the expression and renewal of a community's life force. The community constantly creates new modes of communication from the bright fibers of the old. Its meaning is always of the moment. In the very act of performing the blues, practitioners sublimate their sadness into life-affirming, collective creativity. The ultimate product of this oral/musical conjuration is emergent meaning, created at the powerful crossroads of tradition and possibility.

Getting Schooled in the Love Zone

The Love Zone is encased in siding and cobalt blue house paint and situated on the periphery of Sumner, Mississippi. Sumner lies off Highway 49 like a scattered jack, halfway down the Mississippi Delta's dusty spine and thirty minutes south of Clarksdale. In hot July this part of the highway is lined with lush green cotton plants, bursting with the thick, wet bolls that make up the fabric of the local economy. Wild veins of swamp and kudzu delineate the edges of the passing plantations; the humidity tinges the atmosphere a heavy yellow to match the tan silt layer atop the rich local soil.

Music filters from the dark door of the juke joint. As we drive up in our overheating car, I get the feeling that it will be cool inside. Window unit air conditioners, chained heavily to the outside of the building, grunt in recognition. There is laughter on the other side. I want to be inside more than anything.

I'm an outsider here; I've been an outsider in the Delta all year, inserting my face in spaces that belong to other people, rooms that were not built for me. To the group of elder African American men and FUBU-wearing youngsters gathered before the deep door of the juke joint, I am a potential spoiler, here to self-consciously gawk at their good times, and they are surprised; not even the savviest of the overbearing blues tourists make it to this hideaway. The woman at the door takes our three dollars apiece and smiles gingerly, pointing us toward the bar in the bright corner of the otherwise shadowy cavern. There, the gorgeous owner and bartender takes our order generously, trading our four dollars for two 22-oz. cans of Bud Light, wrapped kindly in layers of printed paper towels for insulation. We seem okay, maybe just lost and thirsty. She hands us a couple paper plates and insists that we pile our plates with the first round of food. The catfish shines gold, the bowl of greens runs deep. The beer is cold, foamy, and perfect.

It's stretched-out Sunday in the Delta, a time for hours to last even longer than usual, when the blues starts as soon as church gets out and lasts long into the night. After lunch, the music begins to kick in. A revolving group of musicians emerge from the crowd, scattered to cool, dark corners painted in words and stars. They assemble, those incredible familiar Delta blues players, part of the handful perpetually touring the local circuit, including Earl the Pearl and Harvell Thomas. Into the fray walks Terry "Big T" Williams, who plugs in and begins to riff immediately. The room becomes electric. Big T works his small

Guitarist, singer and composer Terry "Big T" Williams, who played with Clarksdale's all-star Jelly Roll Kings, is a favorite blues performer in the Delta. Photograph by Timothy Gordon.

crowd by approaching each lady present, looking her in the eye, and playing real close as she dances around his heft, nearly intertwined with his guitar. His trick is to suddenly pull away and rejoin his band, leaving his woman to dance alone or to find a new partner to work up. Big T's signature is "Catfish Blues," the famous old Delta rhyme: "Well I wish I was a catfish / Swimmin' in the deep blue sea / I'd have all! All you good-lookin' women / Swimmin' after me. . . Oh, swimmin' after Big T."[38] The song is played as a chugalong dirge, with a revolving riff that jumps and flails from time to time, like a school of spawning fish. The vibe is utterly sexual and infectious. The way Big T plays the song, it lasts for half an hour. It winds and rings until the entire joint is churning at his command. As the song continues, Big T improvises new melodic phrases that echo previous lines and then changes them slightly. A man shouts approval from his barstool and Big T answers with a similar sound. A woman begins to dance by herself in a slow grind, and Big T responds with a circuitous riff.

As Big T works his way through the crowd, a young man approaches our table. Friendly, robust, and eager, with an oversized T-shirt and white baseball cap perched atop his thick natural, he stands with his friend LaMont, a regular at Red's Juke Joint, and tells me that he has heard I am interested in interviewing Delta rappers. I remember chatting with LaMont a few weeks back about the local music scene.

TopNotch the Villain asks me if I would like to see him rap.

We step outside into the heavy air of the Mississippi night. Giant palmetto bugs and families of mosquitoes fly into our faces as we lean against the posts

Jerome "TopNotch the Villain" Williams. Photograph by the author.

outside of the club, and curious regulars, many of whom we have met in the club, gather around us. TopNotch closes his eyes for a moment, swallows. He pats his chest, beatboxes behind his hand, and then begins to rock back on his heels as he spits a stunning improvised rhyme similar to dozens I have recorded since:

Who's to say my thoughts came from a glass of Kool-Aid
Drunk it up and when I'm sittin' back up in the shade
Summertime for summer rhymes
that I can just spit
For same rhymes the same minds
That make my boys quit

Put that up on your life
And make sure your right time tick
Cause this is TopNotch
And you done heard the lyricist
From a boy
That came from Clarksdale
And made it hard here and
it's hardly felt, thinkin'

that it's hardly the
Air that makes everybody breathe
and then conceive of good feelings
But then again put it back up on your bicycle wheelin's
Took it down from priceless killings
And it's killing your soul

And now I see the cats here
They all out of control
Now let me grab hold of respect
And then put it to paper
But I call collect for fear that
Life is spectacular
Words from the Dracula but don't have them fangs
The only things that I have
Is my pain

So I spit this
From the outside of my heart
To the inside of my lungs
And that the last breath that I spit it
You will hear this song

And every words that I'm copywritin'
they will receive
That it's the knowledge, top dog
From your boy, T.O.P.[39]

Chapter Two

New Blues in the Mississippi Delta

You have Michael Jackson and Lionel Richie and just a variety of music. Even back then, when the blues was real real popular here, every Saturday morning, you know, you would see people outside in the community, barbequin', just drinkin' beer, smokin', and that's how I feel like I got introduced to the blues. Music's been around me all my life, so it's a no-brainer to get in this.
—TopNotch the Villain, Mississippi, 2005[1]

I'm gonner make up the next song up all at once and see what I can do. Now it ain't no song. I ain't got no music or nothing to go with it. I'm gonner see what I can do from the root and branch.
—Sonny Boy Watson, Mississippi, 1968[2]

When I met twenty-six-year-old Jerome Williams at the threshold of the Love Zone that Sunday night, I was inspired to learn more about his work. At that time, he was spending four 12-hour days a week as a telemetry technician at Northwest Regional Medical Center, watching electronic blips on a medical computer screen. The hospital is situated on the periphery of the Brickyard, and it is a source of the few dependable jobs in town. TopNotch had been at it for two years, earning training certificates and new skills as he went. He was even photographed for the local newspaper for bravely putting out a fire on his floor when an oxygen tank exploded. On regular days he would hover in his white coat near the twenty-patient EKG monitor for up to twelve hours at a time, its tiny white dots bouncing in sync with the heartbeats of the second-floor patients. It was his duty to check their rhythms, making sure that each beat fell right in its own time, strong and even.

When he raps, Jerome goes by the name of TopNotch the Villain. He throws a black baseball cap atop his head and an oversized T-shirt over his bulky frame. He is a freestyle rapper, improvising and remixing verse on the fly, adapting his rhythm and rhyme to his immediate environment. Each of his raps is substantially different from the next, composed expertly in the moment. He sets his beat, strong and even, by patting his chest and sputtering with his mouth, and then begins to spit:

Local boy,
Stayin' poster boy
All about the grain
Never worried about some change
Unless I'm a get some a change
Made my chance
Did my thing
Like I did my homework
But it wasn't from the school
But it was from Delta streets I worked

Everything could end my life
And disrespect be put in dirt
Did my hand and shake my hand

Shake my hand
and give the Lord
All the blessing all the praise
But it was my hand they raise

When they saw the title one
Knowing that the title son
Giving me the whole city
Giving me the lock down
Really just to shock you
If you thought about it top down

TopNotch
Hold the bill
Hold the grain
Hold the steel
Hold the mayo
Hold your meal
Hold the flow
Hold your feels

This is back
Through some years
Through some time
Measure points
Making sure
Everybody feelin' they relate to joints
Pulled the cross
Did some thought
Did some thinking
Did some training
Did forever
Then came to bubble out you cranium
Still you're drainin' 'em
With some long type of loop
Everything the Delta said

They had to be fluid, but the
Difference between smart and the
Difference between stupid
It's a fine line and everybody had to go through it
Believe this
When the people come to the hood they receive this
And make sure that nothin' ends your life
but what's prestigious
Achieving it
Thinking that all the thing's the same
Make hood for the love but
Love brings pain[3]

TopNotch's rhythms follow his extended exhalations, long breaths that allow him to rapid-fire poetic verses and then punctuate them with shorter lyrical blasts. He keeps an even 4/4 meter throughout his composition even as he plays with myriad polyrhythms within a piece, some staccato, some rolling over the course of two or three measures. His "receive," "prestigious," and "achieve" lines echo West Coast artist Tupac Shakur's wide-open delivery, rolling up in pitch to accent the repetitive vowel sounds, making space for more chaotic double-time wordplay in the breaks. As I recorded this rhyme during our first interview session together, I recognized TopNotch's ability to weave extended rhymes, thick with meaning, in the moment of performance. In his freestyle, I could hear the

Clarksdalians are known for elaborate and inventive foodways traditions. Photograph by the author.

rhythms of the blues, the complexity of poetry, the songlike phrasing of the West-Coast G-Funk hip-hop collective. The style, in its thick totality, was all his. Jerome and I would meet on his breaks from the hospital. Our interviews became extended conversations. In our second interview, he told me that he wanted to be more involved in my work to document the contemporary music of the Delta. Shortly thereafter, he offered to show me some of the places where he and his friends make music. For TopNotch, sharing his story, his art, and his message with the world is part and parcel of his mission.

After our first few meetings, TopNotch asks me to clear my schedule for a few days so that he can surprise me with a custom-made tour. He wants to show me where his music comes from. I hop into TopNotch's car behind the Filling Station on Highway 49 for my weekend-long lesson. It is just before 9 p.m., a cold day for a Delta October, and the dark streets are abandoned. It is not easy to describe the way it feels to ride in an old Caprice, padded with a bouncy burgundy interior, down these old streets late at night: like suspension in an outer space made of tin, concrete and fine, spongy brown soil. The conversation is personal, then professional, and then interspersed with long moments of cruising silence. TopNotch has become our guide. This convenience store, Top tells me, is where he was almost shot on two different occasions as a clerk a few years ago. His cousin, he continues, was killed by gunfire in a neighboring town in 2001, accidentally shot while pushing a young woman out of the line of fire. In the years since the interview, I have witnessed TopNotch mourn his cousin's death in many freestyle raps, and the tolls of violent death he counts in his songs have continued to grow.

Minutes later, we ride past TopNotch's first childhood home, a modest box in the Clarksdale subdivision of Lyon. It was here that he first learned to rhyme, adapting his own message to the rhythms of L.L. Cool J's "I'm Bad" at the age of five. His mother, Jeweline Williams, was a poet herself and encouraged Jerome to perform for his family and friends. Economic circumstances forced the family to move to a two-room blue house on the overgrown edges of the tiny Delta town of Crowder. He escaped trouble at home by joining the choir at First Oak Grove Missionary Baptist Church, where Miss Martha Raybon, his choir director, encouraged him to improvise new lyrics while performing. Although Jerome's pastor criticized him for "jookin' in the church," the congregation responded with shouts and dancing when the teen led the choir with new lyrics, composed on the spot.

> Yes, they would say, "You sure pulled it out." I'd say that it was not the fact that what we had was not plentiful, but it was the fact that what we had was our song and singing like that. It was the fact that we didn't have anything that made us enjoy making up those lyrics. I think God inspired us—that he was just taking care of his children. When life is too much to bear, he'll help us breathe easy.[4]

After school, he banded with friends and played the dozens, honing his rhyming skills.[5] The most eloquent battle participant was awarded with the respect of his schoolmates and the inevitability of further challenges. TopNotch excelled at the dozens and soon developed verbal battle skills beyond the rhymed couplets featured in the game. TopNotch drives us to meet his cousin Andrew Jones, himself an uproarious jokester, who was TopNotch's sparring partner at school. Drew provides TopNotch and me with a couple beers at his kitchen table and tells me about his cousin's skills during their school years together.

> It had came to the point that [TopNotch] would stand outside, they be sittin' there, after class or whatever, talkin' or whatever. And he'd get to rappin' against somebody else, and . . . he'd start from the month, start with January and go all the way to December. Our eyes would be like [widens his eyes]. And he would just go straight through. This man just put a year out on somebody. Just talk about a year against this dude: "January you ain't this. February, you ain't gonna *be* this. March, you shouldn't have gone against me." And he would just go. Man, he just talked about a whole year. I'd hate to see him five years from now.[6]

Andrew and TopNotch were among the poorest kids in school and learned to parlay schoolyard chiding into an education in quick wit. They tell of a single pair of MC Hammer–style pants, the epitome of late-eighties youth fashion, being rotated between eight family members. Jerome always kept them longer than his allotted share. Although he was constantly teased about his country style and ill-fitting clothes, he became one of the most popular students in school thanks to his social finesse and verbal eloquence.

But the challenges kept coming. Amid a series of job losses and health crises, TopNotch's family fell into a class of poverty that was extreme even by Delta standards. Not long after Jerome's performance debut at the little church in Crowder, economic misfortune forced him to move again. Seventeen members of TopNotch's extended family spent years piled in a tiny Clarksdale project apartment, where they divided the income from a single disability check between the entire group. Another of TopNotch's cousins, Taurus Metcalf, remembers going to sleep each night with a headache from malnutrition during this period; the family was too poor to provide any meals after school lunch. As the children lay in bed with their stomachs cramping, TopNotch used the power of the word to push their hopes forward, according to Metcalf:

> He was rappin' inspirational stuff. "Get your head up, keep pushin'," things of that nature. He used to always rap that when we was little. "Keep your head up, cousin, keep pushin'." So. I still can remember that, so . . . even when I'm married and got kids, even though things happened to me, I'm "keep your head up, keep pushin'," you know, it was just inspirational. It moves you. Keep your blood flowin'.[7]

Even in his childhood, TopNotch found that his poetic and musical skills set him apart from the group. When he used the word to invigorate the church, impress his peers, or help his family reckon with their empty stomachs, he was also taking on the responsibility of leadership. His talent, persistent training, and generosity shaped this role for him early on, and he has accepted the mantle with pride.

TopNotch and I take a break from his self-styled biographical tour to drink a beer—a cold Bud Light bowling pin, wrapped in a light brown lunch sack for insulation—on the corner of a country store in Marks. He wants me to see what people do on a Friday night in the small plantation towns that encircle the small cities of the Delta, and it is not long before I see the benefits of swatting away the mosquitoes outdoors. Every few minutes a car full of friends arrives to buy a case of cans; Friday nights are more often spent at home with close friends than out at the clubs. TopNotch knows them all. He is very popular, known as a friendly member of the community and an accomplished freestyle battler. It does not matter that he moved to Clarksdale thirteen years ago; the constant circulation of the Delta's population allows residents to claim numerous hometowns. He tells me that he has rapped with and against many of these acquaintances on nights just like this.

"Hey, Jerome!" an old neighbor shouts out as they recognize his face in the twilight. Then he looks at me, mildly uncomfortable and wan in a pink plaid shirt.

"Hello, hello," he says politely.

Sometimes TopNotch introduces me as a friend from North Carolina, which results in the friendly but impassive Delta response to social surprises, "Ohhhh. Okay?" Another prompts me to tell more: "All the way from Carolina, huh?"

I tell them that I study hip-hop and they tell me that I have found the right guide in TopNotch. They will have more questions for TopNotch later, when he can take the time to explain our ethnographic experiment and burgeoning friendship out of my earshot.

And just as TopNotch is encouraged to rhyme by these members of his community, he teaches young people in his neighborhood how to flow. Today, friends and neighbors often approach him on the street or at his home, looking for a few pointers for their own rap style and knowing he is willing to teach them. His favorite technique is to challenge a student to engage in an improvised rhymed conversation, encouraging and coaching her style and flow. It is up to the student to insert her favorite rhymes into the context of live performance in a way that makes sense. During one of our conversations, TopNotch's eleven-year-old neighbor, Kevon Jurden, approaches him for a lesson in style. He starts with a memorized verse and then, challenged by his mentor, improvises an appropriate segue to another memorized fragment.

Kevon Jurden: Now I be in my Grandma's house
thinkin' 'bout good things
and I be up in the kitchen tryin' to cook me some pork and beans
I'm a rhyme
Listen if you don't like it you can go look from behind
And I'm a make my cash and you can look from the past
Like a blast from the past I'm gonna last.

TopNotch: And outlast the criminals
and outlast the snakes
keep your hearts in the real
and just don't deal with the fake
Grass for the lawn, baby,

Ain't gotta deal with the snakes
Just do whatever it takes just to make no mistakes.
Set 'em free.

Kevon Jurden: I'm a set 'em free and let 'em know what I came for
And if you don't like it you can go in the house door[8]

During his own late teenhood, Jerome, looking for a way out, joined the military and settled in Fort Rucker, Alabama. The endeavor ended in a crippling back injury for him, as well as a sudden military discharge. Just after his dismissal, Jerome stumbled upon a block party near the base, where he hopped on stage to compete in a freestyle rap contest. He promptly and decisively won, eliciting a huge response from the crowd. It was his first public performance, and it was the answer to his prayers. Upon the announcement of his victory, he was asked his name by the MC, and chose "TopNotch the Villain"—a tag he claims just rolled off his tongue. Like the bluesmen, he chose to adopt a performance (or "other") name, creating his own identity as an alternative to the one on his birth certificate. Tricia Rose finds that "taking on new names and identities offers 'prestige form below' in the face of limited access to legitimate forms of status attainment" for hip-hop artists.[9] The practice of self-naming is a ritual within Afrodiasporic communities, a testimony to the power of the word and an acknowledgment of the tricky nature of identities that are always in process.

Signifying Personal Style

The art and aesthetics that shape TopNotch's verbal style are the result of many years of talking lessons in the church house, at home, in the schoolyard, and over the radio waves. His freestyle is unmistakably developed, the product of sheer talent, relentless practice, and innovation. He is an expert craftsman, able to turn the written word or a visual semiotic into pure rhythm. Not only does he focus on the rhyme and flow of his compositions, he also visualizes his work in terms of stanzas (similar to the blues musicians' "twelve bars"), poetic forms, and shapes. Take, for instance, his use of the following rhythmic vamp, emphasized by its juxtaposition with longer poetic lines:

Words of the talk if the talk got [pause] bigger

You're still [pause] choppin'
I'm still [pause] blockin'

Whether coasts [pause] knew it
They all Top [pause] Notchin'

This is all aggressor, me I'm selector[10]

TopNotch explains this pattern, a rhythm he honed to suit his own rhyming style:

> I have put a little pause in [my rhyming style], like when you start your paragraph, you indent the first line. From lookin' at a paragraph, that's where I got the pattern from, from looking at a paragraph. That's where I developed that style from, believe it or not, honest to God. . . .
>
> No one ever would have thought that I would have used that particular style. . . . When I implement it, they're like "Oh-ho!" They get their head moving, and I know that I got 'em and that it's a style people like, so I just stay with it.[11]

TopNotch's use of intertextual reference to deepen the poetic/rhythmic medium showcases his skill as a verbal practitioner and earns him the approval of his community. He regularly employs aesthetic thought in shaping a rhyme or a rhythmic pattern, sampling from a world of local and popular song lyrics, sounds, and ideas to conjure new meanings and levels of conversation. The result is the amazement and respect of his peers, as well TopNotch's status in the alternative social structures of black Delta leadership. He is rewarded for his eloquence with access to better jobs, invitations to perform, and even a discount at his favorite clothing store. In the Delta, where black life is steeped in the diasporic aesthetics of orality, the ability to create conversation between traditional and emergent styles is held at a premium. "When you got a style, you sample, either from the present or past, you sample, and that's how you develop a style," explains TopNotch.[12]

TopNotch's use of aesthetics suggest further metanarrative context. Barbara Babcock describes this practice as ". . . innumerable devices such as naming, quoting, onomatopoeia, the use of different styles, pronoun shifts, changes in channel or media . . . [and] the intermixture of narrative and song or prose and verse which are implicitly metanarrational."[13] TopNotch employs each of these devices in his work in conjunction with paralinguistic ones, such as gestural and facial expressions, melody, dramatic pauses, and rhythm.

> I guess that's urgency or how the way I feel. You know, you just want to get out there. If I'm speaking real talk, and don't see people move their head or feel like they're not feeling me, I'll change my style to the point where they're like 'Oh,

> man, that man's real fancy, he's just really goin' off!" That would make a person want to change the style. When I kick into another gear, I'm gonna overcome what I came with the last time.[14]

Over the course of my years of work with TopNotch, I have witnessed him perform his rap in myriad social and cultural situations: in conversation with a friend, in staged concert performances with his group, and to a roomful of academics in the halls of the University of North Carolina. The ability to translate his work across these cultural boundaries demonstrates his remarkable flexibility in style and symbolic structure. He tailors his raps in these situations by adding or removing levels and styles of cultural coding in order to make certain meanings in his work apparent to his audience. In this way he obscures, or "signifies," another set of meanings, depending on the level of sympathy and cultural awareness of his audience. In a rhymed conversation with a young neighbor, he will patiently work through simple, boasting vamps about his hometown, while in league with his crew, he will throw out signified references to mutual friends or neighbors, all while maintaining a more accessible narrative for my own ears. I often fail to catch the deeper messages until TopNotch himself decodes them with me as I transcribe and interpret his work. For a recent mixed Delta State University audience, the group tells me that they will "keep it clean" for the performance, focusing on their pop love songs and group dances, even as they point to deeper themes in the course of their rhymes. They save their gangsta tropes for the studio or freestyling in their 'hood.

It is not simply the audience at hand that matters to TopNotch when he rhymes. Through playful remixing of traditional forms, referencing of historical events of the past (he has a photographic memory and can generate any important date in black history), and stylistic sampling he maintains conversation with a number of global networks. He often repeats the phrase "let the world listen right," both in performance and in conversation, demonstrating his conscious awareness of an audience that, although not immediately apparent, could potentially be affected by his message. He repeatedly points out that his ancestors (as well as other figures in African American history) comprise another potential audience for his work, as do future generations who will hear about his raps through recordings and by word of mouth. He has a message tailored to each of these interpretive communities.[15] "The fact that people can read many different types of viewpoints from it is what I'm saying. I'm proud that that particular saying alone can do for a worldwide type of discussion," he says, referring to his global mantra: "let the world listen right."[16]

TopNotch earned his position of leadership through a lifetime of practice, performance, and competition. Every time he elicits a positive response from his crew, every time he rises to the performative challenge, he earns the power to change his community for the better. That leadership means the world to him: after all, he is on a mission.

> I just want to let the people hear what real rap is. It's not about what you're claiming or where you're from, it's just where you want your music to go. If it can reach and inspire a heart, then you know you did yourself a good favor just by puttin' a place in your heart for the person that listens to it. Who knows that a rape victim might need another voice to be heard to let them know life can be okay, even if it's something just tragic like that. If someone's feeling down, kids and things pickin' on them, that voice can be their big brother, you know.
>
> That's another reason why my talent belongs here, you know, it should be known out here. Personally, I would love, push come to shove, you know, hopefully you all can see me one day out here.[17]

In his freestyles TopNotch offers art as a salve for the effects of institutionalized poverty, by demonstrating through transformative word the power speech has had in his own life. He is both eloquent and frank, freely discussing his demons while focusing on his determination to overcome, to rise.

Dell Hymes describes the transformative qualities of performance as emergence: "something created, realized, achieved, and transcendent of the ordinary course of events."[18] Richard Bauman finds that "the emergent structure of performance events is of special interest under conditions of change, as participants adapt established patterns of performance to new circumstances."[19] Emergent cultural expression draws from established forms to speak to the moment at hand. Here TopNotch's self-defined activism comes into fullness: his mastery is manifest in his consistent oral/musical creativity, grounded in a dynamic regional aesthetic. This, according to poet and aesthetic theorist Larry Neal, is the dynamic power of the blues: "since life is change . . . art must be change. There is no need to worry about permanence in the sense that things can be deep frozen forever. The universe is in motion . . ."[20] By eliciting *nommo* in the moment of performance, TopNotch responds to a set of shifting social challenges with the traditional power of the word. The artist's ability to maintain this changing same is the most highly prized cultural resource to the African American communities of the Mississippi Delta.

Freestyle and Make-ups

TopNotch and his peers rap *freestyle*, improvising their rhymes in the moment of performance. TopNotch describes freestyle in terms of process: "That's a whole lot of words come from my head and make it try to make sense." Those words might come one at a time, or already formed into favorite stock phrases, poetic riffs, or popular sayings from current hip-hop hits. TopNotch arranges these fragments into metered phrases, poetic stanzas and rhymes.

> Freestyle to me is like an on-the-spot portrait. And what I mean by that, is that freestyle to me is like an infinitive type of art. I mean, close your eyes and envision something that you like. But when you open your eyes, you can't have it because it never comes. Walk down to the street, and you feel like you can walk a mile but your mile cut short because of a dead end. Try to make a left or a right turn rather than go straight ahead. And that what freestyling is. Freestyling is something that . . . something that you know what you want to say but you can't actually say that to another person because of what you feel you might lose.[21]

The challenge of improvisation creates a performative dimension that allows the artist to prove quickness of wit, mastery of wordcraft, and ability to rhyme "on the fly." Improvisatory technique also allows a performer to rhyme about his or her immediate environment, company, and events. The mastery is in the style and flow of the pastiche, as Keyes describes: "Following African American traditional poetic forms (i.e., the blues and toasts), the couplet rhyme, according to Doug E. Fresh, 'Is just a condensed way of saying something.' Effective rhyming in rap, as with most poetic forms, requires selecting words for both sound and sense."[22]

Delta freestyle hip-hop artists hold the ability to improvise at a premium. While coastal and commercial hip-hop artists often work from the written page, Clarksdale rappers rhyme on the fly, in the course of the everyday. TopNotch describes the informal practice of freestyle rapping in Clarksdale while highlighting its accessibility and meaning:

> From a rapper's point of view, freestyling with other people really just happen. I mean, the most significant part of how it really happens, but when it happens, you just in the middle of it, and what happens to me when I begin to freestyle is that I try to become better than the person that rapping against me. Like my words gotta be crisp, my thought process has to be on point, my aggressiveness has to be aggressive. In this part, I settle for no shorts. Everything is on the line and that's just what's required of me. In a congregation like that, it's over when someone wants a beer. It's funny, but I mean it's true. Someone tells you to cut that racket out, or in some cases, and this actually is a rare case, somebody might get tired. You know in your heart that even if it's a freestyle amongst friends, you knew that you lay it on the line when you got through, and that's when you know you had did your best.

> People recognize real, you know. I mean, it's like, you're going to buy pair of shoes. Now if you can get a pair of Nikes for twenty dollars, you best believe the whole town would recognize that twenty dollars won't buy a pair of Nikes, it'll buy you a pair of Mikey's.
>
> When people give you a little handshake and a hug immediately after you freestyle, it's like a handshake first, and immediately, you give a hug right behind it, I mean, that's real. Most people will do it for trophies to be won, but we do it for that real craft, that means that it's for real.[23]

When a particularly witty reference to the situation at hand is used within an established rhyme pattern by a rapper, his or her crew gets loud, rewarding his skill with an approving yelp or a shouted, "alright, now!" Ultimately, it is quickness of wit within the rap form that determines the winner of a verbal contest. The winner gathers the most riotous reaction of his peers and gains recognition as a master of words, even as the boundaries of such a performance smooth out into the evening's conversation.

The use of a combination of memorized verse and improvised wordplay is central to oral/musical practices of the Mississippi Delta. In *Blues from the Delta*, William Ferris finds improvisation to be the central element in Delta blues style. The blues singers with whom he worked called their improvised verses "make-ups," and deployed them more often at nightly house parties than in the industrial recording studio.[24] Delta blues musicians must create fresh compositions consistently to meet the demands of a lifelong audience: rote repetition will not do for the vocal regulars of the Delta juke joint. Both Delta blues and hip-hop practitioners use improvisation to demonstrate their facility with words and their ability to maintain a dynamic repertoire.

Although freestyle hip-hop is improvised by definition, artists draw from a deep well of favorite vamps, popular phrases, poetry, song lyrics, and oral folklore such as toasts or the dozens in creating pieces. TopNotch, for instance, has a number of his own stock phrases that he inserts into his freestyle pieces.

So I spit this
From the outside of my heart
To the inside of my lungs
And that the last breath that I spit it
You will hear this song

And every word that I'm copywritin'
they will receive
That it's the knowledge, top dog
From your boy, T.O.P.[25]

Because TopNotch performs regularly in a number of varied situations (rather than the static performative context of the popular recording studio) he is free to borrow such verses from himself at will while maintaining his performative originality. Each of his rhymes is unique, and he can rap ad infinitum using combinations of these and improvised verse. TopNotch is also likely to quote popular hip-hop artists such as Young Jeezy, refer to church hymns and prayers, or incorporate blues or soul lyrics fragments into a piece. This technique is called "sampling," a concept defined by Rose as "a process of cultural literacy and intertextual reference."[26] By sampling, Delta hip-hop artists demonstrate their worldliness while simultaneously grounding their work in the familiar regional culture.

This sampling technique recalls the "floating verse" of the blues, in which singers craft song from a mixed bag of communal lyrics and improvised verse. Like the hip-hop artist's sample, these verses are picked up from other lyricists, folk rhymes and proverbs, sermons, and popular song. Delta blues lyrics are used in multiple songs by many singers, pieced together in the moment of performance to suit a particular theme or crowd. The more floating verses a singer knows or can improvise, the longer she can keep dancers moving, and, in turn, the more paid work and community respect she earns. The key to this formula is the interaction between performer and audience in the moment of live performance.

Freestyle hip-hop in the Mississippi Delta is built on the element of interpersonal challenge. When TopNotch and his friends are engaged in verbal battle, a back-and-forth lyrical trade ensues until one competitor falters. These contests take place wherever young people gather in the Delta, between friends and rivals. TopNotch is challenged more often than most because of his status as a freestyle champion in his community.

> In my life experiences, I had all kinds of freestyle rappers whether they want to rap with me or they want to rap against me. They approach me because I'm known to freestyle. I don't have no problem showin' off talents like that. Their clothes be off and they make a wish and they come to rap with me, like, I try to listen to what they say, or what have you, because it helps me determine whether I'm going to be freestyling with them or freestyling against them. They choose their own fate. As a rapper themselves, they feel like they gotta knock of the top dog, they feel who's up top by right. Now, for me to determine whether a freestyle is presented or delivered, whether their freestyle is aiming at me or just aiming at just some particular type structure, I stand alone.[27]

The competition gives rappers a chance to sharpen their own verbal skills, pick up new techniques, and generate new creative styles and themes. Although the tone of a freestyle battle can be fiercely competitive, the element of interpersonal challenge serves to reinforce the bonds of creative community. In *Blues from the Delta*, Ferris reports a similar encounter between Delta bluesmen James "Son" Thomas and Joe Cooper in which floating verses are alternated between the two before an audience. When Cooper eventually fails to recall or invent a sufficiently witty verse in his turn, Thomas, a seasoned bluesman, follows with four verses of his own, winning the vocal approval of the crowd.[28]

The elements of competition and challenge run deeply through African American vernacular culture. They work to sharpen creative skills and determine the social status of performers. Roger Abrahams describes a gathering of enslaved Africans in which a dancer was declared captain of his group. The contest would proceed 'until at last one of the contestants gave up and was hailed 'the best man.'"[29] The best man was awarded a special status in the community. In the same way, the Delta master of words gains status in his or her community by demonstrating a facility with *nommo*, or the "life-giving power of the word," upon which Black Atlantic life is structured.[30]

Both the Delta blues and hip-hop, when performed before (and in collaboration with) a group, are most importantly forms of entertainment that sublimate stress and build community. In his germinal exploration of the social context of blues music, Albert Murray describes these important recreational functions:

> Blues musicians play music not only in the theatrical sense that actors play or stage a performance, but also in the general sense of playing for recreation, as when participating in games of skill. . . . Sometimes they also improvise and in the process they elaborate, extend, and refine. But what they do in all instances involves the technical skill, talent, and eventually the taste that adds up to artifice. And of course such is the overall nature of play, which is often a form of reenactment to begin with, that sometimes it amounts to ritual.[31]

According to Murray, the bluesman is a creative force who takes on both the role of the entertainer and that of the commentator. To Murray, who describes the blues as an active rather than a reactive expressive form, the blues primarily is a music of leisure, dance, and mastery rather than one of defeat or lament. It is tailored more to the Saturday night fish fry than the stereotypical sharecropper's shack.

The prime time for Delta hip-hop artists is also Saturday evening, a time of the week generally dedicated to meeting with friends and having a good time, or (as TopNotch would say) "cuttin' up." Before the clubs open, groups of friends gather, dress up for the big night out, and practice their freestyles over a series of tall beers. They walk to their favorite spots downtown, clowning in rhyme all the way. When a member of TopNotch's crew spits a new rhyme, the others keep the beat, dance, and shout out, approving loudly of well-conceived rhymes and laughing at less successful attempts. The evening is infused with meaning through the artist's style and finesse and his or her interaction with the community, whose participation is necessary to a good performance.

In the performance of hip-hop, Delta rappers find a venue for presentation of the stylistic self through their practices of self-naming. The use of a changing series of "other names" is a staple hip-hop motif in the Delta: a poetic space in which identities themselves are formed, undone, reformed, and remixed:

All the ills,
All the chills
And all the pains from all the years

I can put that like in all the fears
I know you done heard it from
The rap right here
T.O.P. TopNotch the Vill
I love the Vill but
love the Top
Put it on T.O.P. and make sure
That the whole block know about TopNotch[32]

Just as Muddy Waters spelled out the boundlessness of his manhood in *Mannish Boy*, hip-hop artists across the diaspora use poetic play to assert their self-authorship.

The lack of black access to political and economic power has long been a defining feature of the oppressive social climate of the Mississippi Delta, and community members have responded by creating alternative power structures of their own. This performative function of personal expression exists for the blues musician as well, according to folklorist Mimi Carr Melnick: "His boasts provide him with an outlet for his aggressions and frustrations, lend him a means for expressions of protest, and are generally designed to help him be somebody with the greatest possible style and color."[33] The crafting, the playful reformulation, and the assertion of self-made identity is an important function of TopNotch's verbal art: "I'll sum it up in one word: creativity. Style is what you are. It's either gonna make you or break you. There's so much you can say about style," he says.[34]

Freestyle hip-hop, wrapped in thick layers of regional and popular style, creates a safe social space for cultural and political expression by young people of color within a stifling Delta social environment. In the public spaces of the Delta, ostensibly desegregated but marked by rigid social taboo (very little interaction between poor people and planters, little public interracial dating or dining, blacks expected to hold doors open for whites at the local post office), free expression is circumscribed. Rarely, if ever, are the regional legacies of inequality, slavery, rape, slum tenancy, or employee abuse addressed directly in public speech; the results might burn a bridge between the speaker and any hope of employment or housing. The powerful words "race" and "racism" are not publicly uttered, but instead are signified throughout the poetry and performance of Delta artists. James C. Scott finds that "Oral traditions, due simply to their means of transmission, offer a kind of seclusion, control, and even anonymity that make them ideal vehicles for cultural resistance" under hostile surveillance.[35] The music of the Delta, thick with meaning and developed under the pressures of plantation life, is never what it seems from the outside.

This formal trickiness imbues Delta rap with a special kind of power. When asked what genre best defines his work, TopNotch replies, "I call it the gospel truth. I call it education, I call it something I felt that the world needs to know."[36] For TopNotch it is a question of what the music does, not what it is. Similarly, Top Notch and his rap group, DA F.A.M., interchangeably refer to themselves as performers, rappers, and hip-hop artists.[37] TopNotch encourages his peers to use the all-encompassing term "performance" in describing the group's work, coaching group members to couple their rhymes with dramatic movement, expressive dance, and onstage composure. In his own work, Top Notch often frames a rapid-fire spoken freestyle session with a sung spiritual dirge, prayer, or expository speech. He points out parallels between his rap and the blues while remaining cautious about drawing a simple generational connection between the two styles.

Sampling the Blues

The blues is generous; it shares its sounds and structures with all takers, from free jazz to the hip-hop sample. More than anything, the blues is recognized for its passionate poetry, and although its sharp one-liners and clever metaphors are easily reused in a rock chorus or a political speech, its complexities take a lifetime to learn. For Delta practitioners, this means intensive training in the form of active listening, competitive play, and participatory training. And for all the effortlessness with which he spits an improvised freestyle rhyme, TopNotch sets into motion a series of compositional elements with every breath.

> In the South, that's what we're used to, saying the chorus maybe four times or something, then we go mandatory sixteen bars, that's a verse, then we do forty-eight bars, that's three verses, so basically, we do three verses and then a chorus, then we feel like we've finished the product then we add ad-libs. Where if I say the word, if I say "Comin' out this world," someone might say "woooorld," in the background.
>
> Like I said, there's so much stuff that we implement. How we do our song is like how we do our clothes. If we put on a brand new T-shirt, we put on new pants, too. And we better have new shoes. We want our words to represent our appearance. Being in the South, our appearance is important to us. It's what we want to represent.[38]

Most importantly, Delta rappers use the poetic element of rhyme to frame their work. It shapes and is shaped by their lyrical ideas, functioning as point of both challenge and organization. The uniqueness and complexity of a practitioner's rhymes are offset with an even, easy flow, free of accidental breaks or interruptions. A broad vocabulary must be easily accessible. The rapper who can rhyme with finesse (and, in the case of freestyle rappers, on the fly) is a master of words in his community. Rhyme functions not only as an aesthetic tool, but also as a point of reference from which a performer's talent is judged. TopNotch is best known in his hometown for his ability to transcend the couplet form and weave his broad vocabulary into a complex scheme, as demonstrated by the following freestyle selection:

> *This is back*
> *Through some years*
> *Through some time*
> *Measure points*
> *Making sure*
> *Everybody feelin' they relate to joints*
> *Pulled the cross*
> *Did some thought*
> *Did some thinking*
> *Did some training*
> *Did forever*
> *Then came*
> *to bubble out you cranium*
> *Still you're drainin' 'em*[39]

As children, the Delta rappers learned to rhyme from a competitive game called the dozens, in which participants insult each other's mothers with mean rhymed couplets: the tried-and-true "yo mamas." The competitive aim of the dozens is twofold: to more effectively insult an opponent's family while also proving the greater facility with language. The winner is judged by the competitor's ability to improvise in rhyme. The dozens also serves to sharpen the oral skills of its practitioners. The longstanding Delta dirty dozens tradition also functions as a technical training ground for the blues singer, and many of the same basic dozens used by Clarksdale children today were recorded by Ferris in the same neighborhoods forty years earlier. Older male friends of mine in the Delta report that, although the dozens is very much a game, they aged out of the practice as soon as they began to feel guilty about putting their mommas' reputations on the line. A friend tells me that an all-too-true response from a talented sparring partner put him in tears, never to play the game again.

Both blues players and rappers in the Delta cite childhood dozens competitions as a training ground for the lyrical "battle." Alan Dundes found that the social and artistic are infused in the Afrodiasporic practice of the dozens, which he notes functions both as an assertion of masculinity and as a rite of passage for the secular master of words.[40] The dozens not only establishes a framework for verbal creativity; children also use them to determine a social hierarchy. A good dozens player not only coolly withstands merciless insults to his family; he also twists memorized insults quickly to suit the opponent at hand. The dozens also establishes masculine networks of creativity in a deeply gendered plantation society.[41] This does not, however, mean that boys are the only participants in this creative play: lady rapper Kimyata Dear reports that she had to fight to participate in the game and, perhaps because of her talent, was eventually discouraged by the older boys from participating in the schoolground competitions as a preteen.

The complex structure underlying TopNotch's poetry demonstrates both his lyrical sensibility and his ability to shape his speech to particular patterns of meaning. TopNotch, who has become deeply familiar with the structures of the local poetic style, says that he keeps to these patterns subconsciously, almost naturally, as a result of a lifetime of practice. This gives him a basis for manipulating this form, or "changing the grain," in a demonstration of personal style. In the following piece, TopNotch sets his metric/rhythmic motif, and then diverges from it in order to create emphasis (here by adding an extra rhyming line). He then falls back into his pattern, emphasizing his creative work:

But they behave
They sit in the shade
Drink Kool-Aid when it's summertime
And everybody wants to get some of mine

But I'm not like givin' up some of mine
It's some of the time and you can talk
To everybody can make you walk[42]

The Delta blues tends to fall within a pattern similar to TopNotch's, loosely based on the classic twelve-bar AAB blues rhyme scheme. The first and second lines in this form tend to be identical, while the third offers an insightful and/or witty resolution, as in the following excerpt from Lightnin' Hopkins' "Never Miss Your Water":

Never miss your water till your well run dry
Never miss your water till your well run dry
You know you never miss your little woman until she says goodbye[43]

And like their hip-hop descendants, bluesmen and -women used improvisation and innovation to stylize, expand upon, and emphasize thematic motifs. The most successful blues singers modified the AAB format and the couplet to create unique rhythmic interpretations and rhyme schemes, as in this Hopkins sample from "Smokes Like Lightnin'":

Whoa, it smokes like lightnin', yeah but shines like gold
Don't you hear me talking pretty baby,
Smokes like lightnin', yeah but shines like gold
Yeah you know I see my little fair one
Lying there on a cooling board[44]

Here Hopkins uses the rhythmic space within the poetic lines to comment in antiphony to his base statement. He creates a dramatic build, responding to the ominous call of his own lyrics in the heat of the moment. Both the bluesman and the hip-hop artist bring formal poetic line structures alive with dramatic improvisation. This characteristic marks a number of regional expressive forms, from country preaching to the epic, rhymed badman toasts about runaway criminals and savvy pimps. In addition to broader uses of meter, the musical element of rhythm merits attention as an important element of Delta hip-hop. Various rhythmic structures and tempos are employed by Delta hip-hop artists, often within the space of a single piece. Rhythm is used to create variation and emphasis:

Made my chance
Did my thing

Like I did my homework
But it wasn't from the school
But it was from Delta streets I worked

Everything could end my life
And disrespect be put in dirt
Did my hand and shake my hand

Shake my hand
and give the Lord
All the blessing all the praise
But it was my hand they raise[45]

TopNotch doubles his tempo for one stanza with dramatic effect. He showcases his skill at improvising polyrhythms by switching them up several times during a piece in order to frame new themes, build intensity, and emphasize his best one-liners. Similarly, the self-accompanying prewar Delta bluesmen were known to alter their rhythms within a piece to create emphasis. Here Robert Johnson uses a blues rag rhythmic variation for the sake of style and wit:

Hot tamales and they're red hot, yes she got 'em for sale
Hot tamales and they're red hot, yes she got 'em for sale
I got a girl, say she long and tall
She sleeps in the kitchen with her feets in the hall
Hot tamales and they're red hot, yes she got 'em for sale[46]

The blues player and the hip-hop artist alike finish their compositions with a kicker: the accented dénouement. For the blues player, this often takes the form of a stylized musical riff and chordal resolution, an aesthetic winding down that signals dancers to wrap up their footwork without stopping the action abruptly. Although Delta hip-hop is rarely accompanied by a slow drag, rappers tend to signal the end of a rhyme or a rhyming turn with a topical riff that serves a similar purpose: aesthetic resolution. Where a blues player might resolve his or her composition with a change from the IV chord to the I, TopNotch chooses to close with a verbal play on his name. The artist, satisfied with the entirety of his composition, frames his work:

So I spit this
From the outside of my heart
To the inside of my lungs

And that the last breath that I spit it
You will hear this song

And every word that I'm copywritin'
they will receive
That it's the knowledge, top dog
From your boy, T.O.P.[47]

The Rock and Roll of Rhyme

For TopNotch and his crew, rhythm and flow are central to the aesthetics of meaning. These are the spaces of artistic possibility: rhythms within poetic structures, sounds inside and between the words, or overall compositional character. According to TopNotch, these arrangements of sound are the formations by which style and mood flourish.

> People like you, right here where we at now. Being in a car riding slow, I'm rhyming slow. If we're riding fast, I'm bouncing, I'm shaking, the music's crunk loud, oh yeah, we're rapping fast, we actin' bad. If we're sitting around drinkin' beer, we're gonna have that little slur and act like we're sippin' and everything.[48]

When they battle on street corners or practice in backyards, TopNotch and his friends perform a cappella. While their counterparts in urban centers tend to team with a deejay or a custom backup CD for larger dance parties, Delta-based rappers rarely use instrumental accompaniment in the space of everyday performance. Instead, they keep time internally or use an oral beat box technique, creating percussion with their mouths and bodies. Once the beat is set at the beginning of a piece, rappers proceed to punctuate that rhythm verbally. Their voices double as percussive instruments. The rapper's beatbox is a self-contained call and response, an antiphony that gives his or her performance sonic depth and rhythmic complexity.

Early Delta blues artists, when not performing with a backup rhythm section, were also masters of self-accompaniment, using the instrument and/or vocal effects to punctuate their songs. Germinal Delta blues artists such as Robert Johnson and Charley Patton became famous for their exceptional ability to use their guitar bodies and bass strings as percussive instruments, single-handedly supplying the antiphony that characterizes their regional music. Clarksdale singer Son House often sang a cappella, using his voice to mimic a rolling bass drum on the offbeats. Many Delta artists were skilled in the use of hambone, or the patting of the body to create musical rhythm. Often, the percussive sounds of the words themselves were emphasized and molded to form their own rhythmic accompaniment.

Traditional and contemporary masters of words in the Delta combine the oral and the musical in the medium of the talk-melody. Both blues singers and hip-hop artists, like most citizens of the Delta, have strong roots in the Protestant church, where preachers employ a highly expressive, exquisitely ornamented melodic speech. Keyes describes this stylistic link between preaching, the blues, and hip-hop:

> [T]he preacher's most proven stylistic feature is the use of musical tone and chant in teaching (Jackson 1981: 213). Blues singers talk-sing their melodies as well. Thus, it is not surprising that hip-hop MCs describe their verbal performances as "a melody in itself [or] . . . like talking" (Melle Mel interview).[49]

The pentatonic scale is central to much, if not most, African American music in the Delta, and most Delta rappers (as well as many Southern artists in general) prefer the blues/gospel scale as the basis for their vocal choruses and lyrical vamps. Critics who remain focused strictly on verbal complexity as the primary measure of hip-hop merit often overlook the masterful use of the tonal blues drawl in Southern hip-hop, where both the words and the sounds are equally weighted with meaning. In this way, the slow verbal pace preferred by Delta hip-hop artists allows for a host of other aesthetic complexities. Although Delta freestyle artists tend to deliver their verse a cappella, they conceive of their pieces as songs, and their cultural practice as a kind of music. In this way, the rappers blur genre boundaries into an unlimited palate of cultural expression.

Murray describes the musical composition of the blues as a series of vamps, verses, choruses, riffs, fills, call-and-response sequences, and breaks that correlate to elements of poetic arrangement.[50] Although hip-hop artists rarely sing large portions of their rhymes, they use the musical devices of rhythm and vocal inflection to indicate musical movements within a piece. TopNotch employs these techniques in his rap, calling the process "changing the grain." He does this by adding polyrhythms to his delivery, using a stylized second voice, or by stepping back and allowing another participant to sing a chorus. The deep, low minor tones of the Delta blues provide a template for this hip-hop musicality; the pentatonic blues scale is common to most Delta music. TopNotch often cites the Baptist deacon's incantation—the ritual stretching of a few spiritual words ("I know I am a child of God") into an expressive, melismatic chorus—as a source of aesthetic inspiration.

The play of a blues guitarist's fingers on the frets is another medium through which the verbal meets pure sound. In the Delta, guitars can talk. Big Jack

"The Oilman" Johnson makes his sound out certain words, and others begin a musical bridge by begging their instrument: "talk to me." "How the way I'm doin' with my words is how the way he's doin' with his guitar," says TopNotch, comparing his lyrical play with Big T's guitar work. "I mean, I feel like my words and how the way I'm placing 'em to where, you know, not only can they sound good, but just actually to make sense, you know, through logic, is how the way he uses his guitar."[51]

TopNotch attributes his talent with these complex musical elements to his immersion in the blues-infused atmosphere in the Delta. The tradition is everywhere, and it lends itself to new interpretations. According to Murray, the folk blues form lends itself to change through synthesis, extension, and refinement.[52] TopNotch and his clique demonstrate each element of this dynamic quality in their work: in the synthesis of the country blues with contemporary popular hip-hop; in the extension of the blues idiom to apply to contemporary attitudes and situations within the black community; and in the refinement of rhythmic and poetic aspects of the blues to suit the complex hip-hop form.

Delta Flavor, Delta Style

The soul-warming foodways of the Mississippi Delta reflect the deeply interconnected cultures of the crossroads: hot tamales wrapped in corn husks, Italian sausage with sweet chow-chow, delicate Lebanese kibbi, crawfish up from the Gulf Coast, steaks prepared at the Chinese grocery, pork chops, and red velvet cake for celebration. Ribs and barbeque sandwiches are for special occasions and tourists. Soul food, drawn from the scraps of short paychecks, is the richest of all: huge pots of boiled spaghetti, collard greens harvested from the backyard, red beans and rice, a thousand homemade varieties of pan-fried chicken, expertly cooked hog chitterlings and maws and, especially, fried catfish caught along the swampy roads that edge cotton farmland. These heavily textured, delicately flavored meals are made in large order for extended groups of friends, family, and parishioners—a movable community feast assembled from less than little. The element of conjuration is local flavor, and according to TopNotch, it can be found in every aspect of life in the Mississippi Delta.

> As far as flavor, our clothes and the food we eat, all that has to have soul. Like, a blues musician will not come up onstage unless he is well-dressed. Given the fact that rappers are the young, urban folk here in Mississippi, we kinds like our baggy clothes, our jeans matchin' our shirt probably might match the shoes, or I mean, the wristband, the neckpiece, everything has to coordinate, you know. The same reason, the way we dress represents the hospitality that we have. Well,

Abe's Barbeque is known locally for its chili cheeseburgers. Photograph by Andrew Kropa.

> in most cases, Mississippi is known for our southern hospitality. I feel that our fashion of clothing represents that. Most people might feel where, you know, clothes that might not seem appealing to another person. However, when they're trying to get professional, that's exactly what we are in terms of fashion.[53]

bell hooks situates vernacular creativity within a larger context of African American aesthetic practice.

> Aesthetics is more than a theory of art and beauty; it is a way of inhabiting space, a particular location, a way of looking and becoming. . . .
>
> Since many displaced African slaves brought to this country an aesthetic based on the belief that beauty, especially that created in the collective context, should be an integrated aspect of everyday life, enhancing the survival and development of the community, these ideas formed the basis of African American aesthetics. . . . This historical aesthetic legacy has proved so powerful that consumer capitalism has not been able to completely destroy artistic production in underclass black communities.[54]

Couched in an indelible regional culture and bound by heavily stylized folk traditions, the traditional blues and Delta hip-hop share a vivid palate of performative, poetic, and musical expression. In his study of the African American folk hero, *From Trickster to Badman*, John W. Roberts discusses the ability of Afrodiasporic folk culture to adapt to new situations while maintaining its stylistic integrity. "While culture is dynamic and creative as it adapts to social needs or goals, it is also enduring in that it changes by building upon previous manifestations of itself."[55] The blues have been reinvented and renewed countless times during the course of the last century, emerging from the style and flavor of Delta creativity.

Hip-hop is not the first style to push the boundaries of the blues. Early soul music, rhythm and blues, rock and roll, and, now, southern soul music and rap have all been generated by and are generative of new blues stylings. In the Delta the song structures, chord formations, or technologies that separate music into commercial genres (or, for that matter, from other forms of art) are unimportant: when as a song, a story, a foodway, a performance space, or a style is imbued with local flavor, it is the blues. An extended evening of blues performance in Red's Juke Joint involves a host of expressive forms: song, toasts, high fashion and low humor, the twang of a guitar or an impossibly extended drum solo, the richly woven materials of the juke joint interior, and the tastes of expert barbeque chicken and Bud tallboys. In the context of the thick cultural atmosphere of the Mississippi Delta, all of these are the blues.

Well-respected Delta blues musician Terry "Big T" Williams, who was also known as a champion local breakdancer in his youth, describes his blues mentors as both innovators and custodians of the older regional styles:

> I was raised on this kind of [Delta rhythm and blues] music, and I also heard in the background John Lee Hooker, Robert Johnson, Son House, Sonny Boy. You know, I can go on and on with the great guys, but when I met Frank Frost, Sam Carr, and Big Jack, these guys showed me a whole different thing. They showed me love, they showed me understanding. They showed me . . . they gave me a piece of mind that I could always lean on. . . .
>
> I tell a lot of guys that I meet that the music has never been about us anyway. It's all about what the music can do for us. It can make us feel one way, it can make us feel another way. It can calm us down when we need to be calmed down. So music is—this is what these old guys taught me.[56]

This is a deeper definition of the blues, one based on rich community practices—what the music does—rather than generic conventions. The emotional content of the music Big T describes is transposed into a series of creative forms: fashion, fooodways, art, and poetry that intersect in the highly stylized regional aesthetic. Clarksdale is especially known throughout the Delta for its community emphasis on novelty and imagination.

Harvell Thomas (center) and friends at Messenger's Lounge. Photograph by Andrew Kropa.

The inimitable Clarksdale sense of style materializes in many different expressive forms. Renowned hairstylist Ronnie Vaughn at International Hair Design works thirteen-hour days as the weekend approaches, meticulously styling elaborate 'dos for the Delta's most fashionable ladies. These are wild styles that take entire afternoons to press, dye, and curl into unique, flourishing shapes. Meanwhile, customers line up at the Super Soul Shop downtown, a traditional Lebanese-owned store stocked with bright zoot suits and shiny vests. Brenda and Ellis Coleman, regulars at Red's club, fashion a beautiful new set of matching outfits for each weekend's parties from the remnants she picks up as a clerk in Wal-Mart's sewing department. Young people get ready for the hip-hop club with new sets of bright hair extensions, elaborately printed T-shirts, and freshly polished shoes. Some keep it simple and fresh with disposable, gleaming white Ts that they pick up three for a dime at the corner store. The Clarksdale aesthetic in all its variations is complex, deeply signified, and gilded with spiritual flash.[57]

Each of these styles is inexpensive, incredibly fresh, and manifests the changing same that is characteristic of Clarksdale's flavor. Each town in the Delta retains its own sense of place: elaborate car culture reigns up north in Friars Point; country jukin' involves dressed-up overalls and cowboy hats in the plantation towns of Bobo and Merigold; and Indianola is known for its traditional medicine and laid-back atmosphere. Larger towns like sprawling Greenville and homey Greenwood also retain particular styles, influenced by relatively developed economic infrastructures—and both have fostered flourishing grass-roots hip-hop scenes of their own. All of these styles work together to form an unmistakable regional oeuvre, but they also map a diversity of variations and innovations upon blues community life. The blues are defined in terms of what they do in practice rather than a common structure or form.

Clarksdale's creative community, too, allows for the conversation of many variations on and generations of its distinctive style. And while creativity and innovation are key, not just anything will do, according to TopNotch:

> I think of myself like Marvin Gaye: I built on the past to start something new—like the blues in this area. Rap was a new thing when I was growing up. Some of the older generation of musicians in the Delta talk about how there's nothing new about rap. But I think we're building on what they had, not taking from them. They also say that our music is too explicit, but music was all about lovemaking back then. It's true that lyrics can get too explicit, so who's to say that the older people are wrong. Sometimes it's like we're their children and they have to keep us in check.[58]

Each generation of Delta practitioners guards the perimeters of blues creativity while tacitly encouraging young people to push its boundaries. This kind of educational practice, bound in the everyday life of Delta, is central to the preservation of the blues in all its dynamic complexity. At its core are both the capacity for change and the emergent language with which change is set in motion. And although the archiving of the Delta blues as a cultural form is important, it is also important that the critical, academic, and popular establishments accept and foster all its emergent forms created by talented young people of color, steeped in Delta style and worthy heirs to the blues legacy.

A Blues-Oriented Town

After the muddy winter subsides in the Delta, just as the land is planted with cotton, the region awakes to an influx of blues travelers. Juke joints step up their performance schedules as tour buses wind their way from Memphis to New Orleans on Highway 61. Being situated two hours south of Memphis and five hours north of New Orleans makes Clarksdale an ideal overnight stop for tourists on the blues highway. Blues-loving rock group ZZ Top helped publicize the town in a benevolent partnership with the local Blues Museum, and the involvement of actor Morgan Freeman, Charlie Musselwhite, and a series of developers and investors have fashioned the town into a thinly painted blues tourism mecca. Since the late 1990s, Eric Clapton, Aerosmith, and Jimmy Page and Robert Plant have released albums invoking the name of Clarksdale, its crossroads, or its surrounding plantations.[59] *O Brother, Where Art Thou?*—2001's wildly popular cinematic paean to American roots music that invokes the gothic nature of the Delta blues—has drawn the interest of a younger generation of blues fans as well.

Around the same time, blues festivals began to pop up throughout the Delta. Clarksdale, a larger Delta town of about twenty thousand, was among the first in the area to capitalize on potential tourism dollars with its Delta Blues Museum and Sunflower River Blues Festival. The subsequent Juke Joint Festival, which involves a gamut of Clarksdale clubs scheduled into a weekend of nonstop local blues acts, has gained a loyal following. Smaller festivals sponsored by Cat Head Delta Blues & Folk Art, Inc., a local folk art store, Hopson Plantation's annual Pinetop Perkins Homecoming, and festivals in surrounding areas draw in revenue during tourism season as well. The Shack Up Inn/Cotton Gin Inn has become a popular destination for recording artists, photographers, and adventurous tourists seeking to rent refurbished shacks for a "down-home" plantation experience. For all of the international attention, however, bluesman Terry "Big T" Williams insists that the music remains in the hands of its practitioners.

> I'm from Clarksdale, Mississippi. This town grew with the blues, or the blues grew it up, one. I don't know how it happened. But now this town has became a tourist attraction year-round. And the music draws the attraction. If you come to Clarksdale looking for anything other than what we have to add or offer, you came to the wrong place.[60]

I encountered a group of blues tourists-cum-entrepreneurs today as I bought a soda in the local gardening shop. As the Delta blues continues to gain cachet with Middle American blues tourists, a number of investment bankers and real estate moguls have been buying chunks of Clarksdale for tourism development. One heavy investor has reportedly expressed interest in transforming Clarksdale into "the Branson of the Blues." These savvy commercial ventures profit from notions of blues authenticity that preserve in amber the sepia-toned portrait of wailing hardship, "the real down-and-dirty" Delta blues. This results in a fetishization of the poor, old bluesman in the cotton field and the disenfranchisement of those who fall outside of this romantic definition—namely the young black cultural practitioners, such as TopNotch and his friends, who are the creative lifeblood of the Mississippi Delta.

These investors asked me what I was doing here in town, unaware that I had been living and working here for two and a half years. I gave them one of many short answers I have tailored to finesse such situations: I am working on a documentary about local hip-hop artists.

"Oh!" said the shaggy white-haired Floridian. "You won't find any hip-hop here." His shirt was covered in patches from commercial blues festivals across the South and Midwest.

"That's right," said his wife, her swingy ponytail bouncing. "Not one iota. This is a blues town."

"People are blues-oriented in this town," he reiterated, slightly hurt, almost as if I had slapped him in the face.

Chapter Three

A Family Affair

If no one ever, ever takes the time out to listen to a word that I say lyrically-wise, then listen to where I tell you that I come from, because that's the only things I have in this world: is where I come from, and where I'm going.
—TopNotch

As we drive to meet TopNotch's friends in a neighborhood called the Brickyard, he takes a moment to explain to me the concept of *hood rich.* It's a term popularized by Big Tymers, an entrepreneurial rap outfit out of New Orleans, in their song "Still Fly": "Gator Boots, with the pimped out Gucci suit / Ain't got no job, but I stay sharp / Can't pay my rent, cause all my money's spent / but that's okay, cause I'm still fly . . . / got everything in my momma's name but I'm 'hood rich."[1] Hood rich refers to the ability of the poorest members of society to make something out of nothing—an old Chevy with a bright paint job, an inexpensive shirt with shiny gold letters, or the use of humor to alleviate the pangs of poverty.

The young black community of Clarksdale has renamed its hometown as well: *Clarks Vegaz,* invoking the faraway city where luck can change on a dime. In Clarks Vegaz, old Chevys get big brass rims and the club gets packed on Saturday night. In Clarks Vegaz, new white kicks mean everything and the latest jam blasts. Clarks Vegaz is the alternative, a space where the script is flipped. If Clarksdale is a broken old plantation held together with slave-driven nails, named after a slave master, and built for whites on the backs of black sharecroppers, then Clarks Vegaz is a beautiful Afrocentric world, transformed by the word.

TopNotch and I cast into the Brickyard, a black Clarksdale neighborhood named after the piles of rubble that line its periphery. It is Saturday night, the time TopNotch and his peers designate for "actin' a fool" and "cuttin' up" with

Discarded building materials line Clarksdale's Brickyard neighborhood. Photograph by the author.

friends. One of his crew, Small Tyme, has invited me into his parents' living room, a Delta jewelbox of red velveteen and brass picture frames, to take video of the crew performing. The wall-unit space heater is inexplicably turned up to 85 degrees, and a group of young women are in the next room, straightening each other's hair, choosing outfits for the club, and trying to act oblivious to my intrusion. Small Tyme shows me where to set up my camera and Kimyata Dear, a shy teenage girl in a ribboned football jersey, puts a CD of pop hip-hop instrumental tracks on the stereo.

Around six o'clock K-Deezy, Young Buggs, Small Tyme, and TopNotch begin to mill about the room, improvising rhymes over the top of the prefab beats. My footage of the next three hours is unbelievable. A thin blue beam of light shines down from the glass chandelier, and on a good verbal run, the rappers lean forward to break the beam, their faces obscured by shadow and then visible again, lit from above. The four young men, flanked by a group of friends, rap about their favorite video games, their babies, violence in the Brickyard and, most importantly, who they are where they are from.

Behind the sounds of the stereo and the words, these hours are punctuated by gunshots, twenty or thirty of them, spread throughout the evening: an unwelcome antiphony to the celebration inside. They come from close by, not far beyond the front yard, and echo through the streets of the Brickyard that were populated with bikes and kids an hour earlier. The film shows the group

DA F.A.M. at the red-carpet premiere of their documentary: Small Tyme, K-Deezy, Yata Dear, TopNotch, and Buggs Diego. Photograph by Timothy Gordon.

of rappers flinching each time a shot is fired, but no one mentions a word. I do my best to ignore them, trusting TopNotch to warn me in the case of danger. When I ask him about the incident later, he offers no explanation but assures me that I am safe with him. The sounds of gunfire have become more common in the ghettoes of Clarksdale in the wake of increasing gang violence between neighborhood groups in the Brickyard and those in Riverton. TopNotch and his clique are aligned with their neighbors in the Brickyard.

To this group, TopNotch is more than a rapper; he is the master of ceremonies. He sets the tone of each piece by lining a thematic riff for the others to follow. As Kimyata flips through the prefab beats with the stereo remote, the guys, who start referring to themselves as DA F.A.M. about an hour into the session, collaborate on rhymed sequences organized by theme. The entirety of three hours is improvised, and the crew takes turns without a single interruption. Young Buggs, from time to time, sings a chorus as the others chime in. The group dances in unison, cheering a witty line or an off-the-hook rhyme. The crew defers to T.O.P.: they wait for a slight hand gesture or verbal cue to begin a new rhyme sequence, and give him space to jump in at will or solo for a relatively longer period of time. TopNotch, who has helped hone the rhyming skills of each group member, jumps in when one of his crew runs out of rhyme, like a patient, but persistent, teacher. He explains this process to me both as a practitioner and a cultural interpreter.[2]

Well, the beat would start, and we would look at each other, and the person who felt the beat would jump in. Buggs was feeling the chorus, so he would pop right on in with it. That's how it went. . . . Everything that you witnessed this weekend, none of it was planned. No one knew that any of this was ever going to go on but me. I took you through my whole life, and showed you what I do. I showed you the cuttin' up on a Saturday night and the girls shakin' their little Apple Bottoms. . . . I want you to see all that.

Also, I want you to see how we just goes into a hot house and showed you how we could rap off the top of our domes for two hours straight. The first cut was the only cut. None of this was just directed. None of this was scripted or anything. . . . When the camera started rolling, we started rolling. Who ever would have thought? Real talk.[3]

TopNotch thinks critically about his own representation, both in terms of his peers and his potential audiences. With his brand of "real talk," TopNotch is known to many as not only the best freestyle rapper in the area, but an accessible and positive person—a role model. Tonight, Top takes the stage himself as Yata cues up one of his favorite instrumental tracks: "Ready or Not," a song released by New York group the Fugees in the mid-nineties. As the music begins with a minor synth riff, Top looks to his left and right, steps to the middle of the room, and begins to spit:

Look here, your boy got this one now
You know what I'm sayin'
It's TopNotch
I'd like to thank all y'all for coming out to see me this evening
To see my All-Stars
Yes, sir
Ridin' slow with this one, you know what I'm sayin'
I pledge allegiance not to the flag
But the flag of the human race born in the hearts of the struggle
This is love

The rest of the group steps back as TopNotch assumes a position at the head and center of the group, still at the far end of the living room from where the girls and I are sitting. He looks directly into my camera (a cheap model I borrowed from school), which is perched on the arm of a red velvet couch. Top rolls forward onto his toes, hands clasped, and looks up from the ground dramatically. The gunshots have stopped, for the moment. Within two measures of the song's start, the bass drum kicks in. Rather than wait for the beat to sink in, Top swoops his arm and begins to rap without a moment of hesitation. The words just seem to flow.

Thuggin' now
Feelin' like the block's been movin'
Like I say it's how the life I was used to

Man it was nothin' but
three streets and two side views
Like it was South View
But I gave it back and hit it on the bayou

Cannon used to pick us up
Ride us on the trucks
And took us to cotton fields
So we could make a couple bucks

Believe this or not
But when we fill up that rushin'
Wasn't no trees up
but just the sun hittin' and brushin'

Long pants with them long shirts
Hangin' with towels
Wipin' sweat up from my face
And wipin' it from my eyebrows

Lookin' at the cotton
Didn't feel that breeze
But up in the tiny little chapel
We could get that peace

Look-a here, man
I think I was about thirteen
Just to hit it back
And keep us on that monetary scheme

Ain't gonna worry about dreams
'Cause my dreams don't light
But that hustle from that day
Gave me hustle by night

And it's my stripes
I feel like I know that's love
Matter of fact, I give it back,
Super seatback love

Man the people I know then
Is what I don't know now
But I'm glad I stick
with my people sure how
But it's all love
'Cause we came back grindin'
There ain't nothin here
Just a second nick of timin'

But there have been some things
Some things that may be bad
Got a little big
Now my ass is fat

Put a gat up on your block
And make sure it's packed
And I gave 'em TopNotch
And I get TopNotch back

'Cause I didn't want matter-of-fact
Didn't have to flaunt it
'Cause if they taught me that
I'm only headin' [intelligible]

Passin' me a bone to myself
Own to myself
Matter of fact stay lonely to myself

A couple of upper cuts
Are makin' me paranoid
I flip the grain and make the change
And show them boys can be boys

It's the heart of the ten
Matter of fact with the heart

With it then. I gave it all up
So I gave my heart to the man

And if I drink then
I drink for my sane
But this is how the way
It's how the life began

It began for the ready or not
Keepin' that up on the high
And if they ready for block
I ain't worried ''bout 'em talkin'
But then again they lookin' at me and
They still stalkin'
But then again I got the streets talkin'
Man I'm lookin' at the
Sign there says, "S.T.O.P."
Ain't stoppin' me
Show me on the beat

And you can want it
Matter of fact they keep it on the street
Like I stir up the sympathy
Word from the beat

And that color might be red
but I keep it Tarheel
My boys, dogs grinnin'
Just to show my ad-lib

My elbows be ashy
And my shoes at my knees
But that's all right
I still spray a tune out my cheeks

To the O and to the P
'Cause the God at first
Never been a Jehovah
But I dare seen it over

'Cause my witness is business
Hit it up on like a potato
'Cause then they callin' me
The captain was a lieutenant

Man they all just salutin'
Came and took what we doin'
Just to show you this title for
The price of the music

This is all been in love
And I been exposed
Just to took it to the camera show
and then I can blow

Hit 'em up on one more time
and show them my ten toes
'Cause I came from the house
of the 904

Apartment—
about seventeen or eighteen people
One meal just to serve around
And they call that equal

Matter of fact so many sick days
Came like some sick ways
Showin' like the boss
When they caught me by some trick ways

That's alright
'cause it got me key paid
This is why I love it
I love what I made

I know I came from the struggle
Came from the bottom
So when I came back here
I never will forgot

I then came back
But I didn't hear the need
So I had to show the people
This was up my sleeve

Hit it up one more time
And watch me bleed
'Cause they want to see me
process and proceed

Ain't worried 'bout the greed
'cause this is my life
Just like Jeezy said
Man I give up my strife

Ain't worried 'bout the time
The tickin' be tickin'
Ain't worried 'bout them boys
'cause them boys be missin'

See 'em fishin' in the river
Just deliver their thought
just to show you who it is
TopNotch the Boss.
Shyeah!

The music fades out just as he finishes his final verse. The rest of the group cheers him on with whoops and handshakes. TopNotch looks satisfied and excited, brimming with pride; he has shown his skills as a master of words. Later, after I transcribe this footage, I ask TopNotch to help explain some of the references he used in this performance. When I hand him the transcription, he looks upon it with surprise. "I didn't know I could flow like that!" he exclaims. He suggests a few corrections but adds that he is unable to decipher a part or two; he may have been using nonsensical sound to keep his rhythm as he prepared for his next lyrical vamp. In this piece, composed in part in the moment of performance and in part from vestiges of his own previous rhymes, he has embedded his own biography. My interpretation of his poem is embedded in the book font below; TopNotch's commentary follows in bold.

Thuggin' now
feelin' like the block's been movin'
Like I say it's how the life I was used to

Man it was nothin' but
three streets and two side views
Like it was South View
But I gave it back and hit it on the bayou

TopNotch had to move from his childhood town of Crowder, Mississippi after a series of devastating financial blows. His family relocated to the slightly larger Coahoma County town of Lyon, a town so small that it only featured a single through street and two side streets. Here, he made and maintained a strong web of relationships. As an early teen in Lyon, Top became known for his rapping skills and became involved with the Vice Lords, a popular gang in the Delta affiliated with a powerful Chicago group. The lifestyle might appear thuggish to outsiders, but according to TopNotch the group is overwhelmingly comprised of nonviolent members who provide each other with a network of financial support—legal or otherwise. I have met many members of the Vice Lords in my time in the Delta and have had a number of conversations with them about their perceived need for such organizations in the poverty-stricken area. The boundaries of gang affiliation are drawn by both familial and neighborhood ties. According to TopNotch, this shout-out serves a complex of functions:

When I rapped those particular bars, that out my particular hood, or where I was came from. It ain't because I wasn't ashamed of it, but I actually was proud of it. And not to stray from where I was from, and not to be an imposter.

Cannon used to pick us up
Ride us on the trucks
And took us to cotton fields
So we could make a couple bucks

Believe this or not
but when we fill up that rushin'
Wasn't no trees up
but just the sun hittin' and brushin'

Long pants with them long shirts
Hangin' with towels
Wipin' sweat up from my face
And wipin' it from my eyebrows

Lookin' at the cotton
Didn't feel that breeze
But up in the tiny little chapel
We could get that peace

As a teen in Lyon, TopNotch helped his family earn money by working as a cotton chopper with Mrs. Cannon, a neighbor who organized teams of workers for the fields. The youngsters were paid in cash at the end of the day. TopNotch and other male teenagers and adults in the Delta often wear wet towels on their heads and in their pockets in the summer months as a way to keep cool. The style also signifies a brand of country toughness—a commitment to history—prized among many young people in the Delta. Similarly, long-sleeved shirts and loose-fitting pants allowed workers to remain cool in the field and stave off the swarms of mosquitoes for which the Delta is famous. Some young Clarksdale men maintain similar clothing styles throughout adulthood, a complex stylistic signification of identity that echoes the wearing of prison clothes by West Coast youth. Although the fields drained Top's energy, he found renewal in his home church: First Oak Grove Missionary Baptist Church in Crowder.

Also, it illustrated—the reason for the long pants, long sleeve shirts, and the towels was because of no trees around in the cotton field. The sun do give you energy, however it can drain you just as well. I've probably dranken water, I mean, [the sun] causes dehydration, heat stroke, just to name a few. Well, also as a kid, it taught me the value of a dollar. It taught me to work hard for what you want to get in life, determination. It was also men and women, young teenage girls around just as well. The fact that I grew up in it and live through it is why I was talking about it. But a guy that's not from Mississippi can't rap about workin' in the cotton fields, because he won't know exactly what it looked like. That's my history, you know. It's not just my story, that's my history. And if I'm gonna be real with my fans, then the first person I got to be real to is myself.

Look-a here, man
I think I was about thirteen
Just to hit it back
And keep us on that monetary scheme

Ain't gonna worry about dreams
'Cause my dreams don't light
But that hustle from that day
Gave me hustle by night

TopNotch worked the fields in order to keep his family fed and to buy his school clothes. Cotton chopping is a grueling job in which workers use a hoe to cut weeds and stray foliage from the base of the cotton plant. This work is done in midsummer in the Delta, where temperatures soar up to 105 degrees and humidity is often 100 percent. Mites, mosquitoes, and poison weeds pose a threat to workers' health, as does the layer of thick pesticides that coat the land and water. He often describes his work as "hustlin'," whether it involves scraping up money for food or rent by working double-time at the hospital or promoting himself as a rap artist. The latter endeavor involves talking local business owners and venues into allowing his group to perform, and he spends a great deal of time and energy publicizing his work via word of mouth. His passion for his work drives him to practice his art constantly, coordinating recording sessions with his group as well as pay-to-participate Delta rap showcases. Because the economic odds are incredibly tough in the Delta, the art of the hustle—that is, hard work (legal or otherwise) and social finesse—offers a route to survival.

When we were in the cotton fields, we were trying to get the burden off my mom and dad for buying the school clothes. However, the money we made was for survival. Being in a place like that, we still strived to hold our own collectively and made ends meet.

But there have been some things
Some things that may be bad
Got a little big
Now my ass is fat
Put a gat up on your block
And make sure it's packed
And I gave 'em TopNotch
And I get TopNotch back

After suffering from a severe injury from a backroad car accident in his early twenties, TopNotch has been unable to move quickly. He has suffered serious weight gain since this time, which is a point of insecurity for him. He dares challengers to step up to him in the second stanza, to literally point their guns; he is sure that his identity and craft will rise to the challenge.

To go in the world knowing that I'm an overweight person, or a person of a plus-sized figure is quite challenging due to the negative comments from people of opposite structure. So I say to all my people of plus-sized figures, don't let the words hurt the one thing that's going to carry you along the way. And that is your soul. For you have a bird in your cage. Let it sing. I rap what I am and what I see. And I feel good about the fact that my weight has made me a better person. The fact that I'm not happy with my weight—I'm not letting that deter me from me loving me. You gotta start off believing that you're a beautiful person beneath the skin.

Going through a critical day like most people go through, and to be with family and eat. That's depression—that's how some people cope with their depression, their anxiety and things. They eat. I feel like my weight's still on me, because I don't eat right. I don't follow that pattern because it's hard for me to eat more than once or twice a day, and it slows down my metabolism.

I have issues, juts like any normal person. We all gotta deal with problems. At the time I was doing that freestyle, I was explaining my life. I don't wanna hold nothin' back. As a fan, I don't want anything to deprive me and as a rapper, I don't wanna deprive my fans.

It began for the ready or not
Keepin' that up on the high
And if they ready for block
I ain't worried 'bout 'em talkin'

But then again they lookin' at me and
They still stalkin'
But then again I got the streets talkin'

Man I'm lookin' at the
Sign there says, "S.T.O.P."
Ain't stoppin' me
Show me on the beat

TopNotch references "Ready or Not," the Fugees song that provides his musical backup. The final verse involves the kind of complex linguistic play that characterizes African American speech in the Delta. When Jerome hastily entered—and decisively won—a street-fair freestyle rap contest the weekend of his 2001 dismissal from the Army (due in part from an injury), he was prompted to introduce himself to the crowd. Having no official rap name to speak of, he came up with "TopNotch the Villain" on the spot, a name that both echoes his given name (Williams), reflects the quality of his work, and demands a rhythmic delivery. The "Villain," according to TopNotch, also reflects his identity as a lyrical gangsta, schooled in the art of the verbal hustle. He plays with the rhythm and meaning of his "other name" in a number of different ways: "I'm known as TopNotch the Villain, I'm gonna give you a-sexual a-healin'," "T.O.P., TopNotch the Vill" (this one recalls the name of a Cadillac Coupe), or "put it on the T.O.P." His usage in this particular freestyle is especially masterful. "Sign there says, 'S.T.O.P.,' ain't stoppin' me" employs the letters and sound of his name to demonstrate his ability to rise to a challenge. He's T.O.P., not S.T.O.P.

I think the strong part of my raps is emphasized in this particular verse. The very first part of the freestyle. You have me givin' you a little history. In the second part, you get me givin' a critique of myself. And in this particular verse, you hear meeting people know that I'm in my corner, I ain't got nowhere to go, so I'm comin' out fighting. That's my only reason. TopNotch really exemplifies personally what I had already been through—I was at rock bottom—a marriage fell into failing at a career, to almost losing everything that I started workin' out for. That freestyle at that block party was my ticket of redemption. Known as contestant one, the people heard a flow that felt like they could rock and listen to, not knowin' that they would get so much more from it, i.e., understanding, passionate, heartfelt. They got it all from me. As they raised my hand as champion, the MC of the night asked me what was my name, and it was only fitting that I called myself TopNotch.

Every time I listen to that name, I push my buttons to get to that point every single time. It's there for flow, I have to know about it, I have to be on it. Because if it—me not performing at top level—hits the airwaves and my fans sense it, then I'm wrong.

And that color might be red
but I keep it Tarheel
My boys, dogs grinnin'
Just to show my ad-lib

My elbows be ashy
And my shoes at my knees
But that's all right
I still spray a tune out my cheeks

To the O and to the P
'Cause the God at first
Never been a Jehovah
But I dare seen it over

Here, TopNotch shows his skill as a freestyle, or improvisatory, artist by referring to my presence (a UNC-Chapel Hill Tarheels fan) as well as his friend's reaction to this reference. He describes himself on one hand in a self-deprecating way (ashy skin, short legs), but calls attention to his performative skill. Faced with the need to create verse in the moment of freestyle, Top chooses to play off of his name, add on a seeming non sequitur, and then rhyme his last two verses according to this construction: sound, then concept, then resolution in rhyme. The masterful creative process he shows here is remarkable.

I was actually rapping about the blue T-shirt that I had on. As far as red, in Vice Lord terms, means war, but the fact that I had on a light blue T-shirt meant I was keeping it Tarheel cause I was giving a shout-out to UNC. The war is something, hopefully that never ever happens. But being associated with the Vice Lords for so many years, I don't have that problem. People in the hood know that, okay, because I'm not putting on a mirage for UNC, but I'm also not putting on a mirage. In the picture, you're just gonna see me in the blue. I got a black Atlanta Braves hat on, but you know, the fact that people look at colors being gang-affiliated now, it's kinda crazy, though. I was givin' love to UNC, but not takin' away from people's conception that I'm Vice Lords. The elbows ashy, knees ashy, I'm just talkin' about me bein' a kid livin' in a country town in Mississippi.

Hit 'em up on one more time
and show them my ten toes
'Cause I came from the house
of the 904

Apartment—
about seventeen or eighteen people
One meal just to serve around
And they call that equal

Matter of fact so many sick days
Came like the sick ways
Showin' like the boss
When they caught me by some trick ways

That's all right
'cause it got me key paid
This is why I love it
I love what I made

The reference to 904 recalls the small apartment TopNotch lived in for some time in his childhood, in which seventeen or eighteen members of his extended family survived on a single disability check. Besides school lunch, TopNotch and his cousins were rarely able to find nourishment and often went to bed early, their heads aching. In his later teens Jerome spent a great deal of time in the home of his best friend, Timothy "Small Tyme" Williams, and his extended family, the Dears (group members Yata Dear and Keithan "K-Deezy" Dear are also family members). The Dear household was a safe haven for Jerome, supported by the income of matron Debbie Dear, who worked as cook on the gambling boats an hour north in Tunica, Mississippi.

Poor management, layoffs and desperate competition have complicated TopNotch's quest for financial stability. As a result of the soaring unemployment once institutionalized by planters in order to keep labor cheap, job stability is dismal and working wages are just above welfare levels. TopNotch, a talented student and worker without a higher education, has struggled to maintain employment in a society where workers are routinely fired for "insubordination" or "dishonesty" just before they become eligible for benefits, raises, or unemployment.

Now you see why I love what I made? I'm made because who can talk about their history and be just as proud of it as I am? I wouldn't change a thing. I think my trials and errors of life, as far as my trials and errors, no one else could walk that same mile in my shoes.

I know I came from the struggle
Came from the bottom
So when I came back here
I never will forgotten

I then came back
But I didn't hear the need
So I had to show the people
This was up my sleeve

Hit it up one more time
And watch me bleed

'Cause they want to see me
process and proceed

Ain't worried 'bout the greed
'cause this is my life
Just like Jeezy said
Man I give up my strife

The epic tones of TopNotch's freestyle reflect his own history of struggle and transcendence. His childhood stretched from one small Delta town to another, confined by the bounds of poverty and freed by the power of community. His choice to end his performance with a demonstration of his mobility frames his performance as one intended for audiences far beyond our group gathered in the Dears' tiny living room that night.

What I said really did make sense. Just the fact that I've been through it all made a name of myself and still. Yet, people still want me to proceed in life. Like I'm a four-year veteran in the military. Worked at a hospital, and yet still not respected so . . . like Jeezy, man, give me my stripes—I'm well overdue.[4] Give me my stripes in a nutshell means give me my respect, me being a veteran, the stripes on your jacket in the military. But give me the stripes of life, I've been through hell you still don't want to respect me like I'm some type of thug or whatever, you know, just give me my respect, you know. I done survived, you know? But I'm gonna proceed without the permission of no one because I walk this life alone, and at the end of the road, I won't have to walk no more.

Ain't worried 'bout the time
The tickin' be tickin'
Ain't worried 'bout them boys
'cause them boys be missin'

See 'em fishin' in the river
Just deliver their thought
Just to show you who it is
TopNotch the Boss!
Shyeah!

Here, TopNotch calls attention to the artifice of his craft—the music is reaching its final measures, but TopNotch continues casting about for inspired verses until he is ready to stop. He frames his freestyle with a final assertion of

Kimyata Dear in the Dears' living room, where she practices her songs. Photograph by the author.

his identity and an exclamation of pride in rising to the performative challenge. He is satisfied, and the rest of the group pats him on the back, shouts out, and lines up to start in on their next group rhyme session.

It came to me with the words of this last part, it came to me with alliteration, or metaphor, that if you're here for us, great. If you're not, great. So that's the part that when I say the time keep tickin' and tickin', that's what that means. Whether you're here or not, I'm still going to be who I'm going to be, and that's keeping the game T.O.P.[5]

For All My Ladies

Although she remains silent during the course of the young men's freestyle session, I can see that Kimyata Dear knows how to rap—she's been mouthing her own words while the others spit. I ask her, as the men finish, if she knows how to rhyme. She nods, and TopNotch encourages her to perform a piece for me. She selects a particular musical track with which she is obviously familiar, and steps gingerly to the center of the room. While the males nod, standing off toward the walls, sixteen-year-old Kimyata recites a rap she has written about the ravages of drugs on her community. Her chorus, like the verses of her peers, focuses on transcendence: "Open your eyes / Look up to the skies / And you're wise," she says, her voice growing stronger with each line. She has memorized the piece rather than freestyling it, and her poetry is complex and delicate. As she finishes her performance, the guys greet her with shouts and applause, and she steps back into her role as the song selector. She sits down next to me and tells me that she has her own group called Spades Entertainment: three teen girls who sing and rap together.

Months later, she will hand me a demo she made herself in her brothers' bedroom, complete with her own beats and a beautiful vocal track. Her rich singing voice winds its way through the music as she raps:

Yata (in the nasal voice of a bailiff):
All court arise.
We give miss Antoinette life in prison,
Found guilty of murder.

Yata:
I'm a hold it down for my ladies behind bars
For my thug niggaz smoking blunts in the yard
And I'm a hold it down for my hustlas on the streets
And this for my thugs you gets love from me
If wasn't for the pain and sorrow,
Then life wouldn't exist and there wouldn't be a better tomorrow
Yes, I did things and got caught up in the mix
But if it wasn't for those wrongs then I wouldn't be doin' this—hey—

I'm makin' it happen despite who hate me
And I trust no one but the one who made me
God gave me a gift and you can't take it away
And every time he awakes me it gets better every day

And to my thugs keep thuggin' on the block
Stay real don't drop
Count your bread with the hundreds on the top

To my ladies behind the metal gates
Don't cry, wipe your eyes, don't go out that way

All my hustlers take a solo stand
Snitches gotta grip to you like a wristband
But whatever you do
Don't give up keep doin' your thing
Let 'em look, let 'em watch
While your money say cha-ching

Kimyata Dear and her son, Jamarkis Jazez Dear, in the Brickyard. Photograph by Derek L. Anderson.

TopNotch has been teaching Yata how to rap since she was thirteen, when she first approached him with one of her poems and asked for his advice. He told her she had potential and has been working with her to create complex rhymes and a highly stylized vocal delivery. He is especially proud of her work, featuring her on all of the group's recordings.

Yata's poetic skill has been a source of pride for her since she began writing rhymes in junior high school. She learned to write, in part, from her mother Debbie, who has been writing poetry since her own teen years. Yata's talent with verse earned her a number of poetry awards at her school and district. Inspired by TopNotch's rhymes, Yata began to tailor her poetry to hip-hop performance; she had been singing at church and family reunions from childhood and was ready to take it to the next level. At school, both boys and girls respected Yata for her status as a rapper, although she often found herself challenged to prove her skill to the guys before gaining entry to their rhyme sessions. TopNotch has coached her into strengthening her delivery and developing a unique style: tough and feminine, full of poetic imagery and streetwise words of wisdom. Yata directs her rhymes to a female audience and prefers to write and memorize her rhymes before she performs them so that she can get them just right. But it only takes her a few minutes to write a whole song, she says, so she combines the quick wit of freestyle with the polish of poetry. "It hasn't been an easy task," she says. "At first, I was writing poetry, and I had to work very hard to transform it into a rhyme. Not just any rhyme, a rhyme that made sense and a rhyme that was full of character. Once I completed that, I had to work very hard on maintaining the rhyming skills. Now it has become a fun and exciting thing to do."[6]

Like many young women in the Delta, Yata has had to face challenges beyond her years. In Coahoma County in 2004, 76 percent of births were to single mothers, and 21 percent of all births were to single teens. The county infant mortality rates in 2004 were triple that of the national average. A third of women ages 18–24 did not have a high school diploma or an equivalent.[7] And many women, bumped from the welfare rosters by strict state legislation, are forced to work late shifts as cooks or custodians at the Tunica casinos (which are located an hour away by expensive and infrequent shuttle) without childcare. Or they work low-wage hours at the local Wal-Mart, Family Dollar, or chain store, often as on-call workers who must be available to work at any time, with no notice, under threat of losing their jobs.

Yata gears her rhymes toward her peers, for whom the circumstances of poverty are compounded by legacies of gendered oppression.

> I want us women to know that it's more to beauty than just a woman's body alone. We were put here for so many reasons, and we are going with so many challenges, and each of us is born with a special power. I want us women to find what our power is and use it. My lyrics help women see what they don't see about themselves. When I do songs about women and the struggle we go through, I try to help people deal with their struggle and make changes in their daily lives.[8]

When she raps with DA F.A.M. at family reunions and community functions, Yata stands back on the stage, letting the guys bounce and clown up in front. But when her time to rap comes, she is unstoppable, bringing the group's sound and sophistication to a whole new level. She has honed her voice and delivery into a smooth style, rich and always perfectly on pitch.

Yata's production work, patterned after her brother's talent with loop software, has been critical to the development of DA F.A.M.'s recent, more professional sound. She is becoming an expert at putting beats together, checking the new trends on BET and remixing them according to local and personal flavors. She's been singing more on DA F.A.M.'s recordings, too, tapping into her rich, trained gospel voice to create a perfect double-tracked chorus. She even writes rhymes for some of the guys, encouraging them to stay focused on the theme and sound of the song as they record in Deezy's bedroom. She was recently featured as a Strong Southern Woman in a special issue of *Deep*, a glossy southern women's magazine. She was asked to list the traits that made her a leader for the article and decided to write a poem:

> *I am* **patient** *at all times*
> **Dedicated** *to every goal of mine*
> **Competitive** *in any competition*
> *Very* **smart**, *I should mention*
> **Undefeated** *with my rhymes*
> *Very* **talented** *with words of mine*
> **Independent** *is how I live*

A **strong-minded** *person who keeps it real*
A **female rapper** *who raps the truth*
Now don't I sound like a **leader** *to you?*[9]

Yata and I spend an afternoon together each time I come to town, listening to her recent work in the studio, getting our nails done or turning the music up real loud while I give her driving lessons. We share a spectrum of emerging wisdoms with each other. She explains to me what everyday life in poverty is like for young women in the Delta and her dreams for making it out, and she often hands me printouts of poems she has written about her life. Mobility is everything to Yata, who imagines life as a traveling nurse, a job that would suit her intelligence and her desire to see the world.

In the three years since I met Yata as a sixteen-year-old hip-hop hopeful, she has experienced big changes. An unplanned pregnancy at seventeen cut short her plans to get her high school diploma. A series of difficult circumstances placed the responsibility for the child squarely on her shoulders just after her eighteenth birthday. Daily, she balances financial responsibility and child care for her baby, performing the rites of passage expected of a woman her age (learning to drive, studying for her GED, socializing with friends), the process of persistently applying for service-industry jobs in a town with soaring unemployment rates—without a diploma or a babysitter—and her passion for hip-hop. It is not easy. Today, Yata holds her own daily recording sessions in a homemade studio. Toward the vast economic challenges that pervade the Mississippi Delta, she offers lyrical sisterhood and rhymes of hope. In the context of her rap group with Top and her brothers, Yata continues to take the lead with her nuanced poetry and powerful singing voice. For her, the mic is a medium for the expression of her experiences as a young single mother and an alternative representation of women in the rap world. As she records her rhymes in the makeshift home studio her brothers have crafted, she holds her baby, Jamarkis Jazez Dear, on her lap. The sound of her voice keeps him from crying. Although he is just learning to form his first words, Jamarkis pulls himself up to Yata's microphone stand when her beats start to play, dancing and babbling into the mic with enthusiasm and perfect rhythm.

Reminding me that she is a writer too, Yata has asked me for space in this book for her autobiography:

Who Is Yata?

I'm a Southern female rap artist by the name of Yata. My birthname is Kimyata Dear. I know you're wondering why most music artists separate their stage name from their original birth name. Well, I can't speak for everyone, but my reason is because being a rap artist creates another part of me. A part of me that deserves its own name. That's when I created Yata. Yata is a part of me that's able to speak on life in a creative way, which people would not only understand but they are able to rock, feel, hear, enjoy and want to hear more about how I feel on certain situations of life. As a female rap artist, I come hard. Before I go any further, let me define coming hard. Coming hard means bringing forth deep, honest, and understanding lyrics into a song. Hard lyrics bring good entertainment and competition to other artists. I am the best at what I do, not to down anyone, because I enjoy all music of all artists. In fact, I have a few favorites. My favorite female rap artist is Yata. My favorite male artist is Tupac. These two artists were chosen as my favorites because they both have hard lyrics, which means their songs have deep understanding and honest rhythm of words.

Not Yet Famous

My first time ever walking on the red carpet was in my small city of Clarksdale at the movie theatre where we had our first documentary played as a member of my hometown rap group called DA F.A.M. DA F.A.M. is a Southern rap group of four male rap artists by the name of Small Tyme, K-Deezy, Buggs, TopNotch, and one female rap artist by the name of Yata, which would be me. We have been rapping and performing for quite a while, leaving our local fans wanting to hear more great music. We are not yet signed, but with our talent and hit singles, it has to be in the future plans of our lives. But until then, we are still making great music and keeping our fans entertained with wonderful hit singles.

More about Yata

When it comes down to making a track, I do it all. I make my own beats, write my own lyrics, record my own tracks, and enjoy the hit. It was a month that I learned how to work the studio equipment because the guys were always busy, and I was busy writing songs with my free time. No one had time to record me or to make me a beat. Although no one taught me how to work the studio equipment, I played around with it and eventually learned more than I thought I would. Now I make good beats and record five times better. I am 19 years of age. I have a son by the name of Jamarkis Dear and a fiancé by the name of Leroy Houston. These two men have been my greatest strength and motivation in life and to my music career. I enjoy writing music and I have plans on making my own female rap group of three. I don't know what I will call us right now, but it's in the plans. I know the world is waiting to hear my music and waiting to enjoy my performance, so be patient, world, and you will see Yata soon. Until then, I will be in the small city of Clarksdale where I was born and raised.

The Black Ski Mask

TopNotch and his group (including "First Lady" Yata Dear) organized their productions under the name DA F.A.M., in order to signify both their familial bonds with each other and their commitment to and "For All Mississippi," in 2005. They recorded a few songs in a local studio owned by young middle-class white musicians in the Delta, a business built to profit from blues travelers seeking to brand their recordings "live from Clarksdale, Mississippi." Once local hip-hop artists caught wind of the affordable studio, however, they began to approach the owner for recording time. Without an experienced producer to generate backing tracks for the group, the studio technician downloaded sparse, bassy beats from websites offering non-copyrighted prefab music tracks. In December 2005 DA F.A.M. saved just over a hundred dollars and made their first demo. The group picked out a track and sat down to write their verses on the spot. The result sounds more like strains of commercial Southern crunk music than the playful freestyle sessions I had recorded previously.

Small Tyme:
Woooooooooweeeeeeeee!

Ay, it's the FAM know what I'm talking 'bout! We got a ghetto service to Memphis. These niggaz with the dreads in their hair. All the niggaz with the rock face, you know what I'm talking about. Doin' bids. Let's get it!

TopNotch:
Start somethin' finish somethin'. All ready. The chorus like this. Said:

The black ski mask
The black Cadillac
The black ski mask
The black Cadillac
The black ski mask
The black Cadillac

It's murder on this track
It's murder on that track . . .

Small Tyme:
I'm kinda hungry and my mouth need a thirst

That's why I'm out on the corner every day first
Got me on the street I'm actin' like I'm savage
Sellin' everything, oh boy I gotta have it
You small change you never did it big
You never drove a Range you never did this
You never did that you never had no cheese
That's why your pockets flat
You wanna be like me
You wanna drive a Lex but you're so wack
You never fuckin' make it
And if I see you on the block I gotta take it
So call the cops
I ain't runnin' from the law, so fuck what you saw.

[chorus]

Young Buggs:
If a nigga got a problem it's time to murk
If you can't stand the heat then get off my turf. Huh.
We the niggaz that be down to ride,
Down for DA F.A.M. or commit suicide—damn!
We don't claim to be some trill-ass killaz
But the killin' in you will protect your scrilla-huh.
I ain't Nas but I am Illmatic
Loaded guns for the battle cause the streets be tragic
Get 'em wit da shit that they really deserve
And their tips real hollow leave dem holey on da curb
Let you hataz know that we're comin' to getcha
Lettin' out these rounds, "Yo, homey I'm witcha?"
We strapped up man, without the jackets
Frontin' on DA F.A.M., "Hey money, what's happenin?"
We so up in it these hataz can't stand it
We takin' our respect, y'all niggaz demand it

[chorus]

Yata Dear:
When Yata stands the ground underneath the black sky
The only light you see is the white in my eye
I'm dressed in all black in my back windows tinted

And I'm ready to attack
All you suckas get back
Thinkin' that you ready you have no idea
How I make a kick drum far sight disappear
It's magic for the tragedy fall to your knees
Fuck bein' weak I'm one of the realest in the streets
Y-A-T-A yup that's me
It's a lock to the door of the real and I got the golden key
And when I walk no one walks with me
And when I talk no one talks with me
I'm my own army
So get back cause I done already warned you
Step without thoughts and this girl will harm you

[chorus]

K-Deezy:
I first came out the cuts bumpin' Too Short
Then I lean and rock with it 'til I got bucked
You see I'm young and wild but I don't give a fuck
And anybody else talking tell 'em what's up
And if you ain't ballin' you gotta shut up
You see I am the grain and then I do my thing
Blacked all out with the matchin' truck man
It's really massive 'cause this shit insane
Pull it all out and let it marinate your brain
So keep thinking that we're soft, fuck around
You can get your head knocked off
You dealin' with a real baller
So keep your mouth shut and
Stop talking to the cops
Have you runnin' through the hood like Moss
This real ass shit
All you fake niggaz getting' tossed
We already got found in the game and you lame niggaz lost

[chorus]

TopNotch:
Ski mask Cadillac at it you don't want that

Hungry for an ass-whoopin' get your name on this Army jacket
Grounded motherfucka already got me stirred up
Tippy-toe I can fit off the chance it's murda
Rude on the street with a bad nine ghost end
On the rise we can ride Cadillac five deep
All across the Mississippi they don't wanna know about
Playin' niggaz comin' out hard out the fuckin' South
Yata right hand choppa
Left hand choppa choppa
Small don't give a fuck bout none of y'all up on the block
Deezy gotta say throw some grass on the fuckin' spot
Wanna takin' out the trash on the fuckin' nine
A Buggs I made it a hell baby fix
Got you already set and now divide up your clique
Just before you take your last breath here's the last one
Now introducing me, T-O-P, night here I come.
[chorus]

In *Black Ski Mask*, DA F.A.M. uses the script of gangsta identity to stake their claim as southern hip-hop artists. Their lyrics about thug life and ghetto posturing often echo the strains of the thinned-out commercial crunk (critics refer to the pop genre as "crack rap") that misrepresents the southern ghetto on BET and MTV. But the members of the group, each of whom has avoided clashes with the law, tell me that the lyric "murda on the track" refers to the musical track (or song), and that the violent references work to intimidate lyrical competitors. They mix the language of their own violent experiences in the Deep South ghetto with the signified language of rap competition, and create a hip-hop identity with many layers of meaning. Many popular southern hip-hop artists who have experience with the violence of poverty but do not themselves behave violently use a similar vocabulary in their work. The group, who hopes to market their records to peers in the Delta as well as the greater public, has no intention of perpetrating black-on-black violence. They benefit in two major ways from their use of the gangsta posture: an appeal to fans of the crunk and/or gangsta genres (both of which have been phenomenally popular on the international scene) and the use of a coded rhetoric of opposition. Using black ski masks that recall the masked plantation saboteurs of African American folktales, and a black Cadillac that rides triumphantly over those who would stand in their way, they ride right up to, in Yata's words, "the door of the real" and unlock it with "the golden key."

DA F.A.M. coordinate their dance moves for a multifaceted show. Photograph by the author.

Through their personal dissemination of this demo and their regular performance schedule, the group has gained fans in a number of Delta social circles, from young hip-hop artists at Clarksdale High to their extensive networks of family members and coworkers. "Black Ski Mask" enjoyed regular rotation at a number of local clubs as well. For DJ Dr. Pepper, a local DJ and MC favored by Clarksdale's weekend club set, the group is most recognizable for its creative continuities with established expressive styles.

> This is 2008, yeah, and what TopNotch and DA F.A.M. are doing is as the old saying goes, it's what's happenin' today. They like to perform. They're performers, and I think the only influence I would have [as the group's favorite DJ] if it's something they hadn't heard before. You see, if you listen to rap music, it's souped-up soul, and soul is souped-up gospel. So it's really a big circle.[10]

The group used their demo to participate in a local pay-to-play hip-hop showcase at the local VFW organized by Papachasa, a group of Delta music promoters. Dozens of groups gathered to perform a range of hip-hop styles, from old-school gangsta rap in the vein of Oakland's Too $hort to Atlanta's sparse bounce style chants and contemporary R. Kelly–style R&B. Rather than style themselves too closely on these idols, however, the Delta artists stretch and combine styles in their local slang. Backstage, each performer declares his or her affiliation with the "crooked lettaz" community of the Mississippi Delta with shout-outs to Clarks Vegaz, their families and churches, or their extended hip-hop crews. They repeat their cell phone numbers again and again for the amateur cameras in hopes that they will be discovered, admired, and heard beyond the reach of the levees. As each interviewee directs his commentary to those who might see Delta rappers as "slow" or "dumb," it is apparent that these performers have in mind a national, even global, audience with whom they are sharing a first taste of the Delta hip-hop revolution that they hope will come.

Most of the groups who take part in this showcase reference aspects of thug life in their raps, echoing the strains of Tupac Shakur or Snoop Dogg. Many use the deeply signified grammar of "hard" southern crunk, a style based on the complex aesthetics of the underground. Next to professional-looking rappers with sets of shiny gold teeth and expensive pimped-out clothing, DA F.A.M. look reticent in their matching black t-shirts and minimal dimestore pendants; it was the best they could afford. Each group lip-syncs one prerecorded song, and DA F.A.M.'s starts before they are ready. They scramble to catch up and manage to coordinate their dance. Their nervous, friendly faces belie the heaviness of their lyrics. Small Tyme and Young Buggs bump in to each other as they dance on the edge of the stage. Yata hangs back. Her mic, which is supposed to be amplified enough for her to talk over the recorded track, fritzes. The boys pass her theirs as she pushes through her lip-sync and then retreats again. An impromptu member of this posse, the young woman who works at the downtown gas station, laughs as she dances along to the track. "Black Ski Mask," by far the strongest recorded performance of the night, echoes through the emptying dancehall.

The group triumphantly walks backstage from their first live stage performance. They have been performing their entire lives, but the popular stage is new to them. They know there is room for improvement, and there is no doubt in their minds that their next gig will be even better. DA F.A.M's mark on the Delta hip-hop scene has been recorded. Their next moves will require even more sweat.

All in DA F.A.M.

Loath to shell out any more money for studio time, group member K-Deezy learned to use a digital recording program and cobbled together a studio in one of the tiny bedrooms at the Dear house. After becoming ill with Hodgkin's disease during middle school, Keithan "K-Deezy" Dear (Small Tyme's younger

DA F.A.M. performs onstage at Delta State University. Photograph by the author.

brother and Yata's elder) endured years of treatments at Memphis's charitable children's hospital. When he was thirteen, Make-a-Wish Foundation offered him the opportunity to fulfill a dream. Michael Jordan was not available to meet him, so he received his second wish instead: his first computer. Using self-taught skills Deezy programs his own beats on Acid Pro, a PC-friendly music program. Before long, Deezy taped a microphone to the inside of his closet, added a filter made of panty hose and coat hanger wire, and started to record.

The group gathers as often as possible in Deezy's bedroom, where he shuffles and creates rhythms on an outdated laptop. Once he lays down a thick bass line, the group gathers in a circle and begins to write rhymes—they feel it helps them perform in a more polished way than freestyle for their recordings. By the time Deezy's added the song's instrumental hooks, the group is ready to record. They take turns behind the mic, reading their lyrics from a sheet stuck to the wall with electrical tape. Deezy uses double- or triple-tracking to make the vocals sound fuller, for which each rapper records his or her rhyme a number of times, each a little different from the next. When the recording software juxtaposes the versions, the effect is stylized and intense. The group tends to work through at least one song a week, from bumpin' club tracks to slower love songs or ghetto tropes. The most important aesthetic thread running through the entirety of the group's production is that of bass, the deep polyrhythmic resonance that characterizes southern hip-hop.

Timothy "Small Tyme" Williams, the eldest sibling in the Dear family, has been rapping since second grade, when he and Jerome performed a rap during show-and-tell time. Small Tyme puts forth a hard persona in social situations, donning extra-dark shades and an indifferent personality that can be intimidating upon first blush. But he spends his workdays administrating the local Head Start program, where he spends moments between job duties playing rhyming games with preschool kids. Small Tyme's work with the kids gives him a critical perspective on the need for educational spending and after-school programs in the Delta, and he often raps about the need for opportunities for young people in the region, including his own six-year-old son.

> I always speakin' the truth about what we feel and how we feel things are goin' on. Especially with the economics in this town. I mean, we need jobs, we need . . . we don't even have a YMCA in this town here, that's why so much crime goes on in this town here. I think a lot of outsiders don't get it. Don't listen to how the music sounds, listen to what we sayin'.[11]

Anthony DeWayne "Young Buggs Diego" Buggs is more a singer than a rapper, adding his rich vocal vamps to DA F.A.M.'s mix. He's a local basketball star who spends his afternoons on the public court on the border of the Brickyard, and he finds inspiration both in the strains of popular hip-hop and in the church:

> When I hear one of K-Deezy's beats, I get the energy of, you know, whether I should sing this or whether I should rap this, you know, but, as far as the spiritual energy goes, I feel sort of that same thing. When one of those beats is hot, I get the energy to say, okay, let me see what I can bring to it. Sometimes I get the feeling that I need to sing a hook, or just straight up rap it. But I have a little singing influence in me, and so that comes from the church.[12]

DA F.A.M. pulls together the influences of church singing and preaching, poetry, the dozens, and traditional Black Atlantic oral styles to create their contemporary sound; one that has its roots in tradition but belongs entirely to the group, as practitioners, tradition-bearers, and innovators. The group has found its power in the use of traditional forms to speak to personal and contemporary circumstances, according to TopNotch.

> You know, you can't change the whole place, you know what I'm sayin'. That's almost like sayin' things ludicrous. However, you know, pretty much get the people that's willing to listen, you know. People that just want to have some type

> of changes in life or whatnot. And then, you know, you work with that. And maybe then you go out and you get the people that you can reach and could be the people they can reach. And you know, it's a transforming experience. It's, you know, a domino effect thataway. So, pretty much, it all starts from that one person just having the drive, have the idea, have the motivation to get something done, but just need just the manpower or the tools or the right essentials just to get that task completed.[13]

DA F.A.M. is focused on achieving their desires for stardom. In a region where resources are dangerously scarce, the group works collectively to build a reputation and gather momentum through networks of family and friends and consistent self-promotion. Like DA F.A.M., hundreds of hip-hop groups throughout the Delta are recording on affordable home equipment or neighborhood studios set up in backyard sheds. And despite the fact that no Delta hip-hop act has yet been signed by a major record company, the community continues to work to push the levees of the popular market, waiting for the big break.

Cuttin' Up in Clarks Vegaz

After the living room rap session, the group takes me to Annie Bell's, a makeshift hip-hop club housed in some kind of prefab metal garage. The parking lot is filled with older-model cars, a few of which are decorated with oversize rims, sparkling candy paint jobs and spinning hubcaps. The current trend involves coating a classic Cadillac body in flat black paint: the same the military uses to fly their craft undetected through radar. This signification is not lost on a community that has developed a rich culture of private meaning. Nestled next to the club is a little barbeque stand where a dozen clubgoers wait for their orders of fried chicken thigh on white bread or deep-fried tamales.

DA F.A.M. and I line up before the doorman, who seems unsure whether I should be allowed to enter. It is not so much that I look like any kind of official, with my flannel shirt and old jeans crumpled from running errands all day; it is not the threat of my presence, but the fact that I am visibly out of place. I am probably the first white person to ever enter this club, and despite the fact that I felt comfortable deejaying at dozens of hip-hop clubs in San Francisco, I feel conspicuous and intrusive. But TopNotch wants me to see his favorite club and to experience a Saturday night with him and his friends. He explains to the doorman that I am from out of town. The guard tells me to remove my winter hat and nods his head; we pay our three-dollar cover and he moves aside.

Timothy "Small Tyme" Williams is the most accomplished dancer of the group. Photograph by the author.

As I follow TopNotch into the club, I am enveloped by an impeccably dressed crowd of three hundred or so, all of whom seem to know each other and greet DA F.A.M. with total enthusiasm. I buy a round of cold beers for the guys and align myself with the wall. Girls dressed in matched outfits that flash with rhinestones dance and socialize. A deejay to the left side of the red-lit dance stage selects Dirty South favorites on his laptop and conducts the festivities, rapping greetings to arriving regulars and inciting patrons to dance over the heavy crunk bass.

TopNotch stands in the center of the dance floor, dripping with sweat and style and bouncing heavily to the beat, his hat precariously cocked on the edge of his natural. Small Tyme jumps onto the dance floor and begins to work his way across the floor, dark sunglasses adding to his cool swagger. He is the best dancer in the room and neighbor girls from down the street hop up on stage to dance with him. Top, Small Tyme, and Buggs line up at the edge of the stage and bounce in unison, a move they call the Dirty South Sway. Top purses his lips in a mocking face and begins to roll back and forth from his waist with his left pointer fingers on his temple, shaking his head "no." This move, Top explains to me later, is called, "think about it." The beats continue, and the whole room takes part in the celebration. It is Saturday night, time for cuttin' up, and the palpable sense of celebration extends far beyond the rafters of the big tin garage.

Chapter Four

True Blues Ain't No New News

Like I said, we call it the mergin' of blues to rap. Like I said, we gonna transcend it and we gonna tell you what we're talkin' about, with rap emerging from the blues or what have you . . .
—TopNotch the Villain

About fifteen miles south of the Tennessee/Mississippi border, TV signals fade, most cell phones cease to work, and hopes of socioeconomic equality struggle as if trapped under the thick cotton curtain that lines its boundaries. In this part of the world the radio auto-tuner swings almost completely around the dial before finding a weak signal to pull from the air. More than likely, it will find community radio from the closest small town—tiny stations with tiny transmitters whose signals manage to roll over the flat Delta landscape for twenty miles in any direction. From this ether strong black voices emerge in the midnight—each singular, each exquisite.

The first of these to register on the dial is that of West Helena, Arkansas's KCLT 104.9:

"This is DJ Pimp Min-is-ter here with your Friday night sookie, soookie, sooook-ayyy![1]

"Hello, Helena. You're listening to party blues and oldies for grown folks only. Be grown or be gone!

"I'm givin' a shout-out tonight to my partner, Leroy White. Let me hear you say, Leee-roy! Leee-Roy! Party down, party down!"

Keep heading south and KAKJ fades out around the Lyon exit, with Clarksdale's WROX phasing into the dial. DJ Lady Cherry is on the microphone, conducting the night with the coy but pointed demeanor of a master blues vocalist.

"Hello, Clarksda-yullll. You're listening to WROX, the Home of Southern Soul, and I am your host, Lady Cherr-ay. Cherishhhhhhhhhhhh! Cherrycherrishhhhhh! Ain't that somethin'? Ooo-wee!"

George Hines showing an article about Early Wright at WROX studios, Clarksdale. Photograph by the author.

Lady Cherry spins a lover's trifecta of songs, including Theodis Ealey's raunchy "Stand Up in It," Robert Johnson's bittersweet "Come On in My Kitchen," and, inevitably, Kool and the Gang's "Cherish." The next morning George Hines, a longtime regional deejay, takes over the WROX airwaves, busting through the morning air with the enthusiasm of daybreak:

"This is Hines in the mornin' times at WROX, X, X, the station that Early Wright built. George Hines, Hines, Hines on your radi-yi-yo. NO! There is nothing wrong with your radi-yi-yo. We are simply . . . jammin'. I'm like the deejays back in the day: systematic, cruisamatic, rip and read!"

Madd and Marilyn in the Morning, the popular WROX morning radio show hosted by bluesman Bill "Howl-n-Madd" Perry and Marilyn Fontenot, a Cajun journalist and station manager, offers a forum for blues musicians to plug their work and discuss their art. For their seasonal blues summit, the morning crew asked TopNotch and DA F.A.M. to speak about the relationship of their work to the blues. The conversation comes full circle.

Howl-n-Madd: Let me tell you the way I see it. You know, Hip-hop—you know, I mean, you can call it hip-hop if you want to . . . but see, listen to some of the lyrics, you see, and you'll find out that what you're callin' hip-hop, some of those guys has got blues that'll make you go, "Oh, wait a minute, now!" [laughing]
Well, I mean, you know, you can ask, I mean, as . . . the bluesman said, "All music is blues." That's the way I see it. . . .
See, my son, he's also a hip-hop master. And he's got a rap called "Top Notch!" Seriously, seriously. TopNotch, what's up?

TopNotch: Good morning to WROX 1450 AM radio. What's goin' on? Bringin' Mississippi live this morning.

Yes, yes, it's all about Mississippi artists and, uh, blues artists, musicians, I mean about, you know, Mississippi music. Tell us a little bit about yourself.

Well, growing up in Mississippi. I heard [bluesman] Big Jack Johnson this morning on the phone, early this mornin', talking about he's from the cotton field. Well, um, I'm gonna tell you about the cotton fields.

I'm from Mississippi cotton fields.
I'm from Mississippi projects.
I'm from Mississippi all walks of life, I mean, if we're gonna talk about Mississippi, let's talk about Mississippi right.

You ain't gotta stop. Share this knowledge.

Okay. Like I said, I grew up on the blues myself, as a little kid comin' from Mississippi or whatnot. Listenin' to the Saturday blues, dominoes, playin' spades, and all that. It just brought a change into the rap from all that. And I feel like it at a young age, I could put a few words together, make rhymes, you know, make a song of 'em myself. Never knew, just comin' up, like right now, talkin' documentaries and even bein' a part of the rap group you know, DA F.A.M. which stands for "For All Mississippi," and just want that to be known . . .

Mister, mister, look here.
If you wanna talk about Mississippi
You talk about the fields
Like cotton what's in your ears
I'll tell you what's real
About the cotton in the field
I put it on my chest
I'm a bring it to your skills
I did it like this
And then we did it like that
We came to the hood
And we brought it right back
It's Mississippi, baby,
You know where 'xactly it's at
You wanted Clarks Vegaz, just the sound it's back
I put it on my tip-toe
Let me just rip-flows
Let me go here

And show you how we just zip those
Out of the way
And everything
And we gon' pay no bills
But ain't gon' worry 'bout the sound
'Cause the sound is for real
I got DA F.A.M. in here
F.A.M., all Missy
Come with the game
And the game is
All hit me like a hoodoo, slow, silly,
Not sunny?
I play it just like Bugs Bunny,
What's up, Doc?[7]

On Saturday nights DJ Raw holds down the mic at West Helena "Force 2," KCLT 104.9, where he hosts the Delta's premier homegrown hip-hop radio show, the *Saturday Night Get Right*. The small Arkansas town from which the show is broadcast is forty- five minutes north of Clarksdale, just over the thin metal bridge that conjoins the Delta with Highway 49's western stretch. The town, nicknamed Hub City by its young people, represents an important cultural halfway point between the larger towns of the Delta and southern Memphis, and the show's guests hail from both the urban and agrarian reaches of its range. Raw directs potential local contributors to make sure their production work and rhymes are professional and unique, or they will end up on the scrap heap. Their visits with Raw might include a dramatic poetic recitation, the premier of new homemade demo, or a popularity contest between two Delta-produced albums, and each show inevitably commences in a clenching, multi-round freestyle battle over the DJ's preferred instrumental beats. No cussing allowed as he introduces the next competitor: "It's the Rob round, what it do, who are you? Now rep where you're from, who's your crew!"

Although the area has largely been abandoned by its once-thriving cotton and food industries, it remains the locus of the Arkansas Blues and Heritage Festival (formerly the King Biscuit Blues Festival after the town's famous blues radio show), a favorite of the region's most longstanding blues tourists. The festival, held in early October, features traditional and contemporary blues and regional acts, and nourishes the struggling local economy. The influx of local income just after festival time means that local hip-hop artists are more likely to sell their self-released mix tapes in the fall, and DJ Raw's guests direct their listeners to watch for their new albums "come blues fest time." In this way and countless others, the blues continues to nourish the artistic life of the Mississippi Delta.

The Power of the Word

From the church pulpit to the blues radio waves, African American people in the Mississippi Delta create social spaces for the performance of verbal art. The traditions of eloquence, to use Roger Abrahams's term, that define black speech are manifest in every aspect of everyday life in the Delta, even as free political speech is socially circumscribed. The power of the word is at an even greater premium in regions like the Delta, hotspots of tangible, deep-rooted bigotry in which swaths of the population are disenfranchised from institutional and official routes to political participation. Heavily stylized speech, often accompanied by music, allows Delta residents to create power from below as well as to retain life-affirming creativity despite abiding structures of inequality. This language crosses the boundaries of genre, region and era as practitioners draw from the past to create live, emergent meaning. Techniques of oral/musical improvisation remain deeply embedded as the stylized cultural life of the Delta is passed from one generation to the next. From preaching to toasting, the traditional verbal practices of the Mississippi Delta have set the stage for the contemporary development of the region's distinctive hip-hop style.

Although the connections between the blues and freestyle hip-hop are strong, they are only two of many interconnected practices that run through the Crossroads of the Delta. The deejay, preacher, singer, and toast-teller each holds a special status in the black communities of the Mississippi Delta, where the Reverend C. L. Franklin, Fannie Lou Hamer, Ike Turner, Pops Staples, B. B. King, Memphis Minnie, and Nate Dogg each learned to speak. The traditions that nourished the work of each of these masters of words draw from a deep well of diasporic performance styles many scholars and practitioners trace to the *griot* or *jali* of sub-Saharan Africa. This oral historian and musical performer holds a special community status and is enlisted by community members to protest personal trespasses, recite deeply meaningful proverbs, recall tribal histories, and toast festive occasions. Often self-accompanied by a stringed instrument or talking drum, the male or female griot performs in a highly rhythmic, deeply signified poetic style. John Roberts, whose work *Trickster to Badman* represents a comprehensive Afrocentric study of the black heroic tale, finds that the African bardic tradition provides the wellspring of African American verbal art. Roberts traces the history of the black folk hero from the African animal tale to the post–World War II badman. In his documentation of the trickster's symbolic, stylistic, and aesthetic continuity, Roberts describes a diasporic core aesthetic that allows for the incorporation of emergent style and meaning. Roberts cites the ethnographic work of Daniel Biebyuck in Zaire, who found that the West African master of words has many similarities to those of the New World:

> The bard is not bound by a rigid text that he must follow with precision. . . . He inserts personal reflections, proverbs and statements. He digresses to speak about himself, his ancestors, his experiences, clan or caste, his artistry, his musical instruments, his teachers and predecessors, or about certain members of the audience.[2]

The African bard uses a combination of tradition and innovation, memorized scripts and improvisation, and the expected and unexpected to elicit a positive response from his or her audience in the performative moment. In the United States the tradition of rhythmic spoken-word performance continues in myriad forms. Abrahams cites a plantation owner's description of a master of words at an antebellum slave dance, in which a merit-based "captain" conducts the ceremonies:

> "Here a position of real importance may be granted the person who finds himself or herself in the center, for each participant is called upon to helping the project of keeping up the spirit. . . . His leadership enables his followers to have an intense life-affirming experience together." The captain was ". . . usually the most original and amusing, and possessed of the loudest voice," improvising words and music for the celebration.[3]

The earliest manifestations of Afrodiasporic oral traditions in the Mississippi Delta included levee camp work songs and field hollers. The grueling work of clearing the rich, swampy Delta of thick cane break and the earth-moving work of levee building that took place in the years just before and during the Civil War era brought huge amounts of black labor (enslaved and conscripted) to the area. The work was intensive, and men worked with their mules to move earth twenty hours a day. Songs and chants, reshaped by an adept song leader in call and response with his group, helped drive workers throughout the day. Lomax collected a number of such songs from muleskinners in the Delta, including the following example, which may have provided the basis for Son House's "Death Letter Blues."

W. B.:
Well, well, well, well, I got a letter this morning,
That's the way it read:
Hurry home, hurry home,
Your wife and baby is cryin' for meat and bread . . .

B. G.:
Some call me Slick,
An' some call me Shine.
But you can hear my name
Ringin' all up an down the line.[4]

After its clearing and landforming, the rich Delta soil, nourished by yearly floods of the Yazoo and Mississippi Rivers, provided a fertile crescent for the planting of cotton, a crop that requires intensive natural, technological, and human resources. The need for careful planting, chopping (or weeding), picking, and ginning of the cotton demanded massive amounts of labor, and black people came to vastly outnumber whites at the plantation sites. Delta planters, who sought to control their workers through coercion, disenfranchisement, and strict social taboos, established a set of carefully calculated social institutions. One method planters used to retain control involved the implementation of institutionalized lack through debt peonage, a system that kept workers poor and indebted to planters for the most basic of needs. Under this system, black workers could not afford to pay their debts and were bound to their work under threats of violence. This debt peonage was a kind of thick social and economic bondage that, according to Delta residents who lived under the system, represented deep continuities with slavery. Although sharecroppers were ostensibly free, those unwilling to participate by consigning their labor to a particular planter were arrested for vagrancy and brutally forced to work at the plantation work prisons, such as Parchman Penitentiary. Those who transgressed plantation norms were often whipped or hung. A number of my acquaintances in Clarksdale openly trace their lineage to plantation rapes perpetrated by prominent local planters on their "free" houseworkers.

The specifics of cotton planting gave rise to a series of important social facts that would shape the cultural dimensions of the Delta. First, for fear of insurrection, extreme regulatory measures were taken by slaveholders (and, later, plantation bosses) to control the social lives of black workers. This involved rules forbidding free expression on the part of black people. Many musical instruments were banned, church meetings were restricted, and few conversations took place without fear of espionage. Racist taboos and the threat of lynching and rape emasculated potentially oppositional black men and further marginalized black women. Planters retained control by distributing resources including food, clothing, hygienic products, and education minimally; these practices of starvation forced dependence on the vast regional underclass. Most importantly, masters and overseers who feared slave and worker uprisings used surveillance tactics to detect and eliminate resistance. The black population was given little, if any, private space in which to work, worship, or participate in family life. The closely situated shotgun shacks of the Delta, which earned their name for their open floor plan (one could shoot a single bullet through the front and back doors), were freely entered by overseers and officials searching for fugitives and contraband. Communication, for black residents of the Delta, had to take place in the alternative community spaces of the juke joint and the church house and encoded into the shifting and heavily signified use of language and performance.

A second social fact that resulted from the specifics of the Delta cotton industry was the existence of large numbers of enslaved African and, later, conscripted African American workers living together on the peripheries of huge cotton plantations. In Clarksdale's Coahoma County, large tracts of black housing cropped up in the ghetto of New Africa, as well as the edges of the Sherard, Farrell, Lula, Stovall, Hopson, Bobo, Flowers, and King and Anderson plantations. In the shotgun shacks populated by fieldworkers in postbellum years, black laborers throughout the South gathered to hear Black Atlantic folktales about animal tricksters such as Br'er Rabbit or the Signifying Monkey, who used verbal agility to get themselves out of tough situations with stronger animals. These stories not only entertained listeners; they also reinforced the community values of performance, Afrocentricity, and the use of wordcraft to obtain power from below. Tales emphasized the need to keep information away from hostile ears, to mask true motivations behind innocent ones, and to use verbal wit to extricate oneself from tricky situations. The trickster tales flourished into stories about Massa and Old John the slave, who was often caught stealing food or other resources on the plantation. John, unpredictable and oppositional, represented the human embodiment of the animal trickster. Folk legend John Henry also appeared at the soft cusp of the slow Mississippi emancipation: a steel-driving railroad man who used his heavily symbolic "nine-pound hammer" to achieve incredible feats of labor.

In the Reconstruction era, African Americans built a surfeit of tiny white plantation churches for Sunday worship. Missionary and Pentecostal Baptist church services foregrounded the power of music and the spoken word throughout their all-day services. Preachers use the elements of rhythms, improvisation, song, gesture, call-and-response, and the insertion of memorized verse into improvisatory performance to create a vigorous spiritual atmosphere. In my experiences in a number of small black Baptist services in the contemporary Delta, I have witnessed preachers use animal trickster tales, folk proverbs, jokes, spiritual song, theatre and poetry to reach a congregation. The three-hour-and-up church services in the Delta involve a revolving lineup of preachers, choirs, incanting deacons, soloists, and lay testifiers, all of whom use the power of the musical word to inspire and uplift the congregation. Although male pastors and deacons are the most visible masters of words in the plantation church, women participate in every aspect of the Sunday service as preachers, choir directors, soloists, and instrumentalists.

The plantation also became the site of the country juke house, where workers gathered at night to restore their energy through community fish fries, drink, and group celebration. These spaces encouraged constant verbal creativity on the part of participants. Blues lyrics and bawdy toasts, the featured performative styles of the juke joint, each drew from the trickster tradition. Traveling Delta bluesmen Tommy Johnson, Robert Johnson, Willie Brown, Muddy Waters, Henry "Son" Simms, and others played in the plantation commissaries and Jewish and Chinese storefronts in Sherard, Stovall, and Friar's Point. The Silas Green Minstrel Show involved local black singers and comedy performers and enjoyed a lengthy run near the Farrell plantation. The master of words was present in all aspects of the recreational life of the plantation; a realm of positivity and rejuvenation that served to relieve sharecroppers from the rigors of cotton field labor and the brutality of plantation owners.

Perhaps the most important social fact shaped by Coahoma County's cotton trade was the foundation of the town at both the ancient Native American trade crossroads and the waterway of the Sunflower River, a direct tributary to the Mississippi.[5] These transportation routes provided the infrastructure for Clarksdale's development as a capital of cotton brokerage. In antebellum years, the crossing of blues Highways 49 and 61, situated in the center of Clarksdale's New World district, became a destination for traveling laborers, mostly male, who sought to follow piecemeal wage labor after the Reconstruction. In the Jim Crow South these temporary workers needed access to food and lodging, and this black cultural center arose just south of the Illinois Line train tracks. The blues players who had gotten their chops on the plantations translated their work to this cosmopolitan city center. A growing and vibrant black community furnished national musical acts with a ready fan base. Clarksdale became an important stop on the chitlin circuit, and black musicians found a ready audience in the laid-over travelers, migrating workers, and hustlers who populated the New World district. The Dipsie Doodle, New Roxy, and Savoy theatres,

Red Top Lounge, and street corners near the crossroads provided venues for prewar blues artists. Women blues singers including Memphis Minnie (who was, in fact, from the area near the small Delta town of Walls) and Bessie Smith appeared often in Clarksdale.

"Blues talk," the unaccompanied use of rhymed and rhythmic speech, emerged from oral traditions including trickster tales, boasts, and proverbs as well as the new blues aesthetic. The Delta's best toast-tellers gathered around the dominoes tables and dice games of Messenger's game room on old Highway 49, just down the block from the crossroads, to tell tall tales of badmen from Railroad Bill to Dolemite. In slow, stylized, menacing rhyme, the toasters recited extended folk poems, both memorized and tailored to the crowd at hand. Alan Lomax recorded the following toast in just such a juke joint for *The Land Where Blues Began*, his video documentary on the oral/musical culture of the Mississippi Delta in 1979:

Well, back in the jungle it would be
The bad lion stepped on the signified monkey's feet.
That monkey say, "Look lion, can't you see?
Why you stand yourself on my got-durn feet?"

So, the lion say, "I didn't hear a got-durn word you said,
But you say two more and I'll be stepping on your got-durn head."
Well, everyday before the sun goes down
The lion was kicking butt all through the jungle town.

But the monkey got wise and thought to use a little his wit
He say he's goin' to put a stop to that ol' rock kickin' . . . stuff.
So the lion jumped up in a bad rage
Like a young gangsta, full of [inaudible].

He let out with a roar,
His tail shot back like a forty-four.
He went off through the jungle, knocking down trees.
Kicking giraffe until he fell down to his knees.

So, he ran up on the elephant talking to the swine
He said, "Alright you big bad joker, it's going to be yours or mine."
So the elephant looked at the lion out the corner of his eyes
He said, "Go ahead on you funny bunny [inaudible],
and pick on somebody your own size."

The New World district's Red Top Lounge, a classic Delta juke joint. Photograph by the author.

So the lion jumped up and made a [inaudible]
The elephant sidestepped and kicked him dead in the grass.
It messed up his neck. It messed up his face.
Broke all four legs and snatched his you-know-what out of place.

He picked him up and slammed him into the trees
Nothing but that stuff as far as you could see.
So he drug his butt back to the jungle more dead than alive.
[inaudible] that rhyme to that monkey for some more that signified jive.
[laughing][6]

The blues continued to change with times, and the use of electric instruments in the larger clubs downtown, as well as the chugging aesthetic of the moving train, contributed to the creation of a highly stylized R&B sound. Ike Turner and Jackie Brenston, B. B. King, John Lee Hooker, and Muddy Waters all contributed to new musical styles that, although tailored to the hopefulness of a new, more cosmopolitan generation, were deeply connected to the region's cultural roots. Bigger bands could gather in the central nightclubs of the New World district with a drum kit and piano to boot. Many of the songs remained the same as they had been for half a century, but they sounded fresh with the addition of bigger, louder instrumentation. New songs used the Delta aesthetics of rhythm, call and response, and double entendre to speak to a new generation. Jackie Brenston, a saxophonist for fellow Clarksdalian Ike Turner's Kings of Rhythm, sung out hopes for social mobility in the group's "Rocket 88," considered by many to be the first rock 'n' roll record.[7] Groups from the Jelly Roll Kings to the Mississippi Sheiks drew from black Delta minstrelsy (many shared members with the vaudevillian Silas Green Minstrel Show) and national musical trends including swing, boogie-woogie, classic jazz, and urban R&B.

In the mid-twentieth century, radio rose to importance as a social space for African American expressive culture. Black radio was introduced to the Delta as an advertising venue in the 1930s as food, clothing, and agricultural supply companies invested in radio as a means to attract the African American customers who comprised two-thirds or more of the local population. In order to keep black listeners tuned in, stations began to hire musicians and deejays from the local community to act as commentators, record selectors, live musicians, and emcees. These deejays were known to introduce a record and then respond to its verses over the airwaves in a call and response between the static world of recorded music and the engaged live audience. The deejay who could accomplish this talk in rhyme was highly regarded. William Ferris captured this radio deejay style in his 1975 film *Give My Poor Heart Ease*, in which Jackson deejay Joe "Poppa Rock" Louis interacts with a favorite B. B. King record by manipulating its playback:

Joe "Poppa Rock" Louis: [Into mic] The man say, "Why I sing the blues is because I lived it." [Intersperses speech with snippets of B. B. King record]
I know how it feels [Music]
When you're hurt. [M]
Someone must understand [M]
How you feel. [M]
The only way to do it is to say it loud and clear. [M]
Make sure that everyone will hear. [M]
It's the truth the way it is. [M]
That's why I sing the blues. [M]
This is B. B. King [M]
Making a statement. [M]
And a natural fact. [M]
All you got to do is sit back [M]
And dig where it's coming from. [M]
Listen, [M]
Not only with your ear, but also with your heart. [M]
Everybody want to know, [M]
Why I sing the blues.[8]

One of the Delta's most successful early shows was KFFA Helena's *King Biscuit Time*. Hosted by renowned mouth harp player Sonny Boy Williamson (along with guitarist Robert Lockwood Jr. and pianist Pinetop Perkins), King Biscuit broke boundaries by allowing blacks to express themselves musically, in the public realm, with the approval of white advertisers—and eager listeners. In 1947 the first African American deejay in the South was hired: WROX Clarksdale's Early Wright, who managed the station from 1947 to 1992. Wright was a master of rhyme, rhythm, and rap whose quick wit made him the toast of Delta society—white and black. He was best known for his commercial breaks, in which he used the advertising format to promote himself as well as the product in question.

Twenty-one and a half minutes past ten o'clock
I'd like to remind our listener about Young's Repair Shop
Located on Richard and Fourth in Clarksdale
And this is where so many of the people enjoy stopping in
At Young's Repair Shop.
Because as they stop in at Young's Repair Shop,
they're able to get their automobile repaired,
repaired right.
I wouldn't doubt if the Young's Repair Shop, if the mechanic isn't workin' right now.
They works up there, I ain't jokin'.
They have some cars to work on,
People bring 'em far and near to Young's Repair Shop.
If Young can't fix it, you're drivin' in the dump,
That's for sure.
Get rid of it if Young can't fix it.
If you can pay for it, Young can fix it.
What I mean about it, you know like if you need a transmission you can't put it in there,
Well, naturally that car wouldn't get fixed.
But if you can stand [it] to be put in there
Or you can stand for it to be overhauled,
Then Young can take care of it, that's for sure.
That's Young's Repair Shop
On Richard and Fourth in Clarksdale, Mississippi.

Let's see if we can't play you another good number . . .

The Piggly Wiggly store [is] located on the Highway.

And this is where thousands of people have the greatest opportunity in the world
To buy U.S. Grade A cut-up fryers this week for 59 cents a pound.
Ground beef for 99 cents a pound.
You can be en moto while you stop there to buy
Pork sausage, pound side for a dollar 49 cents,
And whole fryers just only 49 cents a pound . . .[9]

As the self-described "Soul Man," Wright used dialect and poetic license to create a rhythmic flow of words and ideas. By employing alliteration, assonance, rhyme, and pastiche, Wright created an influential style of radio announcing while referencing a number of established cultural phenomena. He also employed dramatic techniques such as breathiness, vocal timbre, volume dynamics, control of speed and syncopation, and an occasional burst into song. And while he treated white listeners to a lesson in style, Mr. Early Wright also sent a stylized message of pride and endurance to his community.

In an oppressive, segregated cultural atmosphere, Wright used his position and style to create African American agency in powerful ways. Wright would often promise a free dozen eggs or cut of meat for the first listener to visit an advertiser's business without the permission of the white business owner. When a handful of people showed up at the store, the owner would dismiss the promotion as a trick on Wright's part while enjoying a boost in business, all the while shaking his head. He also used a variety of poetic techniques to garnish his style. "It's the right time of nighttime, Early Wright time . . . Pleasant good evening, ladies and gentlemen, how do you do? This is the Soul Man, to be with you, until I get through. So stand by and don't have no fear because the Soul Man is here." Although local whites are quick to speculate that Wright was functionally illiterate—and therefore could not read the drab advertising copy he so wonderfully paraphrased—he used his style and talent to leverage a position of power and pride for himself in one of the most clenching Jim Crow societies of the South. Wright was responsible for teaching Ike Turner to deejay at WROX, and influenced radio greats Rufus Thomas and B. B. King, who, in turn, have continued to influence global musical styles. Even as the Delta drifted into economic stasis in the mid-twentieth century, the oral/musical culture of its people represented a powerful force in world music.

The advent of the automated cotton picker and use of herbicide to kill weeds in the cotton field brought widespread unemployment in the Delta in the 1950s. Clarksdale's declining planter aristocracy, themselves moving to the comfortable cosmopolitan cities of Oxford or Memphis, no longer had use for the labor surplus they had created. They burned huge tracts of sharecropper housing on the plantations so that their former laborers could not live

Messenger's Lounge, a thriving New World business operated by the African American Messenger family for over 115 years. Photograph by the author.

rent-free. Many purchased or inherited rows of dilapidated shacks downtown to rent at an inflated price to their family's former workers. The black population who chose to remain in the South rather than take their chances in the equally poverty-stricken inner city moved closer to the town centers, but when the train eventually ceased to operate and the importance of the New World district declined, the city could no longer support its people. The old blues Highways of 49 and 61 fell into disrepair, and new bypasses were built outside of town. The civil rights era ushered in a new wave of violence and oppression for black residents of the Delta, and the uneven 1970 school desegregation resulted only in the building of private all-white academies. The streets of the New World district are nearly empty, but the Delta's bright churches and warm juke joints remain, as do the regional radio stations, music, and its inimitable power of the word.

Signifyin' Rap in the Mississippi Delta

The verbal styles that characterize contemporary hip-hop—urban or otherwise—have been essentially nourished by diasporic performance in the agrarian South. Each of the styles transcribed here—blues talk, preaching styles, gospel singing, and storytelling in rhyme—have been prevalent in the Delta in some form since the arrival of black labor in its swampy camps. Nowhere are the raw materials of hip-hop more firmly rooted than in the Mississippi Delta, where oral traditions provide a vital link to historical community expressive modes. Although illiteracy rates are among the highest in the nation, black residents of the Delta retain rich skills of oral communication—practices learned beyond the classroom and within the living context of common culture. Even in a society predicated on institutionalized lack, residents of the Delta retain an extraordinary richness of language.

The use of *rapping*, or rhythmic and musical speech, is essential to performance styles throughout the Black Atlantic diaspora. Blues talk, preaching styles, children's rhyming games, and storytelling are especially prevalent forms of rap in the American South, where messages of survival, opposition, and celebration have traditionally been coded in genres acceptable to white ears. In this sense, *signifying*, the use of one set of verbal meanings to obscure deeper ones, becomes especially important to verbal artists. Signifying through multilayered speech has been especially useful in the Mississippi Delta, where the slightest hint of oppositional meaning was often brutally punished by white overseers. Necessary to this practice is the ability to code-switch, a selective simultaneous use of two languages W. E. B. Du Bois termed *double consciousness*. The ability to speak simultaneously in the languages of the in- and out-groups was critical to the craft of black masters of words in the Delta.

Hip-hop signifying manifests itself in slang, from the use of the traditional term "grain" to describe the status quo (as in cutting a piece of wood along its natural grain, or "going against the grain"—that is, rebelling) to more complicated terms such as "grindin'" or "hustlin'." Hustlin' can mean stealing, and is often interpreted this way by culturally dominant listeners, but in fact it refers to any number of actions that allow the social actor to transcend the bounds of caste using wit, inside information, and hard work. For dominant society, hustling means theft; to residents of the ghetto, hustlin' indicates an individual's drive to survive by sweat and wit. For hip-hop artists, particularly those who identify themselves as gangstas, hustlas, pimps, and playas, the art of the hustle manifest in signifying is the key to social mobility. According to Davarian Baldwin, "The gangsta/playa and the subject matter associated with this icon can now be understood as a strategy, a work in progress. This is a position of maneuverability, which in its present form doesn't endorse the cult of authenticity that must explicitly be a 'pure' counter to the mainstream."[10] Here, signifying necessarily involves the transgression of social norms to create power from below.

In the case of the Delta blues, discourses of creative resistance and transcendence are hidden beneath the language of indirection: a winking lament or a thick double entendre. A paralinguistic cue such as gesture, tone, or facial expression often signals those in the know that a double meaning is being used. In other circumstances, group understandings are strong enough that signifying can be done with no detectable giveaways. Some audience members are able to interpret the deeper meaning while others, due to the speaker's calculations, remain unaware. According to Claudia Mitchell-Kernan, who found that signifying functions as the primary site for meaning-making in African American verbal culture, the term "refers to a way of encoding messages or meaning which involves, in most cases, an element of indirection."[11]

This obliqueness wraps words around meaning rather than working as a semiotic arrow. This might involve circumlocution, or "talking around": the bluesman might ask his woman to "squeeze his lemon." Or a performer might make up an entire story about a mean old snake that has an uncanny—but unstated—resemblance to a plantation boss. When Muddy Waters, the revered Delta-cum-Chicago bluesman, declared himself a "Mannish Boy" in his famous 1955 recording, he was ostensibly directing comments about his sexual accomplishments to potential lovers. But in the context of the institutional emasculation that was part and parcel of black life in the Delta, one can also imagine Waters also admonishing a plantation boss to stop calling him "boy." Waters's use of the rhetoric of hypermasculinity in song created space for his alternative formation of black power and identity.

Themes of hypermasculinity animate Delta hip-hop as well as the blues, and outsiders continue to misinterpret the meaning behind the heavily signified "pimp" and "gangsta" figures. The gangsta/pimp/hustla figure in Southern hip-hop represents the singularly most contested site in popular interpretations of the genre precisely as a result of this symbolic richness. The lyrics can be unabashedly offensive, viscerally hard-hitting, painfully raw. But they are both problematically and effectively embodied by the performer in antiphony to the legacy of racist inscription and projection on his or her own body. Tropes involving violence—sometimes in burlesque and sometimes with disturbing earnestness—tear open space for emergent discourses on race, inequality, and representation that might otherwise never surface. Artists are rarely given credit for knowingly employing, manipulating, or even deconstructing stereotypical ghetto identities through a device Michael Eric Dyson calls *antitype*:

> the expression by blacks of the irreverent meanings of blackness that transgress against received beliefs or accepted norms. . . . Antitypes embody efforts to explore the experiences and identities of blacks who are usually kept—because of class status, lack of power, gender and sexual orientation—from being visible in archetypal black representations.[12]

In the work of Delta hip-hop artists, we see the many ways in which the life-affirming power of the word has been expertly conjured through the use of signification, subversion, and antitype. In the badman of the toasts, the mannish boy of the blues, and the hip-hop gangsta alike, complicated creative figures continue to trouble the status quo. They can be loved or hated, but never ignored.

The substance of the sharecropping society remains intact in the contemporary Delta. As the automated cotton picker was introduced to cotton cultivation in the 1940s and 1950s, planters' insatiable demands for cheap labor were finally met. This left an overwhelming labor surplus that has become the regional socioeconomic legacy. Those in power saw fit to pressure blacks to leave the region and migrate north or west; they had become a liability. But as World War II munitions and automotive jobs disappeared or became full, these diasporic neighborhoods became sated with the urban poor. Many black Clarksdalians who preferred to take advantage of the familial networks and close communities of rural poverty over the violence of urban life remained in or returned to the Delta.[13]

But life in the Delta for the vast majority of black Clarksdalians who remain in the underclass mire involves the constant juggling of sparse welfare checks, check-into-cash loans, fistfuls of pawn tickets (heater in the summer, fans in the winter), and the small but essential dividends of the underground economy. The necessary seasonal tractor, trucking, and ginning work performed by many young men in the Delta prevents these workers from receiving unemployment checks, and the under-the-counter pay for female cooks and housekeepers (and increasingly undertaken by poor whites) will not cover health care or retirement. Even as many Delta planter families, now diversified into groups of landlords, lawyers, and tourism investors, continue to live opulently from the government-subsidized cultivation or sale of their land to agribusiness conglomerates, many Clarksdale parents struggle desperately to properly clothe their children and to supplement the nutritionless, floury boxed food that comes in bulk at the food-stamp-friendly Sav-A-Lot store. These circumstances, along with a lack of access to good health care, take their toll on the bodies of Delta residents. Those who cannot afford to pay tickets for minor traffic infractions are often shuffled into an escalating cycle of legal prosecution and terminal imprisonment.

But in the spaces of the word—in the juke joints, churches, backyards, and living rooms of the Delta—scant resources are redistributed, and the seasonal good fortune of some community members brings a wider sustenance to many. Sublime church feasts and family reunions provide social and nutritional substance, and the arrival of a few spendthrift tourists at the juke joint means that locals can eat and drink for next to nothing. These subaltern networks are built and maintained through creativity and communication, and work in complex and critical ways to foster the life of the blues community. The indispensable preacher, the blues singer, the church choir, the deejay, and other masters of words advertise, draw, and entertain participants at these functions. The event MC is always a respected member of the community, and the better his or her reputation and performance, the more likely an event will successfully attract and distribute community resources. The words and ideas of the master practitioner translate into nourishment in the form of professional connections, group solidarity, offerings of food and drink, and the creativity and education that are necessary for community sustenance. Just as the rhetoric of the badman provided prewar verbal practitioners with a safe space for discourse, hip-hop provides a site for the expression and transcendence of hardship and the radical celebration of self and community. The symbolic world of contemporary Delta rap, populated with grinning thugs, Prada-wearing fly girls, ski masks, Cadillacs, and glistening nightclubs, transforms a socioeconomic reality that closely resembles that of the prewar blues people, and thereby renews the importance of signification through the expression of ideas that "go against the grain" of historical oppression. The MC provides entertainment as well as valuable lessons for survival.

The elements of signifying and indirection, among many others, provide a rich site for the display of verbal creativity. Rather than arrange preformed linguistic blocks on the surface of performance, verbal practitioners use the interplay between surface and hidden meaning to create multiple possible interpretations. Both signifying and indirection form the basis of a highly rhythmic speech, thick with meaning, that has been called rap in the Delta for close to a century. Radio announcers rap between songs, members of the community engage in "rap sessions," or deep conversations, and those needing information ask another to "rap at your boy here." Rap, when it refers to practice rather than commercial genre, signifies meaningful conversation in myriad contexts: a dynamic interaction between artist and community that is relevant to the moment at hand. From the earliest field hollers to the hip-hop "hollaback," the element of call and response, of accountability to audience, is critical to a successful performance. A master of words uses the tools of tradition, improvisation, signification, and indirection to craft a complex and multilayered performance. He or she knows this by the reaction of the audience.

Trudier Harris finds that community expressive practice is collaborative by nature. "When once there seemed to be tellers of tales and listeners, everyone involved in a folklore event these days seems to have equal value to, and responsibility for, the success of the performance."[14] Ultimately, the signifying

Hill country blues musician Robert Belfour and dancer, Red's Juke Joint. Photograph by Andrew Kropa.

practitioner must pack enough meaning, feeling, and innovation into a stylized performance to successfully pique the audience's response. Dancers, too, are crucial to the creative mix of the blues. Jacqui Malone describes the aesthetic work that dancers do from the floorboards:

> The African American aesthetic encourages exploration and freedom in composition. Originality and individuality are not just admired, they are expected. But creativity must be balanced between the artist's conception of what is good and the audience's idea of what is good. The point is to add to the tradition and extend it without straying too far from it. . . . Among African Americans, the power generated by rhythmical movement has been apparent for centuries in forms of work, play, performance and sacred expression.[15]

The master of words at the center of the circle or the front of the room is only one of many practitioners involved in a community performance. The audience provides the enthusiastic response to the performer's call, an antiphony that is necessary to any performance of Delta style. The response itself is a creative act, which is beholden to, but not dictated by, the featured performer. A song lasts as long as the dancers remain on the floor, changing tempos when the foot-stomping dies out, and then the requests roll in. On a given Clarksdale Saturday night at Red's, Wesley Jefferson must tailor his musical set to the requests of the circle of women who comprise the first row of the audience. Dressed to the nines for the weekend, Red's female clientele rally to hear their favorite songs, provide an "alright, now!" to let the performer know he should extend a masterful solo, jump to the mic to sing a verse of their own and otherwise stir the evening's creative pot. Jefferson's fellow bluesman Terry "Big T" Williams will tailor his lyrics to suit his lover, Miss Bobbi Collins, to whom his most heart-rending love songs are always directed.

Even in the seemingly masculine setting of the juke joint or house party, women's participation is central to musical performance. Ferris, in his study of a 1970s Delta blues party, found that the blues talk of female audience members figures prominently into the evening's tenor. In his description of the impromptu Clarksdale gathering, a woman named Maudie Shirley uses her verbal skill to egg the performer on, choose his repertoire and inspire him to improvise verse:

> Midway through the session Maudie Shirley enters the room and challenges Pine Top's male perspective on the blues. She introduces her own verses and replies to Pine Top's talk with phrases like, "You must think I'm a fool, don't you?" and "Well, you got your womens, why can't I have my mens?" Pine Top tries to end "Running Wild" when he says, "I'm gonner finish up," but Maudie insists on her part and replies with "Let me tell you one thing." . . . Using Pine Top's accompaniment, Maudie performs toasts, dozens and jokes for her audience . . .[16]

In the world of Delta blues talk, any performance involves the engagement and collaboration of community. Whether freestyle rap practice unfolds between two teens in a living room or a gospel song stirs a chorus of hundreds, the call and response between performer and audience is critical to Delta oral/musical creativity. The practices of signifying, rhythmic rhyme, music-making, and everyday talk are each contextualized in community, and style and skill are both passed along from master to student and fostered in the thickness of social life. Every conversation is a creation that represents the intersection of tradition and improvisation, self and group, and poetry and flow that characterizes the aesthetic of creativity at the crossroads.

Ain't I a Blueswoman?

The work of female practitioners of *nommo* is rarely documented in mainstream blues histories. A century of (usually white) male ethnographers in the world of black speech and music has focused on the work of male masters of words and contributed to the popular perception that women are only marginally involved in the world of oral/musical improvisation. Lomax's conclusions, based on his short amount of time in the Delta and the work of Dollard, Cohn, Johnson, and other early Delta ethnographers, offer but a surface reading of both the lives of women in the Delta and their expressive culture. The extraction of women from the cultural context of musical development in the Delta (beyond the music of the church) is a mistake made by scores of blues ethnographers.

In his ethnography of the expressive culture of the Delta, Lomax dismissed the role of women in emergent public performance:

> [The blues] was no life for a woman; it was too risky; it took you away from your steady man and your children. . . . These are distractions that women are simply not interested in for very long.
>
> But other factors entered in. Few Delta women sang or composed the blues precisely because they did not live the blues in the sense that their men did. Feminine lives were rock-hard and filled with sorrow, but they did not face alone the danger, deprivation and orphaning of Delta life in as direct a fashion every live-long day as the men. . . . The lives of women as mama's helpers, wives, mistresses, mothers, domestic workers, and churchgoers sheltered and protected them from much of the brutalizing interracial experience their men knew. . . . It was the men, not the women, who created a song style meant to keep a team of mules surging in the collar from dawn to dark.[17]

Lomax's representation of the roots of the blues draws from the masculinized work song, a form that would have been accessible to him during his short visits to the Delta. Surely, fieldwork provided important themes and rhythms to blues formations. But it is also worthwhile to explore the genre's strong connections to practices in which women were collaborators and primary participants, including spirituals, children's games, and folk proverbs. Blues practitioners in the Delta formed their styles in a fullness of context that Lomax may not have recognized in the course of his two brief visits to the Delta. Further, the oppressive interracial circumstances cited by Lomax as a basis for men's blues certainly had their counterpart in the brutal violence against women who worked in or behind the big house. These women certainly lived the blues. And although folkloristic songcatchers have, for the most part, associated popular crossover genres such as the blues and rap with the work of male practitioners in male-centered performance spaces, women are essential practitioners and tradition-bearers of both sacred and secular song in the Delta. Invested ethnographers including John W. Work and William Ferris found evidence that speaks to the importance of the blues in the lives of women, their participation as audience members and performers, and their experiences with the selfsame oppressive institutions that, in part, inspired the men to practice the transformative power of music.

John W. Work, the Fisk University researcher who collected folklore in the Delta in 1941 and 1942, found women and girls participating in a number of oral/musical rhyming styles in Coahoma County. He found girls leading coed groups of children in game song:

> Instead of the lyrical prettiness of . . . typical Anglo-American game songs . . . , most of these songs these Delta children sing are characterized by vigorous rhapsody. In these there is a rapid, highly rhythmic alteration of parts between the leader and the group—true examples of "Call and Responses" chant form. The singing style is ejaculatory and such melody as there is, is usually in measure-long fragments. The group usually responds with a polysyllabic word or short phrase. Thus, these songs represent the definite survival of African musical elements.[18]

Work located Mrs. Bessie Stackhouse, a resident of Clarksdale's New Africa (a sharecropper's ghetto), who was a living repository and practitioner of dozens of such rhyming songs. She encouraged the many neighborhood children under her care to develop their own personal twists on these game songs, which sounded very much like the blues popular at the time. Sang young Florence Stamps in leading the playgroup:

It takes a rockin' chair to rock (Satisfied)
It takes a soft ball to roll (Satisfied)
It takes a song like this (Satisfied)
To satisfy my soul. (Satisfied)[19]

The "satisfied" line is actually sung by the group of children as a refrain in response to each line of the leader's song. Annie Williams provided her own version based on the first leader's motif:

I ain't never been (Satisfied)
I ain't never been (Satisfied)
Went down here (Satisfied)
To the new ground field (Satisfied)
Rattlesnake bit me (Satisfied)
On my heel (Satisfied)
That didn't make me (Satisfied)
That didn't make me (Satisfied)
Mamma can't make me (Satisfied)
Papa can't make me (Satisfied)[20]

Women and girls both know the deeply signified vocabulary of the blues, and are able to improvise their own songs around blues motifs. From a very young age, girls and boys played rhyming games together, incorporating bits of sacred and secular song, popular slang, and gendered challenge and counter-challenge in their performances. Kimyata Dear reports that she often rapped against boys in the schoolyard, but that she was held to a higher standard of performance than the males. This inspired her, she said, to rise to the occasion. She knew she had the flow to compete; her mother and schoolteachers had been teaching her to shape her skills of poetry and performance since childhood. She learned to sing in church and at family reunions and played hand-clapping rhyming games in the schoolyard. Most importantly, she was guided by her own passion for her craft to seek out CDs by popular lady rappers including Gangsta Boo and Lil' Kim.

Not only do women practice oral/musical improvisation, they also contribute to the expressive culture of the Delta as tradition bearers. Mothers, teachers, choir directors, and sisters each have a role in the passing down of performance styles. Their work is more likely to unfold in the home or the spaces of everyday life than on the lit stage. There is much to gain from engaging Delta freestyle hip-hop in the full context of its communal performance rather than relying on the songcatcher's limited stethoscope. Kyra Gaunt, in her germinal study of black girls' rhyming games including double-dutch game songs, finds that girls, in childhood, use rhythmic musical rhyme and improvisation to learn black language patterns. Gaunt concludes that it is only through years of negative reinforcement on the part of males and dominant norms that adult women appear to become ambivalent toward their own participation in popular music.[21] In the Delta, women and girls participate in virtually every genre of musical speech performance, although they do tend to practice some (like leading the gospel choir or bawling the blues) more frequently or publicly than others (such as preaching or poetry). The lady blues singer at the club is likely to have honed her craft in the church choir, in the poetry readings of the family talent show, or in the high-school elocution contests popular in this part of the South.

Southern soul (or "party blues") music, a polished contemporary take on classic blues themes preferred by "grown folks only" in the Delta, offers a stage for scores of popular female singers. Denise LaSalle of Belzoni and Vickie Baker of Vicksburg are especially popular. Mavis Staples and Koko Taylor, both of whom have roots in the Delta, are southern soul favorites on the contemporary airwaves of WROX. Aretha Franklin's father, Reverend C. L. Franklin, was a Delta preacher on Dockery plantation before his migration to Detroit via Memphis. Koko Taylor (of "Wang Dang Doodle" fame) is known to employ the blues boast throughout her performances:

Audience members take turns singing and playing instruments at Red's Juke Joint. Photograph by Andrew Kropa.

I'm going down yonder, behind the sun
I'm gonna do something for you, that ain't never been done
I'm gonna hold back the lightning, with the palm of my hand
Shake hands with the devil, make him crawl in the sand

I'm a woman, I'm a ball of fire
I'm a woman, I can make love to a crocodile
I'm a woman, I'm a love maker
I'm a woman, you know I'm an earth shaker[22]

Barbara Looney, a blues singer from Greenville, is the favorite blues performer in the Delta, and holds court over a band of men including guitar impresario Mickey Rodgers. Her shows, replete with a surfeit of spangles, waving handkerchiefs, and an all-star backing band that responds to her every cue, feature her trademark mix of sultry song and extended improvised oratory. From the cuts, or extended instrumental bridges, of her polished repertoire, Looney conjures lengthy stories, half-sung, about love and loss, feminine empowerment, or retaliatory cheatin'. Like the hip-hop artists who meet on the corners of her neighborhood, she works memorized poetry, bits of popular song, and impassioned vocal vamps into her extemporaneous, masterful, and complex performance. ". . . What a consideration of women's blues allows us to see is an alternative form of representation, an oral and musical women's culture that explicitly addresses the contradictions of feminism, sexuality and power," says Hazel Carby of the potency of women's blues.[23] This is certainly not the domestic wallflower we see portrayed in Lomax's ethnography.[24]

For hip-hop researcher Cheryl Keyes, the issue lies in the limitations of traditional journalistic and ethnographic representation of woman practitioners. "While the majority of scholarly studies on female rappers locate black women's voices in rap, they present only a partial rendering of female representation. These works tend to focus on females' attitudes and responses to sexual objectification, ignoring the many roles and issues of women and female rappers."[25] Emerging young female blues artists such as teen Venessia Young have graduated from Clarksdale's Delta Blues Education Project, a state-funded program that pairs local blues elders (Big T and Mr. Johnnie Billington among them) with young students for the purpose of teaching them traditional methods of blues performance. Jacqueline Gooch, another teenage graduate of the program, has applied her prodigious blues talent to her alternative rock stylings. Throughout the Delta, young women take their turns leading the church choir, coordinating poetry readings for family reunions, or recording themselves singing or rapping at home, as Yata Dear continues to do.

Women's voices are especially prominent over the waves of local blues radio. Lady Cherry, a popular rapping deejay at WROX, received mentorship from an established Clarksdale deejay named Lady Chocolate. In 1992 the self-described "quiet" woman asked Lady Chocolate to lend a few records for her first attempt at deejaying. Linda Johnson explains Lady Chocolate's mentorship, through which Johnson earned the name Lady Cherry: her official entrée to the world of deejaying. "She was the first deejay that I knowed in Clarksdale. I went to her for music, and she said, 'You need a name.' She is dark, and I'm light-skinned, so she called me Lady Cherry." Lady Cherry grounds her style in the past while representing her own personal traits. Although Cherry listened to Early Wright and the other Delta deejays growing up, she credits her style to a less earthly source. "I asked the Lord to guide me and direct me. I didn't try to imitate. That's the soul truth."[26]

Valeria Nelson, a mother and speech pathologist with Mississippi public schools, has carved her own niche in the burgeoning Mississippi "Sip-hop" scene. From her home in Goodman, just on the cusp of the Delta, she has spent two years chronicling the lives of rappers in the region through a series of YouTube videos, meet-and-greets, and entries in her popular blog centered on her life as a member of the Sip-hop community:

> But then again, nobody can ever tell what [rapper] David Banner is going to do. Trying to second-guess him is like trying to predict Mississippi weather. It

might be a cold 40 degrees at 8 o'clock in the morning and then 88 degrees at noon. Can't anybody tell what he will do. One can only count on David Banner to raise hell when he feels like doing it—most times anyway.[27]

As a fan of the music, community member, and organizer for Mississippi hip-hop meet-and-greet sessions for local artists, producers, and club owners, Nelson is currently working on a self-released chronicle of, in her words, "my journey, what I do, and my interactions with people in the world of Mississippi music" entitled *Mississippi Hip-Hop and Rap: A Griot's Tale*.[28]

I wanted to make a connection between the older people and the younger people who make in the music and look at the cultural and social impacts of how music impacts the people. How rap music influences the rest of the culture in Mississippi. The same way you have the church-going people benefit the people here, rap music does as well. It's very strong. Each artist is different: but their intensity, sincerity and earnestness was similar to that of the people in the church. I found similarities in my church culture—in C.O.G.I.C.—to what some of these artists are doing.

At first, it was pretty hard and then I followed the advice of [well-established Jackson, Mississippi deejay] DJ Phingaprint. To make sure that as a woman, I had to show them that I knew about the business and that I was a strong woman. A lot of love has been grown between me and these artists, but sometimes we do have our days. I have to do it as an educator and a mom, and also as a church-going woman. Up 'til now, I have had a real conflict between church-going me and the hood me. I am a better person for it, and have started going back to church. You have to go to God to get directions on how to do things. The rappers stirred my spirit and helped me to get back to church. A lot of the more prominent artists have a strong background in the church and that is still part of them.[29]

A number of young female rappers also populate the world of hip-hop in the Delta, stealing the spotlight at local rap showcases. Lady T, a Clarksdale rapper and coed dozens champ, tells me that she raps over the mic at the local lesbian-friendly hip-hop club, where she is highly respected by men and women alike. In the Papachasa showcase for which DA F.A.M. performed for the first time, a female rapper named Lady Enchantment held the floor down in a crimson fedora and bodysuit, an asymmetrical red-tipped haircut and faux blonde furs: "Put an arch in your back and your hand to the side / Shake it off, baby, and let it ride / Stomp when you walk wit a model glide / Toot your lips up like nothin' nice. Get your bourge on."[30] The backing track is set with a stock old-school jazz sax sample, and Lady Enchantment models the bourgeois-burlesque posture one might take when approached by an inadequate flirt. Lady Enchantment's second performance in the showcase is called "I'm a Lady," in which she calls herself the "Cotton Queen": "Bow down and drop to my feet."[31]

Moms and Second Moms

TopNotch has not told me where we are going as we drive slowly through the unpaved back roads of the Mississippi Delta. Half an hour east of Clarksdale, we roll into Lambert, Mississippi, a tiny Delta town situated a stone's throw from Marks. We park and walk up to a beige, vinyl-sided trailer on a small lot. TopNotch introduces me to his mother, Jeweline Williams, as she opens her front door and invites us inside. Her house is well-lit and cozy, furnished with matching chairs and a collection of stuffed animals and family memorabilia. The walls are lined with family photos.

> *TopNotch*: This God-given talent, may be the case or what have you, your parents just wanna show you off—"Oh, he looks so cute, Oh, he's so cute. Won't you do this for me, baby?" And you didn't really want to do it, you know what I'm sayin', but you can't tell you momma "no" or she gonna whoop you or something, you know what I'm sayin' [joking].
>
> *Jeweline Williams*: He could say all the commercials at a certain age. I remember he just be up in there doin' somethin' and he put it together and then he start sayin' his ABCs backward.
>
> *TopNotch*: Pretty much they say I had a good memory.
>
> *Jeweline Williams*: Just like, he didn't know how to read and go in there, sit on the commode and put the book up like this here, bottom side up, I swear he readin'. And I'm like, come in there and ask him what in the world he doin', he'd say, "I'm readin'." Ask him what in the world it was: "Oh, I'm through now." He'd close the book and get down all nice and beautiful!

Mrs. Williams has placed TopNotch's first-place trophy—the one he won the weekend of his release from the Army—on a well-lit end table of the living room. She's proud of his skill as a rapper—all of her children are talented artists, poets, and performers—and although she declines to take any credit, she acknowledges that she's encouraged them to be their best.

We stop at Jerome's childhood home, not much bigger than a one-car garage, with its windows and door missing. Impenetrable, wild Delta brush, the kind that inevitably hides snakes and chiggers, has grown through its floor and covered its patch of front yard. TopNotch tells me that this was his second home, and I wonder how such a tiny two-room shack could hold an entire family. I think about the way TopNotch negotiates his own history of poverty in his rhymes.

They had to be fluid, but the
Difference between smart and the
Difference between stupid
It's a fine line and everybody had to go through it
Believe this
When the people come to the hood they receive this
And make sure that nothin' ends your life
but what's prestigious
Achieving it
Thinking that all the thing's the same

Make hood for the love but
Love brings pain
But it's overjoy
Speakin' from the choirboy himself
And I know that there was time when everybody needed help

Look at wealth
Wealth brought us back to a broke situation
Everybody thought they couldn't have it
Thought they couldn't make it
And there's some feelings from inside
I know I had to take it [32]

This is a painful site for TopNotch to visit. The brush is waist high now, foreboding, as the windowless shack rots away, unlivable even to poor residents of the Delta. TopNotch pauses for a silent prayer as we approach the house, a reminder of childhood trauma that he chooses to keep private. But the Williams' time in Crowder was also one of creativity and community. Across the tiny Delta township, we pull up to one of many small, dark trailers on a quiet block. There are old cars parked where a tiny front lawn would otherwise be, and a warm yellow light shines from the tiny windows of this single-wide model.

Jerome "TopNotch the Villain" Williams and Miss Martha Raybon. Photograph by Timothy Gordon.

TopNotch tells me I should leave the video equipment behind. I ask him how to lock his car, and he says not to worry: it's safe at this house. We walk up to the front door and knock, and a radiant elder answers. She's tepid, cautious, as she asks us to sit down in her beautiful house. Newspaper clippings and bright children's drawings cover her walls and a rainbow of calico remnants covers the floor.

In Mississippi, TopNotch has told me, young people take on second and third moms, usually older women in the community who help to nurture and encourage young people. Miss Martha Raybon, in whose home we are warm and comfortable, is TopNotch's second mom, and the reason he raps today. "I've had an open-door policy for any child," she says. Miss Martha, he explains, was his choir director at First Oak Grove Church in Crowder, where he joined the congregation at age thirteen. Once Miss Martha got Jerome in the choir, he became the star, improvising new lyrics to the old gospel songs, surprising his mentor—and the congregation—with his ad-libs. The Reverend Henderson may have accused him of "juke jointin'" in the church, but Miss Martha tacitly approved, marveling at Jerome's talent. Explains TopNotch:

> I was thirteen at the time. And what made me just do that all of a sudden is that in practicing, when we were having choir practice, we had a whole lot of people turn out . . . however, the people that was there for choir practice wasn't really there for church. We knew that we couldn't do all of the parts of the actual song [ourselves], so I had to add some things in and had to take some things out. And the whole turnout was that we still got people talkin' about this to this day, so it had to be a good thing. And as much as I took a fussin' about it, sayin' that I

> shouldn't be juke jointin' in the church, they still talk about it to this day. Once you get pushed into a corner, you learn how to come up swinging. Basically that's what it was with the choir and . . . I wouldn't change a thing . . .
>
> [Miss Martha] was more surprised than anything, but the thing was, when I was making up the lyrics, but she would go along with it, and everyone else would go along with it. Some days we pulled a rabbit out of the hat . . .
>
> It depends on who was leading the song. If I felt like that person wasn't coming with it, I'd give them a helping hand. Or I could be leading the song. The songs gospel-wise that I was always into were the struggle-type songs. My all-time favorite gospel song is "Troubles of the World" by Mahalia Jackson. If it don't give you chills up your spine, I don't know what to tell you. It gives me chills up my spine, and I want my rhymes to give you those same chills. . . . It was always on the spot. It's just something that I always just did, and it was a good outcome. It could have went bad, but it was good.
>
> [Reverend Henderson] felt like we were cutting up like black folks in general would on a Saturday night. . . . But I kept it right going, because I felt like I didn't do anything wrong. Once you're rejoicing, who can judge you? I know people who said they caught the Holy Ghost, and I used to think they were playing. So who's to judge? You look at it the way you look at it.[33]

Miss Martha rolls her eyes when TopNotch talks about his rap, saying, "He'll come back to the church—most blues singers started out that way." But her smile indicates her overwhelming pride in Jerome. In deference to Miss Martha, TopNotch challenges himself to avoid using profanity in many of his freestyles. In her home, he makes a point to quote the bible verses and black proverbs she has taught him. He clearly defers to her as a teacher and elder. From Miss Martha, TopNotch has learned to use his facility with words and music to influence his community to positive ends. He sees his chosen hip-hop role as an extension of his part in the choir. He uses his talent to engage the stifling realities of life in the Delta, and to inspire others to create. It is that transformative power, the power of *nommo*, that connects TopNotch's work with that of his second mom and his ancestors.

> We used gospel to get free. That's what I use my rap for. That's why my rhymes have a deep concern. The only way we can be free is by letting it out. That's what gospel was to slavery. That's how they moved from place to place for freedom. This is my cry.[34]

As TopNotch speaks the sentences about gospel and slavery, Miss Martha speaks many of the same words in unison. She has taught TopNotch these ideas and, by adapting his gospel background to his situation, he has done right by her. He is conscious of the importance of this role and includes a didactic element in nearly all of his freestyles, pushing his pupils, as Miss Martha did, to create new meaning in the moment of performance. Miss Martha has also taught TopNotch the far-reaching nature of music, one that has been well understood by black practitioners in the Delta for centuries.

> When young ones come along and whoever wanted to be in the choir, then I would work with them. And, see, just like with Jerome, and the group that I had when he was there. They were eager, and they really wanted to learn, and we would get right in this little trailer. And I remember they were so eager, they come every day wanting to have rehearsal. Whether they knew it or not, there were people on the outside listening to them. During that time.
>
> Back [in the times of slavery], they would use songs just like "There's Gonna Be a Meeting at the Old Campground," letting the slaves know where they were gonna have a meeting that night for church.
>
> "Wade in the Water" would tell them where to wade to to go to the Underground Railroad to escape slavery. So it was used them for a mode of communicating for them to tell where to go, where there would be a meeting for church. Because a lot of them, they were not allowed to have church, so they would have to slip and have church, and when they got ready to go away to freedom, they would have to know which direction to meet up at. So those songs would pass, or as they say, "start in one cotton field and run across to the other one" so that everybody would know where to go, where to meet up at.[35]

Before we leave, I ask Miss Martha if she has any questions for me. She asks if I think Jerome will make it as a hip-hop artist, and I tell her that I do not know, but that he is probably the most talented person that I have ever met. She walks us out to the car and tells me that she prayed about our meeting earlier that day. As we prepare to leave, she begins to sing, in her gorgeous voice, TopNotch's favorite childhood hymn, "Just a Closer Walk with Thee."

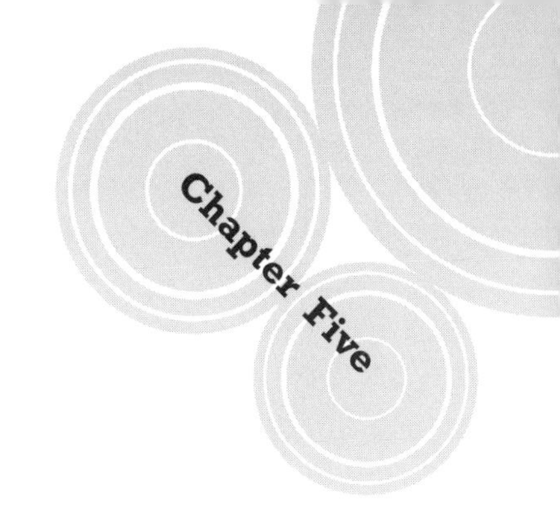

Musical Mobilities

Just as dirty Bill [Clinton] kept the White House close to the outhouse, Southern hiphop's progressive wing was sustaining the brain-teasing verbal panache and shock-of-the-new funk we once snootily considered the sole province of us uppity upsouth cosmopolite muhfuhs. They also proved you could keep it thoughtful and pimpstrollful, goofball and gangsta, conspiracy-theoried and crunk. Being Dirty Southern means never having to say you're sorry for Master P or *The Matrix Reloaded.*
—Greg Tate[1]

The blues crossroads, a symbol of Clarksdale's creative energy, also marks the site of an important global intersection that is as much a part of the regional identity as the rich, spongy soil upon which it sits. The unique cultural convergence that defines the Mississippi Delta can be traced through the town's history as a center for agricultural trade. The suitability of the lush Delta ground for cotton planting led to the arrival of enterprising Anglo development in the years just before and after the Civil War. These planters' ambitious desires for massive land clearing, the creation of a levee system and the labor-intensive nature of cotton planting demanded the massive importation of slave or, after the Civil War, low-wage or conscripted black labor, who retained familial ties to relatives in cities and distant plantations as well as cultural ties to a globally grounded Africa.

As the need for cotton workers grew, Italian, Lebanese, Jewish, Mexican, and Chinese families were brought in to supplement this black labor. Dissatisfied with plantation work and capitalizing on their racial ambiguity in a dualistic society, many of these later immigrants started butcher shops, dry-goods markets, tamale stands, clothing stores, or bootlegging operations. These immigrants were positioned between the black and white social worlds and found a niche in supplying both the planters and their workers with material goods. Clarksdale, enveloped in the vast swampy land of the Mississippi Delta, was situated at the nexus of global influence. The unique foodways, craft, and performance modes of the Delta, resonating under the tin roofs of town and country, represent a cosmopolitan marketplace of multiethnic traditions and practices.

Clarksdale is positioned between Memphis and New Orleans on the arterial "Blues Highway" 61. Photograph by the author.

The Sunflower River and the crossing of Highways of 49 and 61 in Clarksdale were important points of convergence for both the cotton trade and the mass migrations of the early twentieth century. As Reconstruction-era black laborers began to travel throughout the Deep South in search of seasonal employment, the railroad and crossroads became a gathering place for those moving north, visiting south, or staying a while to earn a small income chopping, picking, or ginning cotton in the right seasons. The train ran through the center of Clarksdale and black travelers could approach the segregated window and buy a ticket north to Chicago for $11.50. Black rail porters traded race newspapers and gossip from the big city for well wishes and more gossip from down home. Boarding houses, juke joints, soul food restaurants, gambling parlors, music shops, tamale stands, bordellos, clothing stores, and churches lined the streets of the black downtown. The New World district became an important hub of African American musical creativity, a stop on the chitlin circuit, and a central gathering place for the scores of plantation blues players who lived in surrounding areas.

John Work and Lewis Jones's 1941 study of the records available on Clarksdale jukeboxes shows that African American tastes in the prewar Delta were anything but provincial. Glenn Miller, Sister Rosetta Tharpe, and Louis Jordan were featured prominently, as were St. Louis pianist Walter Davis, Count Basie, and Fats Waller.[2] Jazz critic Tony Russell, in his 1971 reflection on the Coahoma

County survey, was led to ask, "So what of all the blues amidst all this? . . . Of the 108 listings on five boxes, less than thirty are the blues . . ."[3]

Traveling workers, musicians and family members brought records and fashion from across the country. The burgeoning race recording industry acted as a sort of national telephone line as musicians added to new styles, themes, and songs a distinctly local flavor. Many black Deltans listened to the Grand Ole Opry, a radio show that brought countrified versions of black minstrel tunes and gussied-up blues covers in the guise of honky-tonk over the airwaves. Big-band directors such as W. C. Handy introduced the latest in popular dance music to eager Delta listeners. Delta bluesmen and women worked these new styles into their repertoires, and reciprocated by sending their own songs into the market.[4] Peetie Wheatstraw, the Mississippi Sheiks, David "Honeyboy" Edwards, Charlie Patton, Robert Johnson, Memphis Minnie, and many others recorded their brand of the blues for the Vocalion, Bluebird, Paramount, OKeh, Yazoo and American Record Company labels.

Eventually the crossroads that once drew African Americans to the Delta became a means for the great migration away from the South, draining guests and revelers from the streets of the New World district. Retail chain stores drew business down the highway; the loss of industry and agricultural work drastically slowed the stream of visiting performers and audiences to the Delta. But the urban/rural cultural and kinship ties remained intact. Reunions and summer visits continue to bring family members back to the Delta, along with fresh expressions, styles, and sounds. In turn, these visitors invigorate their own expressive culture though the "country" vernacular of their Southern relatives. A Chicago cousin brings a Lupe Fiasco CD to the Delta and returns describing his dinner as "steak and skrimp" in the Delta slang. The Delta drawl, exaggerated by youth in a constant process of linguistic creativity, finds its way back into the big city through a diasporic network that passes words and concepts like the recently-popular "crunk" (a word that describes a hard, bass-heavy club aesthetic) north (and west) of the Mason-Dixon. Renowned Mississippi rapper David Banner's connections in the town, its proximity to Memphis (via the Blues Highway), its walkable neighborhoods, its status as a onetime home to well-known hip-hop artist Nate Dogg, and the thriving underground music network instantiated by the blues account for Clarksdale's reputation as the hip-hop center of the Delta.

Cable television and commercial radio expose Delta youth to the sounds of greater national trends in black music. The old jukeboxes that once made Clarksdale nightlife famous hold records from Marvin Gaye, B. B. King, Whodini, and Lil' Wayne side by side with local hits. Like the blues artists of the New World district, contemporary Clarksdale hip-hop artists choose their styles from a diverse array of influences and then shape them to fit the local aesthetic. Just as the spirituals were used by slaves to communicate from plantation to plantation the arrival of the Underground Railroad or illicit meetings, so are contemporary musical forms used to engage African Americans in the Delta in a call and response with all corners of the African diaspora. The work of cultural practitioners in this area is not dictated by insularity. In fact, it is the result of masterful aesthetic choices—ones made from a world of possibility. In a region where traditions of identity-making and -remaking run particularly deep, artists remain in conversation with global movements by mixing popular trends into local expressive practices.

Hip-hop, an Afrocentric cultural and social movement organized by New York deejay and producer Afrika Bambaataa, was at first a particular subset of a much larger popular stylistic shift from the overproduced disco vocal of the mid-seventies to the more punctual late-seventies rap lyric. In these rising East Coast (and, later, West Coast) rap styles, Delta youth saw both the reflection of their own culture and a fresh set of aesthetic technologies with which to express their ideas. Rather than mimic or ignore the styles of these urban MCs, Delta youth engaged in an extended stylistic conversation with urban black practitioners. Young blues players rapped in the interludes of their performances, their fresh gold chains bouncing on their chests, Delta radio deejays spun the latest dance track from Kurtis Blow, and girls modified the satin jackets and colorful sneakers made popular by inner-city Afro-Rican youth. They infused urban styles with local flavor and re-versioned popular pieces to fit regional expressive modes.

Bridging the Gap

Just as with the blues, genre trouble often comes to bear in endless popular debate over what the constitution of the rap and hip-hop forms must be. These terms are deployed in innumerable ways and in as many contexts, and have shifted over time to signify a series of interconnected meanings. In practice, *rap* refers to the use of the rhythmic, musical spoken word, usually secular, in Black Atlantic culture. Classic blues singers, poets, Black Nationalist leaders, New York hip-hop artists, and rappers from the Dirty South are all rap practitioners. As the New York rap scene crystallized in the popular imagination with the late-1970s release of the Sugar Hill Gang's music, rap was used to label this new genre. Despite this specific adaptation, rap retains its wider use in many of the neighborhoods and clubs in which the spoken word is used. When the Dirty South broke into the popular music scene in the late 1980s and 1990s, its artists used the familiar term to signify continuities between their community practice and the marketing genre. Thirty years after the release of the first rap singles, the commercial term is today rarely applied to anyone but Southern artists, who continue to define themselves as rappers, choosing to remain connected, in name, to their regional creative networks rather than larger market trends or academic discourses.

Meanwhile, another term has come to define certain sounds and scenes emanating from the practice of rap. In the Bronx, where a series of unique social and cultural circumstances converged in the entry of classic New York rap into the popular market, the aesthetics of rap practice continued to shift with a life of its own. In the 1970s New York was folding in on itself financially; overspending had caused the city to cut its sanitation and public safety expenditures to negligible levels. An influx of in-migration from the Caribbean, the flight of the city's upper-middle-class tax base, and a national recession meant massive unemployment and a lack of government support for the working poor. Street gangs cropped up to offer young people protection and community in the midst of the crumbling ghetto. Against this backdrop of socioeconomic depression, neighborhood youth banded together in parks and garages with crates of old funk records and their voices, and set to creating a fresh sound that would speak to their circumstances. Early hip-hop functioned as an opportunity to express dissatisfaction and dreams in rhyme, but more importantly made social space for youth to celebrate dynamic community creativity, as described by Mark Anthony Neal: "Historically African-American youth culture has rarely been driven by ideological concerns, but instead has embraced, appropriated, and reanimated existing structures, organizations, and institutions that African-American youth perceived as empowering them within various social, cultural, and economic constructs."[5] New York rapper Nas's recent hip-hop poem to the blues illustrates the continuities between urban styles and agrarian forms: "My Pop told me be your own boss / Keep integrity at every cost, and his home was Natchez Mississippi / Did it like Miles and Dizzy, now we gettin' busy / Bridging the gap from the blues, to jazz, to rap / The history of music on this track."[6]

DJ Kool Herc, a Jamaican immigrant to New York, drew from the Caribbean sound system and toasting traditions to initiate impromptu dance parties in Bronx public parks. Using two turntables and a mixer, Herc and other DJs created new sounds by looping, cutting, and scratching old records. Over the instrumental breaks, DJs rapped greetings, invitations to parties, and declarations of their own prowess to the crowds. As the DJs became deeply involved in new, technically demanding scratching and mixing techniques, they enlisted MCs to rap over their beats. Crews would challenge each other's verbal skills, and the crowd chose a winner according to which group exhibited the most creativity and finesse. Like the schoolyard dozens, the competitor who could improvise the best response to the jibes of an opponent became the evening's master of words, music, and style.

Rap's first commercial record label, New Jersey's Sugar Hill, drew its most famous artists from the outer boroughs, and brought East Coast urban rap styles onto the popular stage. The label's aim was success on the popular market. Label owners Joe and Sylvia Robinson sought to combine the vernacular sounds of hip-hop street parties with the appeal of polished pop, and their combination of catchy rap styles and reversioned commercial disco tunes immediately caught the national ear. Because the popular interest in rap can be traced to Sugar Hill's catalog, historians often tie the genre inextricably to these record-company representations of the urban ghetto. But Sugar Hill's bright, simple commercial sound is a limited stethoscope to the rich sounds of its contemporary borough neighborhood gatherings and street rap battles, which were stylistically more similar to black vernacular traditions of eloquence than popular disco hits. DJs drew from a well of Southern funk classics, Jamaican sound system favorites, jazz, Puerto Rican bongo beats, and classic rare grooves to create their musical scores.

Under the auspices of Black Nationalist visionaries Grandmaster Flash, Afrika Bambaataa, DJ Kool Herc, and others, traditional black verbal art and musical styles were reversioned to shape the East Coast urban hip-hop moment. Bambaataa, a former neighborhood gang leader who was inspired by new global technologies of rhythm, organized the Hip-Hop Nation, a group of rappers that included the Native Tongues Posse, Queen Latifah, Public Enemy, and others who focused their art on the creation of positive, self-described Afrocentric spaces for the sustenance of black creative life. Connections between New York's hip-hop movement and the greater black diasporic creativity are manifest in the cultural identifications of hip-hop's progenitors. Afrika Bambaataa conceptualized hip-hop as a movement based on a "Zulu Nation," in which multiethnic oppressed people bound together under the power of creativity. Bambaataa's guiding aesthetic principles for this movement were based in the diasporic core aesthetics: polyrhythms, deep bass, stylistic flash, antiphony, and sampling from the old to create emergent meaning.[7] In addition to his intra-diasporic outreach, Bambaataa articulated an intertextual approach to hip-hop, bringing b-boying (or breakdancing) styles, turntablism (or musical creativity), graffiti art (visual aesthetics), and rapping under the hip-hop rubric. But although these practices have come to historically define "old skool" East Coast hip-hop, Southern rappers also stake a similar intertextual aesthetic claim today, according to TopNotch:

> If we want to do popularity, every coast gonna have a sayin' or have a way of feeling that their music is the best music. Popularity says that when the South became popular it has not fallen off. There was a period when West Coast music was the thing, and then the East Coast rappin' about in a dramatic sense, now you got Dirty South rappers, but, I mean, why can't we be hip-hop rappers in the South?
>
> We got cars with candy paint on them, is that not graffiti? You got women and men going to the club to go two-stepping at the movie theatre, and they're not dancing? You got rappers that from the South that's actually sayin' words that come out of their mouths and make a song that makes sense to 'em—is that not lyrics? You have the music bein' played in the club by a guy who spins in the corners all night—is that not DJing? The elements of hip hop—we have all of that in the South. I mean, as hip-hop as been defined![8]

From its earliest days hip-hop styles changed dramatically from moment to moment, even as they retained an identifiable set of aesthetic practices. The disco stylings of the late 1970s became the New Wave sound of Grandmaster Flash, Bambaataa's 1983 robotic electro-funk hit "Planet Rock" (based in Afrobeat rhythms and German prog rock sounds) was eclipsed by the rock 'n' roll swagger of Run-DMC and the mid-eighties Def Jam label. Bebop informed the work of the late-eighties Native Tongues Posse at the same time Puerto Rican youth in New York were releasing a lighting-fast, Latin-infused dance hip-hop called freestyle. Hip-hop spread to all corners of the globe where rap already existed and fused with traditional DJ, song, and toasting styles. Miami emphasized the bass drum and added Afro-Cuban rhythmic flair; L.A. adapted the hard electro-funk dance sound, adding Middle Eastern and techno aesthetics to the mix. Eventually West Coast producer Dr. Dre infused the soaring psychedelic synthesizer sounds of P-Funk into his production to create the nineties gangsta aesthetic. French, Cuban, Puerto Rican, and West African youth mixed the New York style into their own traditions, foregrounding the percussive spoken word where they previously might have sung a verse.

Although black residents of the Deep South are geographically removed from the East Coast urban situation, the early hip-hop movement was not lost on them. Just as the Delta bluesmen once incorporated national jazz and pop styles into their performances, young practitioners in the Delta introduced elements of New York hip-hop into their traditional local rap styles as soon as it hit the airwaves. In one form or another, rap has been a prime discursive and performative tool throughout the history of the Deep South. The medium was only reinvigorated with the emergence of a new urban black expressive culture in the form of hip-hop. Traditional Southern verbal art did much more than work its way through generations of black southerners; it also provided—and continues to provide—a changing same: a wellspring of style for hip-hop artists around the world. To separate the verbal art of the urban North and the agrarian South is to arbitrarily shatter a brilliant and multifaceted whole. For TopNotch this regional style is only one angle of a greater call and response between global hip-hop practitioners:

> Given the fact that down South rappers or hip-hop artists have a tendency to rap about the things that they have or glorifying things that they do more than the other hip-hop cultures—if there's a sudden fact that we're not hip-hop artists because of what you hear in New York or New Jersey . . . ? We all have different styles, and that's great, but the fact that we attack each other region to region, that's a problem.[9]

Many popular hip-hop writers, concerned primarily with contemporary trends in the commercial development of the genre, focused on its development within the urban centers of the U.S. rather than in terms of its diasporic aesthetic connections. The idea that hip-hop practice had its genesis at a particular time and place provides museums and music television "history of" shows a simple narrative with which the mainstream can make some sense of the complexity of black aesthetic practice. Without this historicity, the projects would overrun their boundaries or resist documentation altogether. But these narratives can be harmful, too, lending themselves to commercial caricature. A 2001 Heineken ad released at the height of hip-hop nostalgia featured a scene in which a ham-fisted deejay accidentally invents the hip-hop scratch when a beer is spilled on his turntables: "March 8, 1982/The Birth of Scratching. It's all about the Beer." This narrative both misrepresents pre-commercial hip-hop practices (including scratching techniques) that crystallized in the mid-1970s and removes agency from both the practitioner and the diasporic creativity from which he or she draws. Narrow histories that fail to acknowledge the complex global continuities of hip-hop practice also tend to marginalize the work of southern artists. Their peripheral/inauthentic Dirty South is often only partially represented as the genre's outlying, buffoonish "late-comer."

Michael Eric Dyson describes the nuanced difference between mainstream conceptions of hip-hop and rap in terms of its deployment by critics of certain rap cultures:

> A preference for hip-hop artists who are positive (no cursing, no self-denigrating epithets, no violent references to the ghetto) often overlooks the question of whether they have intellectual depth and the ability to flow. By contrast,

rappers viewed as negative—if for no other reason than they employ the word "nigga" in their repertoire, a charge, by the way, that can be made against many rappers otherwise considered to be positive—may possess these qualities in abundance.[10]

The same categorization Dyson describes is often directed at southern rappers, whose heavily signified music encompasses the joy of the jukes and the realities of life at the low end. This is compounded by the insatiable thirst on the part of popular rap consumers, largely composed of white suburban teens not trained in the nuances of hip-hop aesthetics, for sensational representations of southern black life. But even as southern hip-hop, in the form of crunk or trap, booty-bass and snap, screwed and chopped, trill, bounce, or just plain country-style, is rhetorically posed at the end point of hip-hop history, those who love the music are well aware of its life-affirming powers.

Hip-Hop's Third Coast

Nationally recognized Delta blues artists (and subsequent migrants to Chicago) including Muddy Waters, Howlin' Wolf, and John Lee Hooker used a delivery style that was as percussive as it was melodic, often breaking from sung verse to spoken "blues talk." Waters's "Mannish Boy" and Hooker's "Boogie Chillun" are excellent examples of the use of spoken-word delivery over repetitive instrumental riffs. Much as the looped, extended musical break allowed New York hip-hop artists to improvise rhyme and create a rapport with audience members, Delta blues artists used a guitar dirge and rolling rhythm to structure their improvised narrative. Southern women singers including Big Mama Thornton, Memphis Minnie, Koko Taylor, and Sippie Wallace used rap styles too, to rile up crowds and engage in dialogues of badness. Taylor, in particular, uses extended musical breaks to recite and improvise verse in the live arena. Just north, in Memphis, WDIA Radio deejay Rufus Thomas turned his announcer's cadence into a percussive rap called "Walking the Dog," a song drawn from children's rhyming games and rock 'n' roll rhythms: "Mary Mac, dressed in black, silver buttons all down her back / High, low, tipsy toe, she broke the needle and she can't sew."[11]

Isaac Hayes, who entered the Memphis scene as a Stax studio session musician, wove percussive speech into his soul compositions (Sam and Dave's "Soul Man") and his own recordings in the late 1960s and 1970s, including his lazily-recited "Hyperbolicsyllabicsesquedalimystic," a ten-minute dirge-rap about the fusion of mind and body in song. He continued to nestle a series of raps and monologues in each of his albums for Stax, culminating in his 1971 soundtrack for *Shaft*, in which he depicted a traditional rapping badman brought to cinematic life through Blaxploitation. Although Hayes and Thomas retained enough vocal melody and youthful cachet to qualify as pop singers, their styles helped to update and perpetuate their regional classic toast, rap, and master-of-words traditions. Another of rap's earliest popular appearances occurred with Durham, North Carolina, chitlin circuit comedian Pigmeat Markham's 1968 "Here Comes the Judge," a piece recited entirely in a toasting cadence. The song starts with the bailiff's introduction of the judge to the "courtroom of swing" and proceeds to pillory his austerity and authority: "This Judge is hip, and that ain't all, / He'll give you time if you're big or small . . . / Here comes the Judge! Everybody knows that he is the judge!"[12]

The largest Southern contributor to the classic hip-hop aesthetic is James Brown, whose backing band, voice, and lyrics were sampled heavily in the first decade of popular hip-hop. His most important aesthetic contribution to hip-hop's sound was the *break*, or a section of instrumental music similar to a bridge, in which the drummer (usually Clyde Stubblefield of the JB's) "breaks down" the song's rhythm either solo or with the accompaniment of a spare bass guitar. This intense section of the song provides the dancer with an opportunity to interact with the rhythm, to fill it in the spaces between the beats with his or her style. The concept of the break can also be found in traditional gospel music, where singing stops so that churchgoers can "work out" their joys in dance. In the remixed aesthetic of hip-hop, the break provides the opportunity for the DJ to play extended instrumental sections so that MCs have time to rhyme. By staggering, or "juggling" double copies of a record on two turntables, the DJ could extend the break to last the entirety of a rap performance. The classic JB's break is ubiquitous to the early East Coast "old skool" hip-hop sound. Brown's deep connection to dynamic diasporic styles is manifest in his use of his spangled Pentecostal breaks, screaming blues riffs, and the complex polyrhythms of the Nigerian musicians with whom he collaborated during his 1970 tour of Africa.

On top of the rhythm-heavy instrumentation of his seventies funk, Brown did not exactly sing, as he certainly had on his earliest soul albums. Instead, he drew from preaching and rhyming styles from his childhood in rural Georgia to create his reversioned rapping cadence. The traditional diasporic aesthetics of call and response, polyrhythm, personal style, and repetition are foregrounded in this work. The rhetoric of urban Black Nationalist groups, themselves often only one generation removed from southern life, also worked its way into Brown's rap: "Though I need it—soul power / Got to have it—soul power . . . / I want to get under your skin / If I get there, I've got to, got to win."[13]

H. Rap Brown, the Justice Minister of the Black Panther Party, employed verbal styles he learned in his hometown of Baton Rouge, Louisiana, to shape the rhetoric of the Black Nationalist movement. In his tome *Die, Nigger, Die*, Brown describes speech as a process: "I learned how to talk in the street, not from reading Dick and Jane. . . . We learned what the white folks called verbal skills. We learned how to throw them words together. America, however, has black folk in a serious game of the Dozens."[14] New York Black Nationalist poetry group the Last Poets, often cited among the earliest recording hip-hop artists, drew clear inspiration from the music of the Deep South. They begin their 1971 recording *This Is Madness* with a paean to the timelessness of the blues: "True blues ain't no new news 'bout who's been abused, for the blues is old as my stolen soul . . . I sing the backwater blues, rhythm and blues, gospel blues, St. Louis Blues, crosstown blues, Chicago blues, Mississippi Goddamn! blues, Watts blues, Harlem blues, Hull blues, gutbucket blues, funky junky blues . . . I sing about my sho' 'nuf blues blackness."[15] The use of down-home blues talk as a discursive site for African American cultural expression and negotiation continues today. New York rapper Nas's 2004 hit "Bridging the Gap," for instance, samples his father Olu Dara (a former resident of Natchez, Mississippi, and a jazz musician) to show the continuity of agrarian and urban oral/musical styles.

In 1970s-era New York, black filmmakers employed the oppositional figure of the toast-teller's badman. The "pimps," "hustlers," and "badasses" of the black-written, directed, and produced Blaxploitation genre had their genesis in the traditional black folk hero who retained currency in the agrarian South. Rudy Ray Moore, a classic Blaxploitation genre actor, used material from the toasts he learned as a child in Arkansas to create a heavily signified 1970s pimp character—a rapping, raunchy ghetto Robin Hood who saved his neighborhood from death and poverty. *Black Caesar* (with a theme song by James Brown), Ossie Davis's *Cotton Goes to Harlem*, and *Across 110th Street* each played out the themes of the Southern badman on the streets of New York during its most dismal economic years. The pimp and "hustla" archetypes of the toasts and Blaxploitation cinema were especially meaningful to West Coast rappers, many of whom used the badman antitype to express strength, authorship, and a particular brand of masculinity amidst a devastated racist economy.

Just as popular black performers and revolutionary political speakers employed traditional styles of rhythmic speech to speak to contemporary circumstances, hip-hop's founding moments (and subsequent stylistic shifts) represented a synthesis of established and emergent styles. Black radio styles, which drew upon both master-of-words traditions and new technologies, allowed deejays to comment upon and talk over the strains of popular R&B

hits. In Clarksdale today, the prototypical club deejay style upon which early hip-hop was founded is still popular. A deejay, equipped with two turntables (or in contemporary Clarksdale, double CD players), fades one song into another to create a particular atmosphere, often rewinding and replaying portions of a song in conversation with his or her own improvised poetry. For DJ Dr. Pepper of the Delta Blues Room (a club catering to a "grown" African American crowd), success is not so much song selection but his ability to recognize and shout out greetings to patrons as they enter the club, to utilize or improvise witty rhymes, and to incite dancing. He knows his community well; his family has owned and operated a religious supply store and printing press in the New World district since 1937. He is also a veteran who retired from the army in 1988 after thirty-three years of service. His music and wordcraft is his passion:

> I think the reason that I do fairly well as a DJ is people skills. I've learned over the years that people like to be recognized; they like recognition. Not all people want to be recognized; you have to know the people around you and who to recognize because you might get your nose bloodied if you shout out the wrong somebody—you don't want to do that. One of the mottoes of the Delta Blues Room is that it's like Las Vegas. What goes on in the Delta Blues Room stays in the Delta Blues Room. To be a club jock (and there is a difference between a club and a radio jock because you're dealing with people): the radio jock has a set selection of records that he's gonna play. Very seldom now on radio do you have a request line. Bein' a club jock is real simple. Within reason, you play what the people ask you to play, you play what they want to hear, and really they dictate the show. And remember that you work for them. There's another form of being a public servant.
>
> Over during the forty years I've been doing this, I've done shows with most of the blues artists: Bobby Rush, Bobby Bland, and I think everything as far as black music is concerned, it really started in the church. If you listen to a lot of the original soul music—same music as some of the popular black church songs, different words.
>
> Well, I try to learn from everybody. We pick up something from recording artists, you pick up something from other DJs, and them you combine everything and try to come up with something that's original for you. I think I would attribute my ability to talk well—I listen well. I try to absorb what I hear. And when I say that I'm talking about the blues artists and the lyrics to their songs, and you learn from other people. Little catchy phrases that they might have in their song and you can use it in a show, I guess that's a form of stealing. . . .
>
> It's nothing that you learn, now. Let me put it like this: You listen to other

DJ Doctor Pepper at his family's Church Supply shop in the New World district, where his grandfather self-published religious sermons and poems. Photograph by the author.

deejays, you listen to the lyrics of songs, you listen to the people around you, the guy at the bar telling jokes or whatever, if you want to call that learning. You remember things that strike you. A lot of deejays, I remember we used to have deejay battles to see who is the best deejay, and after I participated in one and it got outta hand, I learned then that nobody can be the best Dr. Pepper but me, so do what you do, and don't worry about the next deejay or his style. Be yourself. That's what makes me the best Dr. Pepper.

Every show is different, you learn from experience—if you've got an older crowd in there, they don't wanna hear what you go to say early on. So what you do is try to set the mood. If you know anything about being a deejay, you know what to play: a little Teddy Pendergrass, a little Bobby Bland, with an older crowd, it's like an old pump—they gotta be primed. The younger crowd, if they already ready to go, you can start doin' a little rap session almost immediately. And if you got a mixed crowd, then you play accordingly: one for the older guys, the older couples, and one for the younger couples, And when you're on the road, I like to get to a club early . . . that'll give me an hour to set up, change clothes, and just listen to what they play on the jukebox and I know where I am then. I don't know—it's just something that you feel, and you feel like it's time to say it, and I've been doin' it so long, it's just natural once you start the show, it's just something that you do.[16]

In the Delta, deejays often work in pairs; one person manipulates the music while another focuses on rapping with the crowd. This is less an imitation of New York hip-hop styles than a practice drawn from local house party and juke joint traditions that call for a master or mistress of ceremonies: a club owner, blues player, radio announcer, or popular host who regulates and coordinates the party through artful talk and a keen social sense. The regulatory role embodied by the MC is also foregrounded in germinal New York hip-hop, as in Grandmaster Flash and the Furious Five's late-seventies classic "Superrappin'": "Take your time and you will agree / That black girl got good security / So when you walk through the door, just do me a favor / Be sure to be on your best behavior."[17] The similarities of contemporary deejay styles in the Delta and those of old-school hip-hop are not lost on Delta club deejays. Many are known to quote freely from the Sugarhill Gang or Grandmaster Flash in the course of a vamp; DJ Dingo of Clarksdale's My Brothers' Sports Bar has a series of Flash-inflected raps he recites over the strains of his own turntablism. In the world of black musical production, symbols, sounds, and styles are freely passed between generations and regions via radio waves, videos, commercial recordings, touring artists, and traveling tradition-bearers. The rich call and response between the practices of the agrarian South and those of the urban centers complicates the linear model of musical development favored by narratives of authenticity.

DJ Dr. Pepper's poetic legacy illustrates the interplay between genre, style and sense of place. His grandfather, the Reverend S. L. A. Jones, was known throughout his community as a talented composer of spiritual verse, sermons, and ceremonial addresses. He owned and operated his own printing press and religious supply store in Clarksdale's New World district in the 1930s, a remarkable accomplishment for a person of color under the harsh Jim Crow laws that prevented many blacks from gaining literacy. His self-published pamphlet, "Addresses for Special Occasions," offers a series of "addresses, responds, obituaries and resolutions" for use in church services, and Jones offers a series of suggestions for the composition of obituaries: "3. Try to be as tactful as possible when reading the obituary before the public, and be sure it's true."[18] He quotes from Kipling and Whittier throughout these published sermons, and he offers much poetic wisdom of his own:

> Death is not a choice; he visits the cradle as well as the childhood. All must come to an end. The redwoods of California which have been standing for all ages must at some time become sapless and die. Flowers grow and produce beautiful blossoms of every hue, but they must in due time wither and fade away. . . . Everything must finish its work, close its books and come to a timely end. Death will visit all ages and all seasons. All life spans are comparatively

brief and without doubt end. Death may many times without warning creep up on people on highways. In the home, Death may appear at any time and at any place. Death aim, and [its] blows are sure.[19]

Jones's verse draws from the rich sense of rhythm and repetition for which the extemporaneous poetry of the Delta is known. The continuities between Jones's impassioned addresses and his grandson's own inimitable contemporary deejay style are many, including the use of a particular motif as a basis for improvisation, a sensitivity to the community's social circumstances, and a shared talent for highly stylized and inventive wordplay. According to the deejay, the genre and technologies of communication may change, but words and rhythm remain as integral to the community life of the Delta as ever.

> I remember when, if there was one television on the block, you're doing good. And the only type of entertainment that you had was each other—you had to communicate even if you were shooting marbles, whatever you were doing. You see now, it's just like me, looking at my laptop twenty out of twenty-four hours a day. People now communicate electronically—they used to communicate verbally.
>
> But I used to do free shows at the schools here in town, and third, fourth, and fifth graders could memorize a rap song word for word and couldn't spell their name, and it's just interest—that's what they like, and that's what they hear at home. If you hear Beethoven at home, you'd know that was Beethoven's fifth. If you hear Tupac at home, that's who you're goin' to associate with.[20]

As the dynamic story of Southern poetry and flow emerges between the cracks of popular music history, a hip-hop story that begins and ends with the Northeastern urban ghetto becomes increasingly untenable.[21] Urban hip-hop artists continue to pull from agrarian aesthetic and lyrical themes to illustrate these historical continuities, just as agrarian artists reference Tupac's urban themes. In KRS-One's "Sound of da Police," the two contexts line up perfectly in the space of hip-hop verbal conjuration: "The overseer had the right to get ill / And if you fought back, the overseer had the right to kill / The officer has the right to arrest / And if you fight back they put a hole in your chest!"[22] Because hip-hop historicization has emanated from New York, the questions of hip-hop authenticity that plague southern artists are rarely applied to urban artists who sample the sounds, themes, and traditions of the agrarian South. Hip-hop practice involves crossing the lines of representation, identity and genre that separate and taxonomize mainstream music. The music's power lies in its deeper aesthetic and thematic continuities—its changing same.

Shops like Boss Ugly Bob's in Memphis specialize in local "mix tapes" for which underground hip-hop artists remix and rap over popular songs. Photograph by the author.

Although many southern rappers tend to identify themselves as such (rather than as hip-hop artists), their self-styled membership in the hip-hop movement is undeniable. Their engagement with the world of hip-hop incorporates global styles with the hustler's marketing savvy as Southern artists make space for themselves in the world of popular music. The first breakthrough for the Dirty South was the arrival of Miami booty-bass in the form of Luke Skyywalker's 2 Live Crew, which fused the sounds of New York electro and freestyle variations with Afro-Latin percussive aesthetics. This music is highly rhythmic and club-oriented. Bass music features less complex lyrics than its New York counterpart, drawing from children's rhyming games and folk dance styles to engage the audience in group chant and dance. Houston's Geto Boys used West Coast gangsta scripts to discuss their experience with southern poverty.

Atlanta group Arrested Development, drawing from their childhood experience in rural Tennessee, built their aesthetic around themes of southern folklife, sampling acoustic/folk instruments and heritage. In 1992, after "3 Years, 5 Months & 2 Days in the Life Of . . ." trying to release their first record (also the title of their album), they scored a pop chart-topping hit with "Tennessee." The group sampled the song's beats from Minneapolis artist Prince while also conjuring the fife-and-drum aesthetic of their neighbors in Mississippi hill country. They reference folk traditions such as double-dutch and horseshoes as well as the kind of immanent spirituality that defines the plantation church:

"Walk the roads my forefathers walked / Climbed the trees my forefathers hung from . . . / For some strange reason it had to be (home) / He guided me to Tennessee (home)."[23] The song created a kind of popular-music niche into which agrarian aesthetics were inserted by rap communities that could not be defined as "urban." In a 1993 article on the group for *Vibe*, bell hooks discusses the cultural connections between agrarian and urban lack communities with Arrested Development leader Speech:

> BELL: People forget that before 1960 many Black people lived in the agrarian South. As someone who has experienced both the urban life of Atlanta and the rural life of Tennessee, how has Southern life inspired you?
>
> SPEECH: I felt a special warmth spending time there while growing up. I felt like I was being embraced down South. I also felt the spirits of a lot of our ancestors who had been enslaved and hanged from trees and who had worked those fields calling me. They gave me ideas and thoughts. Down South, I feel warm, almost as if the ancestors are speaking to me or holding me.[24]

Southern groups including Atlanta's Outkast and Bowling Green's Nappy Roots sample folk tradition in various forms. Whether with an acoustic guitar, a looped blues chorus, or a reference to folkdance, soul food, or church, these groups merge southern experiences with global trends. In their 1996 musical manifesto on the southern hip-hop aesthetic, Atlanta's Goodie Mob teamed with Memphis's 8 Ball and MJG: "Hell, I'm giving you a dose of my knowledge with hot gravy / Jimmy Swaggart, Reverend Ike, and his wife: they couldn't save me / A buttered toast midnight snack with cold water / Too late to thaw the chicken and cook it, so I ain't bothered."[25]

Aesthetic conversations have been taking place across hip-hop's urban/agrarian networks from the moment of the first Bronx breakbeat. Early urban hip-hop deejays, reared on the Memphis Stax sound as remixed by Kingston reggae artists, used funk samples from the deepest South as the basis of their cosmopolitan style. Black communities on the West Coast expanded greatly with the building of munitions factories during World War II, and many families migrated west to these areas from the Delta, Louisiana, Houston, and the plantation towns of the Deep South for job opportunities. The family ties between residents of these areas remain strong today, and artists such as Oakland's Too $hort and Mississippi's David Banner travel freely between the urban West Coast and the South. They carry with them the cultural traditions of the South and their reinterpretations, reinforcing the cultural ties that connect both groups.

The laid-back, West Coast hip-hop style that emerged in the early 1990s shows a strong connection between agrarian and urban aesthetics. Central to this sound was Snoop Dogg, a Long Beach, California, rapper whose parents hail from Mississippi. Snoop Dogg's signature was his slow Southern "country" drawl and his use of extra syllables to lengthen his words. His rhymes drew from agrarian children's games and the badman swagger. Snoop's cousin Nate Dogg, a Clarksdale-to-Long Beach transplant, became the first rapper from the Delta to appear on the national scene. He learned his smooth vocal style in the choir of New Hope Trinity Baptist Church in Clarksdale, where his father remains a pastor. An important figure in the recentering of the hip-hop aesthetic westward was Snoop and Nate Dogg producer Dr. Dre, whose mid-nineties production styles draw heavily from the multilayered, dirgy blues aesthetic. His song "Lyrical Gangbang," from his germinal 1992 release *The Chronic*, samples Led Zeppelin's version of "When the Levee Breaks," a song about the great 1927 Delta flood written by Kansas Joe McCoy and Memphis Minnie.[26]

Nelly, a St. Louis–based rapper with roots in Austin, Texas, employed the sounds of southern rhyming games on his breakthrough 2000 album *Country Grammar*, which set the stage for the direct involvement of southern hip-hop artists on the popular scene. The floodgates for the emergence of (and backlash against) hip-hop from the so-called Dirty South had begun. After the national rise of Atlanta-based groups Outkast and Goodie Mobb, a new southern hip-hop style called crunk rose form the South. Atlanta-based rapper and producer Lil' Jon, a former resident of Clarksdale, synthesized the syrupy sounds of Miami booty bass, Houston's "screwed and chopped," super-slow sound, and the shouted staccato of gangsta styles to create an aesthetic statement of unadulterated southern-ness. The result caught fire on the international market, and the sounds of southern hip-hop superceded the national popularity of coastal styles. In response to decades of coastal dominance in the realm of popular rap, southern artists conjured hip-hop's "Third Coast" as a site for stylistic innovation.[27]

The traditional diasporic badman figure found new currency in the guise of the crunk artist and, to the benefit of southern hip-hop practitioners, continues to catch fire in the popular imagination. A coup for the southern hip-hop legacy was Memphis group Three Six Mafia's 2006 Academy Award win for "It's Hard Out Here for a Pimp," their theme song for *Hustle and Flow*. The film features a fictional Memphis hip-hop artist and domestic abuser who arises from the streets of Orange Mound, Memphis's most challenged black ghetto. Although the film itself raises questions of representation (after all, many southern rappers consciously adopt a performative pimp persona without internalizing antisocial values), *Hustle and Flow* has turned the popular eye toward the work of hip-hop artists from "Memphissippi," a vast imaginary neighborhood where the traditions of the agrarian South meet urban technologies of creativity and survival. When the group appeared onstage to gather their Oscar for their theme song, viewers saw a tangle of twisted clothing and elaborately jeweled grills—a moment of comic relief in the midst of American regalia. But what the mainstream could not see through this heavily mediated representation was the groundbreaking, aesthetically complex work that characterizes hip-hop practice in the Dirty South.

In the wake of this success, the group was invited to participate in a racialized, burlesque-driven MTV reality show about their fictionalized move to the West Coast for a show called *Adventures in Hollyhood.* Although the show's scenario positions the group as countrified, misfit yokels lost amidst West Coast modernity, Three Six manage to flip the scripts of crunk representation to provide their own depiction of the Dirty South. Uninspired by the flavorlessness of the L.A. Scene, group members DJ Paul and Juicy J question whether they are supposed to be rapping about silicone and edamame or waxing on the flavorlessness of white aesthetics. They pull pranks on the disembodied speakerphone voice of their manager, Rosenberg, in an inversion of the music industry's imposed hierarchy. *Hollyhood,* disguised as common reality show fare, represents the group's more subversive plan to establish a space for southern aesthetics and authorship in the commercial realm. Like the most powerful features of Dirty South hip-hop practice, this intellectually driven intervention is hidden in plain sound.

David Banner, Global Gangsta

David Banner (neé Levell Crump), a contemporary Jackson, Mississippi, rapper with a larger-than-life persona—his moniker comes from the "other name" of comic superhero The Incredible Hulk—began his rise on the national popular music scene in the new millennium. His eloquence and intelligence earned him a higher education in Louisiana and a master's degree in business from Maryland, a far cry from the rural ghettoes of Jackson, where he grew up surrounded by the Deep South brand of poverty. Through his early work with Mississippi rap collectives to his international collaborations and unceasing production work, Banner quickly achieved major-label success. New York's Penalty Records caught on to his work early, but when his style did not translate to the label's urban context, Banner turned back to his local community for support. He formed Crooked Lettaz, a group whose lyrical focus was the reality of agrarian Southern poverty and celebration, and distributed his work through his own b.i.G.f.a.c.e. Productions, which stands for "believe in God for all comes eventually."[28] Banner retains his sense of place, appealing to the sentiments of the communities of the agrarian Deep South, and the local context to which he holds so tenaciously is crucial to understanding his hip-hop code.

David Banner chose his "other name" to reflect a brand of badness with a special currency in his home state. What looks like cut-and-paste gangsta rap to listeners from dominant groups is here an alternative script for the expression of black masculinity, based in the folk traditions of Banner's native Mississippi. These toasting and blues-boasting traditions involve a trickster figure—usually a hypermasculine badman, who signifies a kind of "power from below" attained in the context of historical emasculation. Resistance against these racist institutions is signified in the symbolic world of the pimp. At least since Reconstruction era rhymed toasts about "Stagolee" and "Dolemite," African American masters of words have employed the trickster archetype to express resistance, build community, and establish identity. This is especially true in the Deep South, where the expression of Afrocentric meaning has traditionally been coded into musical lyrics and aesthetics in order to obscure it from hostile eyes. When we pull focus from the gender and violence critiques that can be applied to all of American popular culture but are so often aimed exclusively toward black cultural production, we can see the complex of functions Banner's performance might serve.

Eventually, Banner worked his way up the national hip-hop ladder by amassing a string of production credits for crunk artists T.I., Lil Flip, and Yung Wun and scored a national hit with Nelly's controversial "Tip Drill." His success in the production realms of Atlanta and the West Coast earned him a seat at the popular table via a deal with Universal Records, where he records deeply signified variations on the gangsta, pimp, and thug tropes. In "Ridin'," a song from his album *Certified*, Banner raps the following lyric: "I'm from a place where you gotta let your nuts hang / Where them crackers used to cut your stomach open just to let your fuckin' guts hang / Right there in front of the kids / I might as well split your wig 'cause that's just what the master did."[29]

John W. Roberts, author of *From Trickster to Badman*, a sociohistorical exploration of the black folk hero, describes the badman of slavery times in terms of his methodology in sabotaging the order of the plantation: "They sought through open defiance, violence and confrontation to improve their lot in slavery regardless of the consequences of their actions for their own or the slave community's welfare."[30] Not only does the badman flaunt the law, he is a potential danger to those in his own community who would stand in his way. But when these localized traits cross the boundaries between local and popular cultures, artists wrap these oppositional messages in layers of illusive meaning. Enmeshed in and hiding behind Banner's lyrics is another message entirely.

While on the surface "Gangster Walk" appears to celebrate black-on-black violence, Banner is in fact referring to a masculine dance popular with young men in the dance clubs of the Deep South, a creative outlet for the expression of black masculinity that draws from traditional diasporic dance styles. In "Ridin'" Banner goes on to lay bare the activist possibilities made possible by his hip-hop persona: "But now I'm the new Nat Turner / Spreadin' something to the kids / Like Sojourner, Man, the truth."

The entirety of Banner's work is draped generously in heavily signified language. His first two solo albums, for instance, are entitled, *Mississippi: The Album* and *MTA2: Baptized in Dirty Water*. He also uses the popular medium of the music video to further explore the relationship between text and meaning. In his video for "Like a Pimp," he is seen running from white supremacists, tearing a noose fashioned from a rebel flag from his neck. In others, he is seen struggling to avoid eviction, walking through the poverty-filled streets of Jackson, or referencing civil rights abuses through his video imagery and costume. Robin D. G. Kelley, in his germinal exploration of the historical race rebel and his contemporary manifestation, the gangsta rapper, finds that the badman posture affected by many hip-hop artists resonates far more deeply than its surface tropes: "Whether gangsta rappers step into the character of a gang banger, hustler, or ordinary working person—that is, products and residents of the 'hood'—the important thing to remember is that they are stepping into character; it is for descriptive purposes rather than advocacy."[31]

Given Banner's deep roots in blues and gospel practices, his use of the badman figure as a creative outlet recalls in slow, menacing, stylized rhyme the trickster toasts of old that are still performed by young men in the rural South. The crossover between the traditional oral toasts and pop music performance involves new layers of signification and translation. In *Mystery Train*, Greil Marcus traces the thematic and performative translation of the *Stagolee* badman figure from vernacular oral performance to the popular music of Lloyd Price and Sly Stone.[32] In Mississippi the role of the badman was often assumed by the blues musician, the region's preeminent master of words. Like Muddy Waters, Banner draws from the local to create his signified world. In a thematic nod to the Muddy Mississippi, in fact, he named his second album *MTA2: Baptized in Dirty Water*.

In the video from Banner's "Cadillac on 22s," we see Banner walk away from the murder of a young girl and into a shirt reading, "RIP Emmett Till." Fourteen-year old Chicagoan Till was the victim of a 1955 lynching in the Delta town of Money, Mississippi. His purported crime was whistling at a working-class white woman, and his white killers, who openly confessed their crime, were absolved in a courtroom circus. Banner also repeatedly name-checks

Medgar Evers, the Jackson NAACP leader who was shot dead by a white supremacist in 1963. The video depicts the hanging deaths of Andre Jones and Reynold Johnson, two young Jackson men hung in a 1990s epidemic of unsolved Mississippi prison murders; Banner raps before their ghostlike images and removes the noose that hangs before them. He has spent cultural capital rallying for the exhumation of Till's body, justice for Jones and Johnson's murders, and funding for after-school programs and Katrina victims. His life-affirming action in the black neighborhoods of Jackson is palpable. In a May 2003 interview with the *Jackson Free Press*, Banner strikes a chord similar in tone to fellow Jackson native Richard Wright's *Native Son*:

> They don't have nothing to do in Jackson. They don't have any recreation. On top of that, when you do have events, the police patrol a little bit different than when white kids have events. It's like that's what they expect and what they want. That makes us upset; it's almost like a challenge. This weekend, I was driving my Dodge Viper, a $90,000 car, and I stopped at the mall. I had to run back to my car because I left something; I got there, and Narcotics was running my license plate. They're telling me subliminally that they don't want us to be successful. That pressures kids. If kids have nothing, they're not scared of jail. You have to give them some type of positive enforcement. Negativity is all they know.[33]

Banner demands that the nation and the hip-hop industry pay attention to the call of the Dirty South. When David Banner shouts that he is the "new Nat Turner," he is keying a performance of black masculinity that begs deeper interpretation. From trickster to pimp to thug to gangsta—to activist—the badman makes cultural space to critique Mississippi at its deepest and darkest levels, according to his mother, Carolyn Crump:

> "Remember *The Incredible Hulk* television show?" she says. "Dr. David Banner was a very well-educated, refined, humble person. But when people messed with him, what did he turn into? The Incredible Hulk.
>
> "Same with my son. He's humble, educated, fine and decent. He just becomes a whole 'nother person when he steps on stage. But it's all good because of the message he's trying to get across. . . .
>
> "He's a lot of people, but he's true to each of them."[34]

Thanks in part to Banner's efforts, Till's body was exhumed for the collection of further evidence in 2005. Banner hopes to see Till's murderers prosecuted posthumously. In "Mississippi," Banner's alternative state anthem, the artist uses words and rhythm to send a message loud and clear to "the home of the blues, the dirtiest part of the South" in which, he claims, "a flag means more than me."[35] For TopNotch and his peers, Banner's work is the ultimate regional inspiration:

> Let's take Hurricane Katrina for example, David Banner's was one of the first names you heard of giving back to Mississippi in general, the places that got hit the worst. When the global name hip-hop was in trouble by the White House, it was David Banner who was sticking up for the global name of hip-hop as a whole, whether the White House wants to blame something for the miscues and the negativity of what's going on the world today, and they want to place the blame on hip-hop. The true people that knew better really stood up for that and that's when I knew that I really had to do something local. So the purpose of my Delta hip-hop conference was just that.[36]

The Don Imus hearings in spring 2007 represented the (re)eruption of the elements of love and theft, blame and pity and naturalized xenophobia that trouble the relationships between dominant culture and emergent black creativity. This white radio announcer, a well-to-do baby boomer, pointed a finger at the Southern iteration of hip-hop as the cause of his racist and sexist remarks about women athletes of color, claiming that the very words he was using were generated by the black community. This swift defense deflected the blame from Imus's own casual hate speech and back to the partial representations of hip-hop that are so often projected on nonwhite bodies. Imus's approach resonated with the hegemonic discourses of American common sense. Talk show hosts, talking heads, and Congressional representatives alike overlooked Imus's transgressions and took another opportunity to call black male hip-hop artists to the stand.

Hip-hop academic and minister Michael Eric Dyson, New Orleans hip-hop artist and entrepreneur Percy "Master P" Miller, and David Banner were invited to testify before the House Subcommittee on Commerce, Trade and Consumer Protection, led by Illinois Congressman (and former Black Panther) Bobby Rush. They were questioned about the use of violent and misogynistic language and images in hip-hop for a hearing entitled, "From Imus to Industry: The Business of Stereotypes and Degradation." Tellingly, both rappers brought to the hearings are from the Deep South, and although Master P adopts a revisionist line on hip-hop lyricism, the trio managed to eloquently address issues of representation, embodiment, performativity, and complexity in hip-hop practice. Dyson insisted that these popular misinterpretations emerge from a misunderstanding of the complexity of hip-hop practice embodied by Banner's work.

> LBJ cussed like a sailor. Richard Nixon—they got the tapes—cussin' like a man goin' out of style. They're still the presidents of the United States . . . Look at

Richard Pryor, who used cursing in a very creative and interesting fashion, and yet he spoke about some of the most powerful social problems that prevailed in American culture.

Here's what we have to come to grips with: To be positive is not itself a virtue if it's not accompanied by serious, powerful art that forces us to reflect upon society. All art should not make you feel good. Some art should get in your face. Some art should be irreverent. The point and purpose of art is not simply to make you feel warm and fuzzy. Some art ought to make you change your bigoted ways . . .

But I think if we're looking for either/or, black-or-white answers, that's not it. . . . That's the convergence of complexity that manifests our conflicted lives. And I think that hip-hop at its best, again, both reflects the pathology that needs to be rooted out and provides an answer—a scalpel of rhetoric to dig into the body of the problem and see what the reality is.[37]

Later the committee directs its criticism toward Banner, who, like Dyson, attempts to subvert the positive/negative dichotomy that undergirds mainstream misunderstandings of Southern hip-hop practice. Banner explained the hidden cadence of his hip-hop activism even as his questioners failed to engage the texture of his art. "Have you ever *listened* to my music?" the artist asks the congressman who insists that Banner's ghetto-centric lyrics are inconsistent with his social activism.[38] Banner continues: "My message is very consistent, actually. I call my music a bible with a *Playboy* cover. I start here and I end at a different place."[39]

In her novel *Beloved*, Toni Morrison describes the action of a whip on the back of a woman, a slave, whose skin raises hard scars in the shape of a chokecherry tree. The branches of this abiding symbol of violence and transcendence extend to the practice of Southern artists today.[40] On his back, in a symbolic reclamation of skin where the scars of slavery were inscribed, Banner has thickly, permanently, tattooed the name of his troubled state, a signified rootedness to which he is fully committed:

"One of Mississippi's problems is that we have people who don't come back and change some of the things that pushed them out to begin with," he says.

"I understand why things happen in Mississippi, positive and negative. And if somebody doesn't stop this circle of pain, it will happen the rest of our lives.

"Let's stay here and get it right. I don't really have no choice, do I?"[41]

Meanwhile, Banner's music pumps from the trunks of thousands of young people in Mississippi: "Lord they hung Andre Jones, Lord they hung Reynold

Johnson / Lord I wanna fight back . . . / I dunno if I can take this world right here no more / 22 inch rims on the 'Lac, I guess that was yo footprint in the sand carrying us on yo back."[42] Banner's commitment to the local—to the kind of community empowerment engendered by Mississippi leaders Medgar Evers, Fannie Lou Hamer, and the churches, brother- and sisterhoods, and breadbasket organizations that have sustained the region in the worst circumstances—has not been lost on the current generation of 'Sip-hop practitioners. TopNotch cites Banner's influence in describing his desire to remain in the thick of his home community:

> If I was to leave, and I really don't see myself leaving per se, it's not in the immediate future, but if I was to leave, it is to get what I can get as far as more revenue and more stock and bring it back home to Mississippi. As a rapper, I know there will be shows that will take me to different places in the world. But home is exactly what it is. Anyone can live in somebody's house, but there's nothing more gratifying than just to be able to live in your own.[43]

Gnarled grill growling in the Mississippi sun, Banner rallies to increase afterschool programs, exhume the bodies of lynching victims, and bring attention to the institutionalized lack upon which racial dynamics are structured. Banner broadcasts his richly signified message, drawn from a deep well of regional expression, to new audiences far and wide, and his songs often feature an interlude in which he calls out to his urban relatives: "This is where your grandmamma came from!" or shout outs to his friends and collaborators throughout the Delta, the Dirty South, and the national hip-hop scene. Banner is said by residents to ride his tour bus through the poor Clarksdale neighborhood of Riverton, where he has family and artistic collaborators. He ended his album *Mississippi* with a shout out to Clarks Vegaz, a point of pride for TopNotch and his crew: "I thought it was real real proper that a nigga ended this album in the Delta. Yeah. I'm up in Clarksdale right now, you know what I'm talking about, yeah. Greenville, Greenwood, Itta Bena. Man, I've been to the Coast. Man, I've been to Starkville, tryin' to out this Mississippi shit down . . . God bless, I love all y'all. Thank you for visiting Mississippi."[44]

Bass Is the Place

Even as popular styles change, southern hip-hop continues to reflect its deep sense of place. In the Dirty South, regional style is expressed in the liminal space where language meets rhythm. Only very recently have Clarksdale rappers begun to record. Thus, the main mode of hip-hop production takes place in the realm of the local community. While many Clarksdale youth listen to popular crunk music at the club or in their cars, rap is a part of everyday life that does not require a premixed soundtrack. Nightly, young people meet on street corners on a walk to the barbeque stand or a friend's house, often challenging each other to a friendly rap battle. Sometimes this happens over a soundtrack created by beats on a nearby car stereo. Other times, a battle unfolds much like the dozens, only the rhymes focus on each rapper's representation of himself and his crew rather than the opponent's mama. They weave verse fragments, catch phrases, and rhythms from the popular radio station into their thick local vernacular.

After school Jerome and his friends watched rap videos on BET, fascinated by what their urban counterparts were doing with rhyme and music. They soon began to fit their rap with the beat of popular black media, creolizing urban hip-hop culture with Delta oral culture. Soon, according to TopNotch, they adapted the pop form to the vernacular culture of the Delta:

> On street corners, everybody would get in a little huddle and everybody would spit a freestyle verse. And basically that's what I wanted to show you, that we still do that now . . .
>
> We all emulate styles, that's how we grew up. We just do it off the TV, or hear the radio, or hear people rappin' that don't fit the song, we'll rap over 'em freestyle. We got people out there who want to challenge each other with freestyle battle duels . . . Just degrading another rapper for your personal gain, I was never really for it. So as a freestyle artist, I just put in words that people never thought about. . . . Getting in freestyle huddles, that's what we took from New York. Or freestyle dancing . . . the difference is that we did it southern, like southern cooking, everybody in the world know about that soul food cooking: it's good for your soul. Maybe it wasn't good for our health, but it was good for our soul. . . . We made it southern and we made it happen, even when we messed up, we thought that it was great—we didn't care how people how the way people thought it would sound. We did it our way.[45]

TopNotch, inspired by the rappers he saw on TV, continues to develop his rhyming skills. He dreams of his voice coming through radios worldwide, changing his challenges into opportunity, his "doubts into diamonds."[46]

Just as the work of the griots found new permutations on southern plantations, traditionally southern oral/musical styles make their way to the urban centers of the North and to global popular culture at large. Today, New York artists such as Mims and West Coast rappers including Oakland's E-40,

K-Deezy makes beats on his PC using Fruity Loops software. Photograph by the author.

Senegalese-American singer Akon, and Jamaican dancehall artists incorporate southern bass, speech patterns, and slang into their repertoires. The recent Bay Area Hyphy movement, for instance, shares a particularly hard, slangy vocabulary with southern hip-hop, along with dance moves that resemble both New York's Afro-Rican B-boys and southern burlesque club styles. These rappers shout out their allegiance "from the Bay to the 'A'"—Oakland, California, to Atlanta, where local crunk practitioners have developed trap, snap, and bounce rhythms. Houston artists continue to mine the deep layers of their super-bassy screwed and chopped sound. Regional artists from Timbaland to Triple Six Mafia[47] have become top global producers. And in the neighborhoods, schoolyards, living rooms, and clubs throughout the diaspora, young black people gather and rap, remixing all that they have heard, all that they are, and all that they want to say in the realm of rhyme.

In spring 2008, a collective of Clarksdale teen rappers calling themselves Money Mission Entertainment posted a song called "Crank Dat Clarksdale," a localized parody of Atlanta rapper Soulja Boy's popular 2007 dance/crunk hit "Crank dat Soulja Boy," on the Internet self-broadcasting site YouTube. Rather than sample the original song, the group used (Belgian-developed) Fruity Loops software to produce a spare techno-rap backing track for their community reversioning of Soulja Boy's narcissistic song: "We got our own dance, no more pop, lock, and drop it / And e'rybody hit the floor, no standing back and watching / Lean down touch your toes, find that Money Mission pose / (All) Crank dat Clarksdale."[48] The song is accompanied online by a nearly five-minute video of a group of teenagers dancing an elaborately choreographed group dance to the song in the gymnasium of Clarksdale High School. The video ends with the five high-school boys dancing in a ring, recalling the ancient diasporic rhyming games that local children continue to play. In another track called "Get Wit' It," Money Mission rapper Trill Fields suggests that people "be hatin' cause my chump change is a college tuition!" His name also suggests a Delta in-joke on the tropes of southern "gangsta" rap: *Trill* refers to a certain thuggishness often associated with street life, but *Fields* points back to Clarksdale's agrarian context. Meanwhile, thousands of other global hip-hop practitioners release their own stylized YouTube versions of Soulja Boy's song, from the dashiki-clad African "Niger[ian] Boys" to a group of Chinese grade-schoolers dancing for their national New Year gala.

The global cultural networks manifest in the online movement of Soulja Boy's Atlanta crunk to Africa, to Clarksdale, Mississippi, and back through traditional Afrodiasporic dance styles have been present from the earliest days of life at the crossroads. Mark Anthony Neal points out the rich diasporic networks established by Pullman porters on passenger trains before and during the Great Migration, and the subsequent development of spaces for agrarian southern community (juke joints, rent parties, and the urban blues) amid the high-rises of the city.[49] This diasporic conversation, Neal finds, is also evident in the New York production of Memphis-born, Detroit-raised singer Aretha Franklin's Delta-drawn soul, or the WattStax festival in Los Angeles, which celebrated the Memphis sound that has always infused West Coast urban-migrant community creativity. Anthropologist James Peacock describes these networks in terms of a grounded globalism exemplified by the practices of the American South: "Imagine Southern Identity as a kind of geist, a spirit or cultural complex expressed in the myriad ways noted . . . Globalism infuses that identity, which is also infused with localisms (which themselves reflect older foreign histories); the whole gradually takes root in the regional setting."[50] The power of the crossroads, characterized by the grinning figure of the storied trickster devil, emerges in the intersections of deeply southern Delta cultural practices and vast global movements.

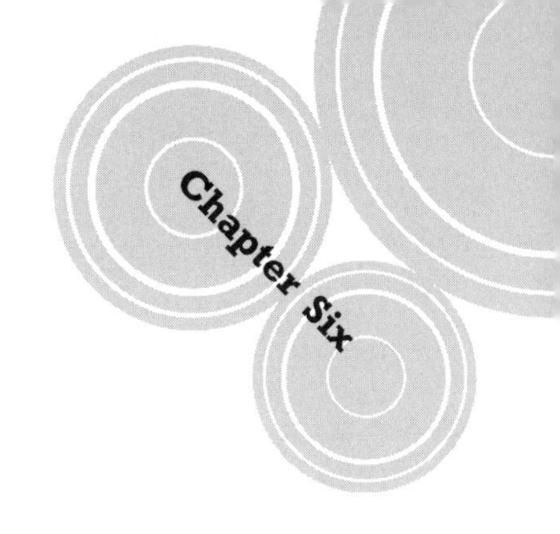

The Undivided Road

Don't stress; innovate.
—TopNotch the Villain

East Tallahatchie Street traces the vestiges of old Highway 49, a thin east-west stretch across the southern Black Belt. It is a lonely nighttime path that cuts from Hopson plantation to the New World district, a route used only by locals to bypass the two-lane highway. Few lights reveal the crumbling road ahead, pockmarked with potholes and gaping divots. A rotting sofa lies broken across the right half of the road. Garbage lines its banks. I pass Red Panther Chemical, the site of a massive toxic spill in the late 1960s. It is defunct now, surrounded by a concrete lot and a tall chain link fence. The side streets that cross this route hide lines of tainted water, believed by many locals to contribute to the high cancer rates in the area. The federal Superfund environmental cleanup program broke open this road a few months earlier to cart away the carcinogenic soil beneath, and a few blocks of pavement are a paler, smoother grey than the rest.

My headlights shine on a hand-painted note taped to an old traffic blockade and nestled in a patch of green roadside to my left. "FREE Greens Just Help Your Self," it reads. Three faces appear in the night: a poor man and woman in old clothing. His head is covered with a damp white towel. She holds a long baby in her arms and looks exhausted. I imagine they live in one of handful of shacks scattered throughout this route—tiny vestiges of housing built for sharecroppers at the turn of the century without running water, electricity, or glass windows. Wrecked cars from the highway linger on dirt mounds in their front yards. According to local civil rights activists, Martin Luther King led residents of the area past these very houses to Marks, Mississippi, where the group commenced the 1968 Poor People's March on Washington. Residents of these houses, too poor to buy vehicles, often walk miles to and from home by this treacherous route daily. Drivers must be careful to drive slowly down the road; its overgrown edges make it impossible for pedestrians to walk anywhere but its tattered lanes. The cracked concrete makes for a slow ride.

As my car approaches the crossroads, I look in my rear view mirror. A large white van of meandering tourists follows behind me, trailed by a third vehicle. I rarely see other travelers on this road and know the group is on their way to the New World district juke joints that have opened after a local blues festival. I am stopping by one of these shows to see T-Model Ford, one of my favorite Hill Country bluesmen, perform before heading back to North Carolina. My radio is tuned to WROX, and southern soul music filters from my windows. I hate leaving Clarksdale, a place where I have built the most meaningful friendships of my life. But I do not belong here, and this town does not belong to me.

I stop at a crooked sign and a group of overgrown railroad ties. I am at the old crossroads again. To my right, down old 61 (a decade ago it was renamed after Dr. King), is a chicken wings stand that advertises four flavors: "MILD," "HOT," "HONEY GOLD," and "MISSISSIPPI BURNING." A block down to my left is Messenger's, the old juke joint where plantation workers and hustlers would shoot dice and tell outrageous toasts. Ahead of me are the last vestiges of the road that I am on: a dirty, fading path that terminates East Tallahatchie Street. After the crossroads, it passes a dark juke joint on the left packed with Brickyard residents and then crumbles into dust at the dark railroad tracks.

I turn left at the old crossroads and park half a block down, just before the Messenger's storefront. The moment I open my car door, red and blue lights flash in the dark sky. I turn around to see two officers approaching the big white van that followed me down Tallahatchie. They tell me loudly to get back in my car as well. A large-bellied cop, his skin the color of sand, approaches my window.

"Have you been drinkin'?"

"No sir," I reply.

"Well, where were you before you drove down here?" he asks, his belly nearly touching my door.

I have the feeling that I should come up with something to say, but what? I do not know how to answer. "At the Commissary, sir." I'm shaking, confused.

"Get out of the car."

As quickly as that, I am bent over the trunk of my car and handcuffed, pushed into the back of the waiting car. I am alone, and can just barely dig my phone from my pocket and make a call. I get Tim's voicemail and leave a message to tell him that I have been arrested. Then I call TopNotch. I do not know what he can do to help, but I feel he is my best ally in this. He tells me to stay calm and that I will be okay. The officer approaches the car and I hang up, put the phone back in my pocket. I see him arrest the driver of the big white

Free Greens on East Tallahatchie, Clarksdale. Photograph by Timothy Gordon.

van, and I recognize two of its passengers—tourists from area blues festivals. Then I see a tow truck hitch up my battered old car and tow it away. I have just started graduate school and am down to my last seventy-five dollars, my gas money for the ride home.

It is a three-block ride to the station, and I say nothing as the officer drives me slowly to our destination. As I am ushered into its fluorescent cinder-block basement, I see a number of white blues tourists waiting in handcuffs in the holding area. I do not know what is going on or why I am here. I catch a glimpse of the jail cells down the hall. They are scraped nearly free of paint in patches where prisoners used their fingernails to scratch out messages. Dingy sheets line cardboard mattresses. I am terrified.

We are moved into a smaller cell in our handcuffs. I see a tourist I know, Mark, who was in the big white van behind me. He has been drinking a little. He is calm. I realize I have been swept up in a drunk-driving sting, set up for tourists tooling around the black side of town. They drive from the countryside blues festivals to the downtown juke joints, and many have a few beers along the way. In my entire year of living in the Delta, I never knew anyone to be arrested for drunk driving. Tonight is different.

But why did they not ask me to touch my fingers to my nose, ask me to recite the alphabet backwards, or have me blow in a machine before they arrested me, let alone read me my rights?

We stand for half an hour, handcuffs intact, before the officers line us up and guide us two by two into a room with a massive Breathalyzer machine. A wiry little white officer sits on a card table next to the machine, smiling. The barrel-chested, light-skinned black man who arrested me lines the far wall, scowling. Mark looks at me nervously. I am nervous too. I do not understand the logic behind my arrest and do not trust anything the cops have in store. They tell me to blow.

Moments later, a look of bemusement crosses the little white guy's face. "I guess she wasn't drunk after all!" he chortles. But the handcuffs stay on.

My handcuffs stay on as Mark blows a bit over the legal limit for driving. His handcuffs stay on, too. We wait for half an hour alone in the room until he is led away. I am alone now, handcuffs intact. The deputies begin to fill out pages and pages of paperwork, finally asking me for identification. They pull out a traffic citation, place my name in the upper right-hand corner, and fill out an unspecific offense: "Careless Driving." The handcuffs stay on.

The cops begin to process Mark's paperwork. It takes over an hour, and I sit silent. The clock reads 11:45, almost three hours since my arrest. I wonder about my car, about my bags and my stuff. I will not make class in North Carolina tomorrow. Finally, the shorter cop unlocks my cuffs and tell me to follow him. He points toward the back seat of his car. "I couldn't let you walk out in this bad neighborhood by yourself." He drives me up a ramp that runs from the swampy riverside to the side of Sunflower Road, where the white van's passengers are waiting for us. Eventually, Mark is released, and we make our way to the tow yard to rescue my car. They lend me the hundred dollars to get me out of tow. I hug them goodbye and enter the tow-yard office. Alone with the tow-truck operator in a tin garage off Tallahatchie, I feel uncomfortable. He is too close. I shove the money in his hand and rev up my car as he finally opens the garage door.

There is no way I am going to drive back to Chapel Hill tonight. I am shaking, nervous, and lonely. I get behind my wheel and drive down to Red's juke joint, where a smattering of patrons are finishing their last drinks of the night: an older black couple with perfect coifs who make beautiful matching outfits from discount remnants; a friendly younger woman in a tight tank top; and my favorite dancing partner, Mr. Tater, a local bluesman with a thick country accent and a wonderful smile. Red grins behind his deep red sunglasses and asks me where I have been. I start to bawl. "Red," I say, "I was arrested!"

Red pauses for a moment and looks at me. He hints that my North Carolina license plates might have been a sign of opportunity for the tow company operator and his friends. And then Red moves to the center of the room, his booming voice rising above the low blues on the stereo.

"I'm sorry that this happened to you. But let me tell you what it's like to live day-to-day in Clarksdale, Mississippi," he says, and then commences into an intense, time-stopping oratory, detailing each time he has dealt with the law. He tells me that he has had to live his whole life prepared for the moment when a person is just going about his business, and then a finger is pointed. A grown man in Mississippi only has so much control over his own body, he says, because it can be handcuffed at any time, for any reason. I am sipping a beer now, slowly, as I absorb Red's midnight sermon.

The couple at the bar shouts back at Red as he speaks, "Right on." Mr. Tater agrees vociferously. I am feeling so much better, but still kind of sick, like the days after an immunization shot. The truth hurts, but it makes me stronger. The red lights of the juke joint warm us like a fire.

The Good, the Bad, and the Trust Me

When Tim and I first arrived in Clarksdale, we were swamped with invitations to tea or nightcaps from local whites. They were curious about who we were, why we had come to Clarksdale from California. They offered us management jobs at their restaurants and places to stay. Some of our new friends were kind and supportive, relieving the stress from our big move with humorous stories of Clarksdale's past, beery trips to the levee, or canoe journeys down the Mississippi River. They took us to local juke joints and showed us where to find Robert Johnson's multiple graves. They became close allies as I dove into my research, sharing their own knowledge of local history to round out my understanding of how the Delta works.

A few white practitioners of southern hospitality, however, particularly those with deep investments in the racial status quo, were not so kind. Their enthusiasm lasted approximately two weeks, until our political views and intentions to work with the local black community were made sufficiently clear. Their front-porch sweet tea sessions dried up, and Tim and I were relieved not to have to find ways to handle the racist comments and ideas that overshadowed their afternoons. Some residents of Clarksdale's historic "big houses"—those described by former Clarksdale resident Tennessee Williams in *Cat on a Hot Tin Roof* and *A Streetcar Named Desire*, were clearly not interested in aiding interlopers.

I lost my job as a journalist at the local paper directly after covering the ideas of local black middle school students regarding the war in Iraq. I received no explanation—just a replacement sitting at my desk on a Monday morning. At a role-playing mock presidential election at the school, John Kerry won two-thirds of the vote. The students expressed their support for any candidate who would bring their cousins and siblings home from the war. Nearly all of these students from Clarksdale's poorest neighborhoods know a soldier personally: many young Delta men and women look to the military for employment and educational opportunities not available in their hometown. But angry online responses to my article from local whites cropped up:

> Fed Up Nov, 03 2004:
> This only shows how our tax dollars are being wasted in the hood.
> -----------
> [Name Removed] Nov, 03 2004:
> These kids will grow up looking for free cheeze too, unless they quit thinking like their parents. I suspect the writer of the article injected a whole lot of their opinion in this. Thank God they were 100% wrong . . .[1]

The day the story ran I received a call at my desk. The voice on the other end, sounding vaguely familiar, told me, "We don't like outsiders here." I could not put my finger on that voice. The backlash to what I thought was a straightforward article astounded me. I was also still reeling from an incident weeks earlier, in which a strange white "politician" appeared at my desk to discuss his candidacy for the state legislature. His behavior toward his black "driver" in the newsroom seemed odd, as did his comments about race. "I want to stop racial and social profiling against blacks, rednecks, and college students by punishing cops who make bad arrests with ninety days of jail time," my notes quote him as saying. I had a feeling. A quick web search turned up his involvement in the defense of Sam Bowers, a KKK Grand Wizard convicted of the 1964 slayings of three civil rights activists in Neshoba County, Mississippi. I was worried about mentioning this connection in my article, but decided not to hedge. Nothing came of the incident. But all this talk about race was wearing out my welcome at the paper, which is largely sponsored by wealthy white business owners.

After my departure from the paper, the social pressure continued. One professional local white woman told a waiter at a local restaurant—a young black man who was involved in Clarksdale's hip-hop community—that I was with Child Protective Services and should be avoided. She had apparently expected the word to circulate to my consultants and cut short my project. I received word of this rumor immediately; I had already gained the solid trust of the family in question.

A March 2007 Page 1 op-ed piece on the tragedy of Clarksdale's nominal school integration (in 1970) by the current editor of the paper sums up the taboos I had inadvertently transgressed:

Grange Cemetery's tombstone angel, a Clarksdale landmark made famous by Tennessee Williams in his play *Summer and Smoke*. Photograph by the author.

I was asked recently what were the biggest changes that I had seen in Clarksdale since my early years as a child. Without question, I answered, the destruction of our neighborhood schools by the federal courts in 1970. That single one move began the slow deterioration of the Delta that is now in its 37th year. It hit this area harder than any earthquake that ever trembled or shook San Francisco. Since 1970, thousands of people have been smacked hard in the pocketbook, attempting to pay for both public and private education. When it was no longer feasible for them, most of these folks just packed up and moved to other areas of the state or country where the livin' was a little easier . . .

With the advent of legal alcohol sales and liquor by the drink, restaurants were the first to offer alcohol to those who dined. But by the early 1970s, bars and honky tonks sprung up and offered liquor by the drink. . . . With this newfound way of socializing, lifestyles began to change and change drastically. Women no longer were "prudes" like many of them had been tagged previously. These same women began to wear pants more often than not, discarding dresses they had worn for a lifetime. And being around men in bars at night, unfortunately even changed their language habits and the way they spoke. Through the sixties, women never cursed in public and most men respected them enough not to used [*sic*] four-letter words in their presence.

The legalization of alcohol some 40 years ago has changed our lives drastically and it affected us in a thousand other ways.[2]

A view from the author's front door, Coahoma County, Mississippi. Photograph by the author.

The "integrated" public schools of the Delta were largely abandoned by whites, who self-segregated their children in private white academies. The rejection of the principles behind the Brown v. Board ruling of 1954 is a common cause discussed on the contemporary gilded front porches of Clarksdale.

Tim and I could not find a rental house in town. For reasons we did not immediately recognize, white landlords told us that there was nothing for us in a town half-full of abandoned housing.[3] We eventually found a spot near Highway 1, on the periphery of a large plantation, where the wealthy remnants of the planter family, as well as the families of their white overseers and black workers remain in minimal housing. We rented half of a rotting duplex with an open septic system in the shadow of the old cotton gin. In return for our rent, our working-class white landlords offered not to, in their words, "rent the other half to niggers." An extended African American family lived through a patch of cane break near the roadside. The father of the family had been working on a nearby plantation in exchange for a small paycheck and housing, but when he fell out of favor with management, he was told to move. Because his pay had been too minimal to save rent for a new place to stay, the family remained for months, trying to patch a deposit together. In the meantime, the plantation boss cut off water and power to the house. They stopped by our house sometimes to get water for their infant's formula or to collect the turnip greens that grew in abundance in our yard. Their two school-aged girls kept their poverty a secret at school and did their homework by candlelight. When the family did suddenly move, they left Tim and me plastic bags of perishable condiments as a goodbye gift.

One night in a local blues club, a robust young woman climbed the stage to guest on a bluesy version of Donny Hathaway's "The Ghetto." I did not hesitate to tell her afterward how much I appreciated her interpretation of one of my favorite songs. She introduced herself as Jacqueline Lenard, a nurse practitioner and director of a free health clinic in Shaw, Mississippi. She explained that she had been called by the Spirit to move from Seattle and open a family clinic for impoverished Delta residents. Her family had left the Delta for safe ground a generation ago; some of them had been witnesses to the infamous murder of Emmett Till. She invited us to her nearby church, Pleasant Grove Missionary Baptist, which was situated on the next plantation over from our rental house. There, we began to meet members of the local black community within the context of community and worship.[4] Miss Jacqueline would lead the choir in her own styling of the popular gospel tune:

How you gonna pay your rent
When all of your money's spent?
Say you got a light bill due
And you got a gas bill too!
Jesus will work it out![5]

On weekends Tim and I road-tripped to little juke joints in the country or asked locals where to find the blues. We made house visits to friends in the community and caused a stir when we invited our friends, black and white, to our house for parties. Even as we forged strong relationships, we dealt with stares, comments, and alienation. All the while we were learning the language of the Mississippi Delta at church, in conversation, over the waves of WROX, and through the blues. Finally, we were invited to the little house parties and gospel practices and living rooms of those who became my friends and consultants. The spring after our arrival in the Delta, I was introduced to TopNotch at a little juke joint down Highway 49.

In my four years in the Delta, I have been able to find a place for myself in Clarksdale's musical community. But I could not just drive down Highway 61 and shimmy my way inside. It was only through series of interactions, conversations, and reputations that I was accepted in my role as an ethnographic collaborator. Scores of journalists, filmmakers, promoters, and researchers have paraded through the Delta since it gained its reputation as "the Birthplace of the Blues." Their process usually involves setting up a paid interview or two with well-known bluesmen James "Super Chickan" Johnson, "T Model" Ford, or David "Honeyboy" Edwards and a visit to the tourist spots that fill with blues travelers on summer weekends. Some write films or books about the Delta blues experience. Over the course of my research in the Delta, a number of major investors have bought up the bulk of downtown. A Hollywood movie star has teamed with a local white businessman to spur the local tourism industry through an upscale soul food restaurant and a clubby "juke joint" where the stage is raised five feet above the tourist crowd. The story of the birth of the blues has the most cachet for those who dream of saving it from death.

And there are those who just love the music. Under the bright blues crossroads marker at midnight, they seek a touch of blues conjuration.

I did not have a particular project in mind when I arrived at the crossroads. I knew that I wanted to learn more about this music that had nourished the American sound. The more I made my way through the Delta, the more I realized that the Delta was telling me to listen. I had to give it "Delta time," a term locals use to mean that things happen according to the priorities of fate. I had to stop imposing my own ideas about the blues, the lines of authenticity and difference that bound my understandings into a little box. When I listened, I heard the blues in the voices of the radio deejays, in the tomes of the church incantations, in the sounds of the kids rapping at the end of every Delta street. My many nights in the juke joints shook my assumptions out of me. I had to come to terms with the fallacy of my expectations. Finally, I had to experience the power of the word in Red's juke joint the night of my arrest. It was all that I had, and it healed me.

Collaboration Conversation

When I arrived in Clarksdale with this utopian vision of getting to know the blues, I did not realize that I was about to engage in an extended ethnographic project, fraught with the burdens and tricks and privileges of representation. As these five years of ethnographic work crystallize into a series of short documentaries, articles, and this book, the weight of this responsibility pulls at the edges of my work; my experiences and relationships are more than its pages can hold. But my commitment to my friends, family, and consultants in the Delta also provides the weight of the book's momentum. TopNotch trusted me to step into his life as a collaborator and interlocutor, and he has sacrificed much to enter into this ethnographic relationship. I relish the moments, in interviews,

Co-director TopNotch the Villain reviews daily takes from documentary filming. Photograph by the author.

in presentations, or in our everyday conversations when he nudges me to pass the mic and step aside so that he can share his own wisdom.

Robin D. G. Kelley points out the implications of the ethnographic strange-making that characterizes dominant studies of Black Atlantic culture, highlighting the practices of representational "othering" that intercept the possibility for new intercultural understandings. This can be traced through the history of ethnographic studies of the dozens, which reduce the practice to a series of ritualistic, behavioral texts rather than recognize the everyday affective, aesthetic, and social commitments of its practitioners:

> My purpose, then, is to offer reflections of how the culture concept employed by social scientists has severely impoverished contemporary debate over the plight of urban African Americans and contributed to the construction of the ghetto as a reservoir of pathologies and bad cultural values. Much of this behavior not only conflates behavior with culture, but when social scientists explore "expressive" cultural forms or what has been called "popular culture" (such as language, music, and style), most reduce it to expressions of pathology, compensatory behavior, or creative "coping mechanisms" to deal with racism and poverty.[6]

As an ethnographer, I am committed to critical questions in cultural research, analysis, and representation, often in collaboration with people and groups whose subject positions are distinct from my own. Contemporary ethnographic work, centered in the deeply contextual realm of practice, is an exercise in writing culture: the crafting of practical representations of communities in which we have positioned ourselves as participant observers. This ethnographic work with hip-hop artists in the Mississippi Delta attempts to intervene in discourses on the pathology of black musical practitioners and to transform dominant ideas of blues authenticity that restrict public resources to these artistic communities. But even as I struggle to speak across the boundaries that separate, the lines of difference that underline ethnographic work come sharply and persistently into focus. Words and categories threaten to hijack my representations. I often feel bounded by my need to textualize, to grasp, and to make sense of things and, in turn, to communicate with others who may not have similar experiences.[7]

Ethnography necessitates strategies of representation. According to Soyini Madison, critical ethnography:

> . . . takes us beneath surface appearances, disrupts the status quo, and unsettles both neutrality and taken-for-granted assumptions by bringing to light underlying and obscure operations of power and control.[8]

Critical ethnographers seek new methods, modes, and media for this purpose, remixing the representational structures of our texts as we imagine the consequences of deploying the discursive strategies of each representational approach. We write and rewrite culture, broadening and refining our practice. We investigate the registers in which we go about this transformative work both within and without the academy by critically engaging with established cultural representations.

Ethnography represents a route by which subaltern voices can make space in dominant frameworks. Works such as John Langston Gwaltney's *Drylongso: A Self-Portrait of Black America* and Louise Meintjes's *Sound of Africa!* use critical ethnographic techniques to document self-representational and subaltern expressive practices, respectively. One useful strategy for the transformation of established frameworks of knowledge might involve what James Clifford calls a "polyvocal" approach to representation, in which ethnography becomes collaborative, interactive, and productively unfinished.[9] A polyvocal representation allows for a multiplicity of voices to shape and reshape the frameworks by which we understand ourselves and the "other"; in discourse together, we speak across difference. Rather than hang our work on the idea that we can sort out rules and orders that define the communities with whom we are working, then, we might envision a chorus of productively unfinished—even conflicting—understandings that draw power from, rather than circumscribe, the unknowable.

As an ethnographer, I can shape a story, elicit it in the fullness of its context, experience it as a participant, and describe it as an observer. But ultimately, I owe it to my consultants to give them space to represent themselves. They mean too much to me as community members, friends, and adopted family to do otherwise. As a woman ethnographer, I bring to the table my understanding of what it feels like to be looked at by strangers. I have tried in all I have done to never let my gaze hit the side of anyone's face. My photography and my writing, I hope, allows my consultants to gaze back into the camera, to offer self-representations. I believe it was my willingness to engage the community of the Mississippi Delta on this level that led me to the Love Zone to hear TopNotch rap on that hot summer night.

Further, critical ethnography requires a commitment to reciprocity: a collaborative exchange of ideas, time, and energy that ultimately transgresses the line between "researcher" and "researched."[10] TopNotch and Yata, especially, have remained intellectually engaged in this project as collaborators, critics, and partners. TopNotch has visited UNC three times to lecture university classes and perform. He has developed a considerable following on campus, and cooks buckets of soul food for his new college friends each time he visits. He met a student in one of those classes, a Ph.D. student in French literature from New Orleans, and fell in love. He has been laid off from his job at the hospital and has since found work with the local Head Start program and as an intern at the new B. B. King Blues Museum in Indianola. He has also made the decision to attend community college full time. He wants to learn digital technology, but he is also excelling in his speech class. We will continue to collaborate on projects, including this manuscript. Our partnership is less a material this-for-that than a dynamic intellectual freestyle, building over the years into a common vocabulary with which we can talk about the cultural practices and social issues of the contemporary Delta.

Since Yata had a baby in February 2007, a healthy boy named Jamarkis Jazez Dear, she has been working hard to get her G.E.D. and driver's license by summer. She knows she will be a great mom and is already teaching her baby to rap. Jamarkis sits on her lap as she records her rhymes on her family's computer. She is struggling to find a job and hopes to enroll in a four-year college within the next few years. She recently asked me if I think that this book will help her to become known as a rapper. I told her that it is unlikely that an academic book will get her a video on MTV, but that I believe that she can use this work to build her reputation, to apply for college, and to feel good about herself and her talent. The next day, she sent me this poem:

THANKS Ali
BY: Kimyata L Dear

A kind hearted person came to visit my home town
Where a lot of excitement and talent was found
Who would have known one lady will help introduce our skill
Thanks for knowing how important it had to feel
To make front page of our newspaper, and walk down our first local red carpet
I want to thank you so much for getting DA F.A.M. started
I have a good feeling that this was all in the LORD's plan
To send someone like you to give Clarksdale a help in hand.
To a woman who has been so kind and true
From: DA F.A.M.
To: you

The creation of this book involved nearly five years of ethnographic work, and in the process I formed deep bonds with many of my consultants and collaborators. TopNotch has spoken to more than eight college classes over the span of three trips to the University of North Carolina, rapped for a story on his work on NPR, and has been featured in a number of local publications. In 2008 he sent a handwritten note to Delta State University, a school half an hour south of Clarksdale, suggesting that they hold a Delta hip-hop conference:

> To clear the negative streotype about hip-hop and bring forth all local talents in hip-hip-hop from around the Delta and surrounding counties. To bring togetherness from all and possibly play and perform local music inbreaded from the Mississippi Delta. . . . To give an understanding of where we are taking this music. To acknowledge other music other than blues or gospel, but not to take anything from it. To give a clear understanding of where hip-hop comes from. . . .

The First Annual Delta Hip-Hop Conference, held in February 2008 through the generosity of the Delta State team, was a resounding success, drawing local students, poets, spiritual hip-hop artists, and Memphis rapper Al Kapone into its fold. DA F.A.M. performed clean versions of their best new songs.

The most glorious moments involving this project came with the premiere of the short documentary TopNotch and I directed together (along with my UNC colleague Brian Graves) at Delta Cinema, a small, formerly segregated movie theatre in Clarksdale on January 18th, 2007. The local paper, briefly under a hip-hop-friendly editor, featured a story about their work on the front

(Possibly Projected)

Delta Hip-Hop Conference

Mission Statement: To clear the Negative Stereotype about Hip-Hop and bring forth all local talents in hip hop from around the Delta and surrounding Counties. To Bring togetherness from all and possibly play and perform local music inbreaded from the Mississippi Delta.

Overall Achievement: To have this Conference annually. To start Delta Music Awards (DMAs) in all Categories of music. To give an understanding of where we are taking the music. To acknowledge other music other than Blues and Gospel but not take anything from it. To give clear understanding where hip-hop comes from. To have a successful Conference.

Jerome "TopNotch the Villain" Williams's handwritten proposal for the Delta Hip-Hop Conference at Delta State University.

page with the headline, "Bridging the Gap from Blues to Rap." The group gained press throughout the state for a showing of our documentary at the old Coahoma Cinemas, which drew together two hundred locals including the state senator, a few bluesmen, a churchful of schoolkids, family members, and blues journalists. The local tourism magazine took photos of the group standing under their name in lights. I sought out a long strip of red carpet at a discount store in Chapel Hill and, after the thirteen-hour car ride to the Deep South, laid it out across the cracked Delta pavement. DA F.A.M., Martha Raybon, Red, the documentary crew, and our friends strutted down the carpet in our best clothes. We toasted plastic flutes of sparkling grape juice and hollered throughout the whole film. Photographer Troy Catchings of the Clarksdale *Press-Register* photographed the event, as revelers stood in front of the bright vintage marquee: LET THE WORLD LISTEN RIGHT. The film features Big T and Miss Martha, as well as performances by DA F.A.M., who continue to gain popularity throughout the Delta. They have recorded more than twenty songs now and are performing in local rap showcases and workshops. The music is getting better and better, and the group now sounds more like a polished pop hip-hop act out of Atlanta than a homemade enterprise. After his graduation from school, TopNotch hopes to start a record label through which he will release his own group's music.

TopNotch the Villain, who will receive half of the profits from this book, asked for space for his own entries in these pages. As he looked over the first

The author, co-director Brian Graves, and co-Director Jerome "TopNotch the Villain" Williams at the Clarksdale premiere of their documentary film, January 2007. Photograph by Timothy Gordon.

draft of this section, he told me over my fuzzy cell phone connection last summer, he decided that he had something to say beyond the poetry that he had already generously shared.

> Ali, to have worked with you for the time presented to us is nothin' short of inspirational. From a freestyle rap to a couple interviews, to class teachings, to performances, to documentaries, to possibly a book, and imagine we only gettin started. Time, devotion, dedication is how we gotten here so far, but you have always seeken extra miles, and that a world of things will describe this feature. I know you will be successful in everything you do. Never be discouraged to the point that you become unfocused. Always remember the times we have been together in struggle always guttering it out. Stay blessed, let God direct your path, and always keep the game T.O.P.
>
> Now for the people that's reading the book.
> In advance, I would like to thank you for reading a book that is based on my life and what I am trying to become. It is in my mind that you will enjoy what you are about to read or already have read. Hopefully, this is one step closer to realizing a dream. Dreams are made for you to believe them and achieve them. Everything is possible with God being first and foremost. Without you reading this, this would not be possible for me. So keep dreaming and keep the game T.O.P.
> TopNotch the Villain signing off.[11]

At the Delta Blues Room, TopNotch and his friends are recognized immediately. DJ Dr. Pepper, who was the first local deejay to play the band's music, is sure to send them shout-outs throughout their time spent at the club. They are gregarious, rushing to the dance floor together to take over the line dance sequence or to lip sync their own songs as they boom over the system. Dr. Pepper singles them out again:

I'm talking to, uh, hey brother, I want you to stay on the floor
Let me see DA F.A.M.
I want to introduce you guys
This is Clarksdale's own rock DJs
And you know what I like about 'em
They got a little Jesus in 'em
They got a little rock in 'em
This is F-A-M
Now let me ask you guys:
Would it be alright
if tomorrow night,
I play something off of their CD?
Would it be alright
If I start tomorrow night?
Huh?
Be alright. Be alright.
That's what I'm talkin' about.
Let's give our main man a hand
Here—DA F.A.M.
I'm gonna get somethin' straight tonight . . .
(Come on here! Get it right!)
I'm gonna get somethin' straight tonight.
First of all, from you, I can play some of your music tomorrow night.
I think you got somethin' on your mind . . .[12]

In TopNotch's estimation, this project was well worth the "guttering it out" we had to do over the years. In the collaborative space of good ethnography, at the crossroads of our experience, in our passion for music and deep support for each other, my friends in the Delta and I have crafted a call and response of trust and reciprocity. TopNotch the Villain continues to gain fame as a rapper in the Delta. Local blues bands often call on him to join them onstage, where he improvises rhymes over their songs. He is excited about this book's release and hopes to use his share of its profits to start his homegrown record label.

Clarksdale's classic New World district crossroads. Photograph by the author.

Miss Martha was called by the Spirit to preach. Her face lights up when she talks about her vocation. She has joy to spread and people to teach, and her first public sermons have been a success.

Life in Clarksdale continues when I am not there. In the moments when I realize the little disconnections that separate my academic life from that of field and family, I feel like an observer—an outsider to the community to which I have become so attached. But I return to the Mississippi every couple months and find myself folded right back into the groove. Or I bring the lessons the Delta has taught me into conversation with my academic business, especially the wisdom TopNotch imparts when I am nervous about my work: "Don't stress," he says. "Innovate."

The last night Tim and I spent in the Delta before moving to Chapel Hill, Red told us to come down and join him for a drink at his club. We had been through a trying thirteen months in the Delta, and we were nervous about our upcoming move. We had finally started to settle in, to run on Delta time. As we drove up to the club, however, we could see that something was going on. Big old vans, shiny bright Chevys, and certified clunkers lined Sunflower Avenue. Red was waiting at the door, eyes smiling above the rims of his red sunglasses. The door to his juke joint was propped open, and a crowd awaited us inside. It was a group of friends, gathered together to sing us out of town. Mr. Tater was ready to dance, and Wesley "Junebug" Jefferson and Big T pounded out the sounds of our favorite Delta blues songs. The rappers we had met just a few months before were there, too, giant cans of Bud in their hands, insulated in swaths of paper towels. Around midnight, Junebug took the room down and sang us a few new verses—an improvised song about Tim and me driving a broken old van from California to spend some time with the blues in Clarksdale.

The next morning, we were ready to go. We drove up to the crossroads, looked back in the direction from whence we had come, and chose the opposite path.

In the Word, We Are Healed

On any Sunday morning at the Delta "church time" (just after 11 a.m.), it is possible for a visitor to the Delta to join the community in crossing the holy threshold of St. James C.O.G.I.C. Temple. Looking out toward the street from its doors, one sees the crumbling old crossroads to the west. To the east, the tombstone angel bends its wings toward the ground. The Church of God in Christ, or C.O.G.I.C., is a Holiness denomination that was consolidated in the Mississippi Delta in the mid-twentieth century; its roots run deep into the rich soil of the New World district. Bill Ferris took a great deal of photographs and Super 8 footage of the old Clarksdale C.O.G.I.C. church in the 1960s, which he released in the form of a short documentary entitled "Black Delta Religion."

The usher seats us front and center in the large white church, which today is about half-full with its congregation of about a hundred fifty. The choir is just beginning its selection for the service, a contemporary gospel piece executed with intensity and careful precision. The harmony is complex, and the song fills the tall bright church without the aid of microphones. The choir is exceptionally bright and crisp, balancing practice and passion in its resonant sound. Christopher Coleman, a friend in his early twenties who works at the Delta Blues Museum, stands out in front with his ringing tenor. The service is being broadcast on WROX, the local blues radio station that belongs to the Lord on Sunday mornings.

The service turns to a healing ceremony; the choir and band continues to play a quiet spiritual dirge as the deacon calls troubled worshippers to approach the altar. The gathering group includes three preteen girls, the matron with whom they are sitting, a very pregnant woman, and an elderly sister of the church dressed in her uniform of Pentecostal red skirt, white suit coat, and elaborate white headdress. The deacon confers with each believer in hushed tones and then places his hand on her forehead, furrowing his own brow as he

Clarksdale's Church of God in Christ sits on Martin Luther King Street in Clarksdale's New World district. Photograph by the author.

concentrates deeply on his words and rhythms. Over and over, he repeats his request for God to purify the blood, from the top of the head to the soles of the feet. He asks this of God in the word, he repeats, in the word, and in the blood, we are healed. The devil will no longer bother or try to confuse this woman. This woman will be healthy, and Jesus will purify the blood and the heart from the top of the head to the soles of the feet. In the name of Jesus and the word of God we are healed.

Each believer shouts for joy as she falls backward and then recovers with the help of the deacon and the female ushers in nurses' uniforms, who lead her back to her seat. The healed continue to shout and jump long after the event, and some run graceful laps through the bright aisles of the temple. The young girls sit in the front row and hug each other, each with her head on the shoulder of another. The sister in red is final receiver of the ceremony, and she prepares to receive the sacrament solemnly as her thick glasses fall far down her nose and her corkscrew braids bounce around her shoulders. As the deacon implores the devil to leave the sister's mind from confusion in the name of Jesus, the woman begins to run in place, stomping her legs with absolute intensity. She faces the sky with her fists at her collarbones, pulling at the air in a kind of begging gesture. Her eyes are closed as the deacon works his word and his hands, asking Jesus to purify the blood in the word made flesh.

As the deacon finishes his work, the sister in red falls sharply backward into the arms of the ushers. The choir sings louder as the stage clears for Bishop Scott's mighty sermon. As the service comes to a close, we are asked to introduce ourselves and, after doing so, are given hugs and kisses by a number of the congregation.

Conclusion

Let the World Listen Right

If the crossroads marks the path across the realms of the living and the dead, then music represents the life force of the blues community of the Mississippi Delta. The title of this book comes from a conversation TopNotch and I had in the earliest weeks of our collaboration. For him this project represents a way to build an audience for his art—to strengthen the connections between his community and those both within and outside the South. He plans to stay in the Delta to use his voice to rally for new job opportunities, improved educational funding, and recognition of the voices of young practitioners of the living blues. His raps entertain, tell stories, solidify friendships, and make and remake identity. Most importantly, they transcend the difficulties of daily life under the Delta's dire circumstances, and they lead others to do the same.

The feeling he gets when he really starts to flow in his raps, when the words just come together and the rhythm catches, is the same feeling he had when he used to sing at church. No matter what is going on with his unstable job, his health, his friends, or his family, he forgets it all when he feels the Spirit. I can see it on his face when he is rapping; I get caught up in it, too. This, in his characteristic rhythmic flow, is how he describes it:

> Now in my raps or what have you, how the way it transcends, or how the way I catch this Holy Spirit or what have you, is that I catch this, I just keep rappin', and the more I start makin' sense and the more you begin to feel it, the more crunk, you know what I'm sayin', you get, you know what I'm sayin' or what have you . . .
>
> The more live, the more, you know the energy start a-flowin', and it's like, for me it comes like from my toes and it goes into my feet and it goes like to my

ankles, and it goes to my shin to my calf to my knees to my thighs to my hips to my waist to my belly to my heart to my chest to my throat to my brain. And then once it gets to the point where you can't hold it in your body no more, it just all comes out in one big ol' blur and it's just beautiful music.[1]

I have watched so many people in the Delta, many of whom I consider friends, some of whom I love like family, experience the trials of life at the crossroads. Violence, illness, addiction, obesity, unemployment, depression, teen pregnancy, and abuse are the bruises of the Delta brand of American poverty. But no challenge can tear the bonds of community in the Mississippi Delta; these ties are twisted from the fiber of the word.

Throughout the Delta, rhythmic oral/musical performance takes place anywhere community gathers. But nowhere does the power of the word ring more clearly than the pews of the Baptist church. In the pulpit of the Crowder, Mississippi, Pleasant Grove Missionary Baptist Church, Pastor Allen Johnson delivers his sermon with dramatic expertise:

If you don't get into the word, he already got you beat.
That's why you don't bother with him
He already got you
He's goin' with somebody else
That's tryin' to learn the word of God
Why?
Because he know that
the word
The word of God is what he's afraid of
He's not afraid of you
He's afraid of the word of God
He took Jesus
And put him on a pinnacle
And took him to his weakest spot.
He knew he was hungry
And fasted for forty days and forty nights
He knew he was hungry
and tempted him with these things
take time to think about what you're doin'
take time to get it right
Take time
To line up the word of God with your lifestyle
And this is what God wants up to do

To line up the word with our lifestyle
And when we line up the word with our lifestyle
Then God will hear your prayer
and answer your request
He tell us that's what your weakness . . .

You gotta live and walk in the word.
It doesn't matter
what the drug addicts say.
It doesn't matter
what the pimps say.
You gotta live in the word.
Because the word will.
Keep you.[2]

Miss Martha Raybon finds a similar feeling when she is hitting the ringing notes of a favorite gospel song, such as Mahalia Jackson's "Troubles of the World":

Soon I will be done with the troubles of this world
Troubles of the world
Troubles of the world
Troubles of this world
Troubles of the world
Soon I will be done with the troubles of this world
I'm goin' home to live with God.
I'm goin' home to live with my God.

Miss Martha taps a deep spiritual power when she sings at church. It is her relief from the rigors of the week, from her struggles with the bills. She loves her assignment as the church choir director, to share the power of the Spirit with the young ones so that they can carry their song beyond the confines of her trailer, beyond the walls of the church. She smiles when she describes the power of song in her life:

> When the Holy Spirit take over, ooh, you have . . . you're just out of control. You don't know . . . you know, ooh. The singin'. And a lot of people will tell you, the power that go with you singin' that song. And how it made them feel and how it makes you feel. It makes you feel, a lot of times, that'll just make you forget all cares, all worries, all everything.[3]

Like Miss Martha, Yata finds that the power of the word engages and exceeds the issues of everyday life. In the creative space of rhyme and song, she feels "lifted up."

> Like when you rappin', you just let yourself, let yourself go. Same thing like people do in church. When you feel a song, you just let yourself go. And usually when you do that you rap better or sing better because you just rappin' or you singin' from your soul, which really just lift up everything, and it just comes out better result than not feeling your song and just rapping to be rappin'.[4]

Miss Martha reports that when Jerome attended choir practice as a child, his group did not realize that her neighbors were standing outside of her trailer, listening to their voices. Today, TopNotch knows that his voice and his message can cross the firmest of boundaries. They are made to do so.

Field Work

We had been filming in the Mississippi Delta the entire month of July, dragging our heavy equipment through hundred-degree humidity and dusty Delta silt, and we were tired. After dozens of interviews, long days of driving down back roads, and fifty hours of rich footage, we were still unsure how we wanted to end our short documentary on hip-hop in the Mississippi Delta. TopNotch and I had been collaborating for two years in an effort to represent the music of young people in the Delta to new audiences in an accurate light. With the help of another UNC graduate student, we committed our summer to co-directing a multimedia portrait of the contemporary musical landscape of the region. The labor was exhausting in the thick summer atmosphere, but we were driven by the opportunity to share our work with a wider audience.

We spent the day recording TopNotch freestyling rhymes about various aspects of life in the Mississippi Delta for use in the film's soundtrack. Meanwhile, I was preparing to pack up and head back to North Carolina in just a few days to begin the editing process, unsure about how to structure our film. We debated different ways to end our documentary that afternoon, hoping to mine a climactic moment from the footage we had already taken.

To our surprise, with less than an hour of natural sunlight remaining, TopNotch suggested that we set up our cameras in a cotton field nearby. I felt unsure about filming TopNotch in that setting; I told him I was concerned about breaking the stereotypical image of the Delta artist in the cotton field. Top insisted. Our tiny crew duly packed up our gear and headed to a hidden corner of Hopson plantation in hopes that the industrious managers would not discover our presence. Top stood twenty feet into the field as our two cameras began to roll, paused, and then launched into a breathtaking twelve-minute improvised performance centered on themes of race, labor, spirituality, and nature. In this radical remix of the cotton field trope, TopNotch set himself to, to paraphrase Ellison, finger the jagged grain of history to craft his own powerful representation of self, community, and artistry. This is his work.

By the time he finished, we had both sensed an audience far beyond those of us in the cotton field that day. Top's movement, tone, breath, style, and rhythm combined with his words to create a performance that cannot be contained in a simple transcript. His crimson cap and shirt, lined with silver streaks, popped against the rich green of the flowering cotton fields. TopNotch's verbal art alone, improvised in the moment of performance to speak to audiences real and imagined, is thicker than the soil beneath his feet, ploughed by stolen labor for 150 years.

[spoken]
Cotton field.
In my past life, in my ancestors' life, this is all they had right here.
They had one another, they had love.
And the reason why I just had to bring you out to the cotton field simply because:
in order for me to know where I'm going, I must know where I come from.
It's the cotton field. So now the world, I want y'all to listen and listen right.
This is what we used to do when we was in the cotton field.

So if y'all watchin', y'all bow y'all heads for me.

Heavenly father, I'm glad that you showed us a better way from the days of the past but it seems that with our mindset, we're gonna head back right there.
I hope you lead us in the way whereas the righteousness is always gonna triumph over evil. It's possible.
Let them know that, you know, that Martin Luther King, Malcolm X, Sojourner Truth, Harriet Tubman, just to name a few, didn't have to go through what they went through just to see that our lives not to be free.
That, you know, we can hold hands with many hands of America. Blacks, whites, Asians, Chinese, all colors of God's spectrum.
And Lord, we can only do this through, you know what I'm sayin', in your son Jesus Christ's name.

So with that in mind, I pray now and forever more. Amen.

Cotton choppin'.

As the wind blows in Monday's mornings
Sunday nights 'n' getting ready for early Monday mornings
Seein' me ridin' on the trucks in early mornings
Back in the days up when the cotton got (m) chopped by them hoes
All perspective
Never worried about bein' a ho
Just the difference between me and (m) bein' on my toes
Got whips and chains
And I know they got bars in backs
And they still got a part of that
They like scarred I see
Bloody tears
Many through years sufferin'
Knowin' that they cryin' many tears and they up
And never place the stuff
I know they gave this up
Just to only make it to church
Let me give (m) you a hymn
Where they speak it
I know troubles of the world
They will never long to see it
It will be done

Let me cry these awful tears
From the mornin' sun
And I'm a raise this above until my days are done

I cry tears 'cause I know
Blood shed and bloody red
Thoughts of man, people and
My ancestors dead here
They got grace and pick 'em' more
I never seen pick up trees
But they burnin' with me
Best believe they gon' live through me
'Cause I can bring 'em back to my memories
I cried tears you best uh believe
Thatta I would love to fight for here
I got my right through here
I put my stripes through here
I even do two years of my life for this here
'Cause I did two years of my life here

Grabbin' my same hoe
Walkin' down the line
Seein' Johnson grass and oh, baby it's mine
Milkweeds they were growin'
No cotton for certain
But now I have to go and close the curtain

Now as the night fall
It creeps down into
Now that we walkin' right down dead in the center
Now we used to make twenty-eight dollars in the day
Now let me take you back before the days
When there were just some nickel and some quarters
Knowin' that good and well
It couldn't support families and daughters
I know, understand, it taught us
They didn't want to see us read and write
but that's okay we gon' read
and I'm gonna tell you what life was like
hard streetin'
I'm thinkin' that it's all completed
I don't wanna see my sentence not completed
I add a period to the life that I live and be
You wanna feel the cotton choppin' through me

It's more than T-O-P it's more than whatever you cry
It's gon' be whatever these tears that up in my eyes
I had too many f'ckin' family members that dead and died
Try pressin' through knowing that they been crucified
Livin' my life
I live this life sworn of the sword they never like see me
So now I got to bring you some more
Giving me more I give you my strength every day
It just lookin' up into the sky and the Lord I pray
Just hopin' that you live your life through my babies
Cryin' me baby maybe
Isn'ts and maybes

Now I see uncle and uh uncle Jed
Seein' these people and they lookin'
All over their head
Nappy head and they seeing some roots
Stanky still getting booted

But they gettin' burned by the sweat it's pollutin'
And I know they came up with solutions
But just the fact that they didn't have the means or the materials to do it
Some of 'em
They tried to break free
And only thing they saw
Was a foot cut off like Baby T
Now you wanna look for Kunta Kinte
I got words that'll make you say like
Ooh, it won't be okay
I don't spread my butter with no Parkay
It's all day when I say they all grey
You won't wanna see the real truth?
I got your real truth
Aunt Jemima
Sally Sue
Now Joseph let me speak my life you HOVA

You wanna take me out now that I know-uh that it's over
My troubles of the world it will be done
I know this a challenge and my challenge down to one
Because we done made from the ways of the holocaust
Shed no tears
I'm a shed through years
Man careers done tried and crucified and lies
ain't gonna see it
But they gonna see this up in my eyes
I bring pain
I know that there's trouble with this game
But I just don't see a damn thing's gonna change
I make it my business just to talk about livin' for witness
This gonna be my choppin' cotton
Forever for livin' this
I feel this
And you gon' see it through my eyes it's gonna bleed
Don't ever worry 'bout what you see
I know my little ABCs
If it's backwards then I give you WXY and Z
Like Y are you Z in on me?
Better get your Z's up because I think they need what?
Everybody in the world gonna need Jesus
But I'm givin' you a false pretendin'

Ain't gonna worry 'bout you sinnin'
I'm gonna worry about the beginnin' words you endin'
I'm lookin' for your fold 'cause you're not my friend
Understand that this game can end
It's like money and dreams back
I believe it's goin' to spend
You cannot say that
Tellin' me the loss from the gravy
It's so thoughts are crazy
I had to pray just to make me make it
And I believe it's the chance I take
Cotton choppin' exclusively for baby it's gonna be okay
I've given you my church hymn
and this is my cry
this is my cry
this is my cry
But it's not over people
It's not over
This is a song that I just have to take you to
Y'all know what I'm sayin'
I gotta take you to church with me
Gotta take you to church with me
You know I'm sayin'

It's like songs like those
I got in my head I still got in my head
I'm a put it to your head
I hope that you like it, you know what I'm sayin'
It goes like this:

[sung]
I know I am a child of God
I know I am a child of God

[spoken]
I end it right there
Can't give you too much more
Can't give you too much more
Then you might think I can sing
I'm just a rapper
I just know about life
I know about my life

I know where I came from
And as it so happens,
This was our place and home right here
Know what I'm sayin'
When the upper class members were eatin' steak
And all the good fine foods
They gave us the little fatback
They gave us the hog maws
They gave us some chopped up greens
And guess what?
We made it a blessing anyway.
It's called soul food today
But I just call it somethin' that we used to live
And survive off for every day

Now.
Really, you heard the truth from me, you heard the cotton field, you done heard the cotton chopper. You done heard Mississippi.
Don't never, and I mean, don't you ever believe that Mississippi is all about the blues.
This Mississippi right here.
It's air, it's fresh, it's divine, it's all me. The truth. It's the truth.
This is where a whole lot of blood, a whole lot of tears, and a whole lot of memory will always stay in these cotton fields.
I guarantee you won't see nobody walking through these in the night.
I guarantee it. Guarantee it.

Let the world listen right.
Just let 'em listen right.
All my ancestors get up, y'all can walk through me.
You can walk through me.
So I walk through the valley of death
So I fear no man and no evil.
You can walk with me.
Sojourner Truth, you can walk with me.
Harriet Tubman, you can walk with me.
Kunta Kinte, you can walk with me.
Martin Luther King, you can walk with me.
Malcolm X, you can walk with me.
All my peoples you can walk with me.
All my indentured servants, you can walk with me.
All my brothers and sisters, you can walk with me.

Jerome "TopNotch the Villain" Williams. Photograph by Timothy Gordon.

For everybody that just believe they went through some hardship and some hard times
You can walk with me
We gonna walk this together
This is my dream
This is my brother's dream

He want to see us hold hands, man woman and child, breathe through the life of the ways of the man.
You're only a murderer if you don't feed knowledge to the person that's comin' behind you. It's a generation. You can't never short them out in their malnourishment. It's knowledge for their brain and their soul.

It gives them a reality, it gives them a to chance to think and give them a chance to believe. It gives them a chance to move on when things is just not right.
Like I said, you can walk with me. You can walk with me.

Everybody come out the field,
The breeze is over.
They'll listen right through me
They'll listen right through me.
They'll listen right through me.
Now listen.[5]

Notes

Front Matter

1. bell hooks, *Yearning: Race, Gender, and Cultural Politics* (Boston: South End Press, 1990), 112.

Introduction

1. These unemployment figures may be overly optimistic; many terminally unemployed, undocumented and seasonal Clarksdalians are not included in these statistics.
2. Molefi Kete Asante, *The Afrocentric Idea* (Philadelphia: Temple University Press, 1987) 83–86.
3. Ibid., 87.
4. Jesse Jackson used this term to describe the Delta after his 1985 visit to the region.
5. See Clifford and Marcus's important book of the same name.
6. See James Cobb's comprehensive social history of the Delta and of Clarksdale in particular in: *The Most Southern Place on Earth: The Mississippi Delta and the Roots of Regional Identity* (New York: Oxford University Press, 1992).
7. The title of Alan Lomax's popular 1993 Delta blues ethnography.

Chapter 1

1. Cornel West, "Prophetic Christian as Organic Intellectual: Martin Luther King, Jr.," in *The Cornel West Reader* (New York: Basic Civitas Books, 1989), 482–83.
2. Many thanks to Robert Birdsong, a Clarksdale fireman and historian, for his historio-geographic tours of Clarksdale.
3. Theodis Ealey, "Stand Up in It," from *Stand Up in It* (Ifgam Records, B0001XAKLA, 2004).
4. The Delta Blues Education Program pairs accomplished blues musicians with grade-school and high-school students. More information can be found at www.bluesed.org.
5. Robert Farris Thompson, *Flash of the Spirit: African and Afro-American Art and Philosophy* (New York: Vintage, 1984) 19.
6. As quoted by his brother, Rev. LeDell Johnson, in David Evans, *Tommy Johnson* (London: Studio Vista, 1971), 22–23.
7. Ibid.
8. Of the generation of blues musicians who began to record for popular audiences in the era between World Wars I and II.
9. Robert Johnson, "Me and the Devil Blues," from *Robert Johnson: The Complete Recordings* (Columbia/Legacy C2K 64916, 1990).
10. Author interview with Obbie Lee Barnes (Puttin' Hatchett), January 4, 2008.
11. Son House, "Death Letter Blues," from *The Original Delta Blues* (Sony B000007T4P, 1998).
12. In Cobb, *The Most Southern Place*, 265.
13. Many of these conditions remain present for Delta residents today, who are in the midst of an obesity epidemic thanks to the unavailability of fresh and affordable produce. Fruit and vegetables are particularly lacking at food stores that cater to the large percentage of the population who subsist on food stamps.

14. From Charley Patton's "High Water Everywhere—Part II," transcribed in Robert Palmer, *Deep Blues* (New York: Viking, 1991) 76–77.
15. In Cobb, 277. See also W. C. Handy, *Father of the Blues* (New York: Da Capo, 1991).
16. Alan Lomax, *The Land Where the Blues Began* (New York: Pantheon, 1993), 14.
17. See Alan Dundes's analysis of Dollard's "The Dozens: Dialect of Insult," in Alan Dundes, ed., *Mother Wit from the Laughing Barrel: Readings in the Interpretation of Afro-American Folklore* (Jackson: University Press of Mississippi, 1990), 277–94.
18. Charles Keil, *Urban Blues* (Chicago: University of Chicago Press, 1992).
19. The Blues Brothers, "You Can't Play the Blues in an Air-Conditioned Room," on *Red, White and Blues* (Turnstyle B00000E959, 1992).
20. Origin unknown. Available at ieee-huntsville.org/y2003/lw0306/lw0306blues.html.
21. See Greg Tate's book of the same name, *Everything But the Burden: What White People Are Taking from Black Culture* (New York: Harlem Moon/Broadway Books, 2003).
22. Roger Abrahams, *The Man-of-Words in the West Indies: Performance and the Emergence of Creole Culture* (Baltimore: Johns Hopkins University Press,1983), 24.
23. Albert Murray, *Stomping the Blues* (New York: McGraw-Hill, 1976), 74.
24. Ibid., 68.
25. Ibid., 258.
26. John W. Roberts, *From Trickster to Badman: The Black Folk Hero in Slavery and Freedom* (Philadelphia: University of Pennsylvania Press, 1989), 12–13.
27. For a journalistic history of popular music and the Delta, see Elijah Wald, *Escaping the Delta: Standing at the Crossroads: Robert Johnson and the Invention of the Blues* (New York: Amistad Harper Collins, 2004).
28. Frank-John Hadley, "Hip-Hop Meets the Juke Joint: Adventurous Artists Attempt to Resurrect Blues from Its Death Bed," *Down Beat—Jazz, Blues & Beyond* 72, no. 2 (February 2005).
29. Ibid.
30. Terry "Big T" Williams, interview, Clarksdale, Mississippi, July 13, 2006. From the short documentary *Let the World Listen Right* (Brian Graves, Ali Colleen Neff, and Jerome Williams, 2006).
31. See David Evans, "Techniques of Composition among Black Folksingers," *Journal of American Folklore* 87, no. 345 (1974): 240–49; Jeff Todd Titon, *Downhome Blues Lyrics: An Anthology from the Post–World War II Era* (Champaign: University of Illinois Press, 1991); Paul Oliver, *Yonder Come the Blues: The Evolution of a Genre* (Cambridge, UK: Cambridge University Press, 2001); and Samuel Charters, *The Poetry of the Blues* (New York: Oak, 1963).
32. William Ferris, *Give My Poor Heart Ease* (film, 1975). Available at www.folkstreams.net.
33. Lawrence Levine, *Black Culture and Black Consciousness: Afro-American Folk Thought from Slavery to Freedom* (New York: Oxford University Press, 1974), 5.
34. Ibid., 444–45.
35. Portia K. Maultsby, "Africanisms in African American Music," Joseph Holloway, ed., *Africanisms in American Culture* (Bloomington: University of Indiana Press, 1990).
36. Cheryl L. Keyes, "At the Crossroads: Rap Music and its African Nexus," *Ethnomusicology* 40, no. 2 (1996): 223–48.
37. Ibid.
38. These lyrics have been used by myriad blues singers throughout the twentieth century, including James "Son" Thomas, Muddy Waters, and contemporary singer Robert Belfour.
39. Jerome "TopNotch the Villain" Williams, performed as part of an interview, Clarksdale, Mississippi, September 3, 2005.

Chapter 2

1. Jerome "TopNotch the Villain" Williams, interview, Clarksdale, Mississippi, September 3, 2005.
2. William R. Ferris, *Blues from the Delta* (Garden City, NY: Anchor Press, 1979), 62.
3. Interview, 10/03/05.

4. Interview, 10/09/05.
5. William Ferris recorded scores of the dozens in Lyon, Mississippi, in the late 1960s, many of which are familiar to TopNotch today. Available through the UNC-Chapel Hill Southern Folklife Collection.
6. Andrew Jones (Jerome "TopNotch the Villain" Williams's cousin), interview, Lambert, Mississippi, October 8, 2005.
7. Taurus Metcalf (Jerome "TopNotch the Villain" Williams's cousin), interview, Clarksdale, Mississippi, July 6, 2006.
8. From an impromptu performance recorded by the author on July 6, 2006.
9. Tricia Rose, *Black Noise: Rap Music and Black Culture in Contemporary America* (Middletown, CT: Wesleyan University Press, 1994), 36.
10. From an improvised performance in the Brickyard, Clarksdale, Mississippi, October 7, 2005.
11. Jerome "TopNotch the Villain" Williams, interview, Clarksdale, Mississippi, October 9, 2005.
12. Ibid.
13. Barbara Babcock, "The Story in the Story: Metanarration in Folk Narrative," Richard Bauman, ed., *Verbal Art as Performance* (Prospect Heights, IL: Waveland Press, 1977), 73.
14. Interview, October 9, 2005.
15. See the work of literary theorist Stanley Fish, particularly his book *Is There a Text in This Class? The Authority of Interpretive Communities* (Boston: Harvard University Press, 1982).
16. Interview, November 25, 2006.
17. Jerome "TopNotch the Villain" Williams, interview, Clarksdale, Mississippi, September 3, 2005.
18. Dell Hymes, "Breakthrough into Performance," "*In Vain I Tried to Tell You*": *Essays in Native American Poetics* (Philadelphia: University of Pennsylvania Press, 2004), 81.
19. Bauman, *Verbal Art*, 42.
20. As cited in Houston A. Baker, "Critical Challenge and Blues Continuity: An Essay on the Criticism of Larry Neal," *Callaloo* no. 23 (Winter 1985), 70.
21. Jerome "TopNotch the Villain" Williams, interview, Clarksdale, Mississippi, April 7, 2008.
22. Cheryl L. Keyes, *Rap Music and Street Consciousness* (Urbana: University of Illinois Press, 2002), 126.
23. Jerome "TopNotch the Villain" Williams, interview, Clarksdale, Mississippi, April 7, 2008.
24. Ferris, 63.
25. Jerome "TopNotch the Villain" Williams, interview, Clarksdale, Mississippi, September 3, 2005.
26. Rose, 89.
27. Jerome "TopNotch the Villain" Williams, interview, Clarksdale, Mississippi, April 7, 2008.
28. Ferris, 67–70.
29. Roger D. Abrahams, *Singing the Master: The Emergence of African American Culture in the Plantation South* (New York: Pantheon, 1992), 96.
30. Asante, 83.
31. Murray, 87.
32. Jerome "TopNotch the Villain" Williams, interview, Clarksdale, Mississippi, September 3, 2005.
33. Mimi Carr Melnick, "I Can Peep through Muddy Water and Spy Dry Land: Boasts in the Blues," in Dundes, *Mother Wit*, 268.
34. Interview, October 9, 2005.
35. James C. Scott, *Domination and the Arts of Resistance: Hidden Transcripts* (New Haven: Yale University Press, 1990), 161.
36. All interview excerpts from a phone interview with Jerome "Top Notch the Villain" Williams conducted on November 26, 2006. TopNotch had reviewed the video and transcript of his performance that same day and had been asked to reflect on its meaning.
37. The distinction between the group members' alternating self-described status as rappers and hip-hop artists is contingent upon whether the group is describing their work as southern popular "rappers," freestyle practitioners engaged in rap battles, or in the context of their status as members of the global "hip-hop" community, which they often invoke in our interviews for this book.
38. Interview, October 9, 2005.

39. Jerome "TopNotch the Villain" Williams, interview, Clarksdale, Mississippi September 3rd, 2005.
40. Roger D. Abrahams, "Playing the Dozens," in Dundes, *Mother Wit*, 297.
41. See Levine, *Black Culture and Black Consciousness*, for a deeper discussion of the potential functions of the dozens.
42. Jerome "TopNotch the Villain" Williams, interview, Clarksdale, Mississippi, September 3rd, 2005.
43. Lightnin Hopkins, "Never Miss Your Water," on *Lightning Special, Vol. 2 [Original Recording Remastered]* (JSP Records, B000OV123O, [YEAR]).
44. Lightnin Hopkins, "Smokes Like Lightnin'," *Smokes Like Lightnin'* (OBC, B000000XYR, 1995).
45. Jerome "TopNotch the Villain" Williams, interview, Clarksdale, Mississippi, September 3, 2005.
46. Robert Johnson, "They're Red Hot," *Complete Recordings*.
47. Jerome "TopNotch the Villain" Williams, interview, Clarksdale, Mississippi, September 3, 2005.
48. Interview, October 9, 2005.
49. Jerome "TopNotch the Villain" Williams, interview, Clarksdale, Mississippi, September 3, 2005.
50. Murray, *Stomping the Blues*, 224.
51. Interview, July 3, 2006.
52. Murray, *Stomping the Blues*, 214.
53. Interview, April 7, 2008.
54. bell hooks, *Yearning*, 104–5.
55. Roberts, *From Trickster to Badman*, 11.
56. Terry "Big T" Williams, interview, July 13, 2006.
57. For more on the deeply signified aesthetics of the black diaspora, see Robert Farris Thompson, *Flash of the Spirit.*
58. Jerome "TopNotch the Villain" Williams interview, Clarksdale, Mississippi, September 3, 2005.
59. Eric Clapton's *Me and Mr. Johnson* is an album of Robert Johnson covers invoking many Delta blues tropes and landmarks; Aerosmith's *Honkin' on Bobo* references a plantation just outside of Clarksdale; Page and Plant's *Walking into Clarksdale* features a song of the same name and is, in fact, very critical of the local gambling and tourism industries.
60. Terry "Big T" Williams, interview for film *Let the World Listen Right*, July 13, 2006.

Chapter 3

1. Big Tymers, "Hood Rich," *Hood Rich* (Cash Money, B00065UJJ, 2002).
2. See Abrahams, *Singing the Master.*
3. Interview, October 9, 2005.
4. Young Jeezy is a popular southern rapper whose lyrics deal with street life.
5. This commentary was provided by TopNotch via phone conversation with the author, September 20, 2007.
6. From interview with author for an article in *Deep* magazine, August 16, 2007.
7. Statistics provided by the Mississippi State Social Sciences Research Center.
8. From interview with author for an article in *Deep* magazine, August 16, 2007.
9. Ibid.
10. DJ Dr. Pepper, interview, Clarksdale, Mississippi, August 3, 2008.
11. Timothy "Small Tyme" Williams, interview, Clarksdale, Mississippi, July 15, 2006.
12. Anthony DeWayne "Buggs Diego" Buggs, interview, Clarksdale, Mississippi, July 15, 2006.
13. Jerome "TopNotch the Villain" Williams, interview, Clarksdale, Mississippi, July 12, 2006.

Chapter 4

1. Transcribed from TopNotch's appearance on *Madd and Marilyn in the Morning*, WROX, Clarksdale, Mississippi July 19, 2007.

2. Roberts, 124.
3. Abrahams, 105–6.
4. Lomax, *Land*, 244.
5. Thanks to Clarksdale fireman and tour guide Robert Birdsong for his firsthand knowledge of the county's topography.
6. In the documentary film *Land Where the Blues Began* (Alan Lomax, 1979).
7. See Nick Tosches, *Unsung Heroes of Rock 'n' Roll: The Birth of Rock 'n' Roll in the Wild Years before Elvis* (Cambridge, MA: Da Capo, 1999).
8. Ferris, *Give My Poor Heart Ease.*
9. From a recording of a 1980s-era broadcast from Wright on WROX made by white teenage Clarksdalians.
10. Davarian Baldwin, "Black Empires, White Desires: The Spatial Politics of Identity in the Age of Hip-Hop," in *That's the Joint! A Hip-Hop Studies Reader*, ed. M. Forman and M. A. Neal (New York: Routledge, 1999), 174.
11. Claudia Mitchell-Kernan, "Signifying," in Dundes, *Mother Wit*, 311.
12. Michael Eric Dyson, *Is Bill Cosby Right? Or Has the Black Middle Class Lost its Mind?* (New York: Basic Civitas, 2006), 33.
13. Nicholas Lemann explores this process in depth in his excellent history of Clarksdale–Chicago migration, *The Promised Land: The Great Black Migration and How it Changed America* (New York: Vintage, 1992).
14. Trudier Harris, "Genre," in *Eight Words for the Study of Expressive Culture*, ed. B. Feintuch (Champaign: University of Illinois Press,[YEAR]), 113.
15. Jacqui Malone, *Steppin' on the Blues: The Visible Rhythms of African American Dance* (Urbana: University of Illinois Press, 1996), 26–36.
16. In Ferris, *Blues from the Delta*, 111.
17. Lomax, *The Land Where the Blues Began*, 361–62.
18. In Robert Gordon and Bruce Nemerov, ed., *Lost Delta Found: Rediscovering the Fisk University–Library of Congress Coahoma County Study, 1941–1942*, by John W. Work, Lewis Wade Jones, and Samuel C. Adams, Jr. (Nashville: Vanderbilt University Press, 2005), 99.
19. Ibid, 104.
20. Ibid.
21. Kyra Gaunt, "Translating Double Dutch to Hip-Hop: The Musical Vernacular of Black Girls' Play," in *That's the Joint*, ed. Forman and Neal, 251.
22. Koko Taylor, "I'm a Woman," *Deluxe Edition* (Alligator Records B00005UF1W, 2002).
23. Hazel Carby, "It Jus Be's Dat Way Sometime: The Sexual Politics of Women's Blues," *Radical American* 20, no. 4 (1987), 12
24. See also Angela Y. Davis's excellent 1999 contextual exploration of the lyrics and performance styles of women blues artists in her *Blues Legacies and Black Feminism* (New York: Vintage, 1999).
25. Cheryl Keyes, "Empowering Self, Making Choices, Creating Spaces," In Forman and Neal, *That's the Joint!* 273.
26. Lady Cherry (Linda Johnson), WROX deejay, interview, September 18, 2005.
27. southernfriedreflections.blogspot.com/.
28. Available through Nelson's MySpace page, myspace.com/mssweetiemississippi.
29. Interview, September 14, 2007.
30. From the Papachasa Showcase Party (Clarksdale V.F.W. Hall) DVD, Papachasa Ent., February 24, 2006.
31. Ibid.
32. Jerome "TopNotch the Villain" Williams, transcript of freestyle rap from interview, Clarksdale, Mississippi, September 3, 2005.
33. Jerome "TopNotch the Villain" Williams, interview, Clarksdale, Mississippi, October 9, 2005.
34. Notes from visit between Jerome "TopNotch the Villain" Williams, Martha Raybon, and Ali Colleen Neff, Crowder, Mississippi, October 7, 2005.
35. Interview, Miss Martha Raybon, Crowder, Mississippi, July 19, 2006.

Chapter 5

1. Greg Tate, "Love and Crunk: Rowdy Big Boi and Fly Andre 3000 Divide and Conquer the Dirty South Book of Hiphop Rules," *Village Voice*, September 30, 2003.
2. In Gordon and Nemerov, *Lost Delta Found*, 311.
3. Ibid.
4. Elijah Wald explores these popular influences in the Delta in *Escaping the Delta*.
5. Mark Anthony Neal, "Postindustrial Soul: Black Popular Music at the Crossroads," in Forman and Neal, *That's the Joint!* 371.
6. Nas, "Bridging the Gap," *Street's Disciple* (Sony B0006B2AFQ, 2004).
7. See Thompson, *Flash of the Spirit*, for an exploration of Afrodiasporic aesthetics.
8. Interview, May 13, 2008.
9. Ibid.
10. Dyson, *Is Bill Cosby Right?* 36.
11. Rufus Thomas, "Walking the Dog," *The Very Best of Rufus Thomas* (Stax B000RIWAQC, 1996).
12. Pigmeat Markham, "Here Comes the Judge," *Here Comes the Judge* (Blues Journey B00026K8YK, 1991).
13. James Brown, "Soul Power," *20th Century Masters: The Best Of James Brown* (Polydor B00000JMKD, 1999).
14. H. Rap Brown,. "Die, Nigger, Die," in Dundes, *Mother Wit*, 354–55.
15. Last Poets, "True Blues," *This Is Madness* (Celluloid B00000JWSB, 1995).
16. DJ Dr. Pepper, interview, Clarksdale, Mississippi, August 3, 2008.
17. Grandmaster Flash and the Furious Five, "Superrappin'," *The Best of Enjoy Records* (Hot Productions B000001QIX, 1990).
18. S. L. A. Jones, *Addresses for Special Occasions* (self-published, n.d.), 14.
19. Ibid., 14. This selection has been edited lightly for printing mistakes and minor punctuation errors.
20. DJ Dr. Pepper, interview, Clarksdale, Mississippi, August 3, 2008.
21. See Chang, *Total Chaos*, for an exploration of the global practices that converge in dynamic hip-hop practice.
22. KRS-One, "Sound of da Police," *Return of the Boom Bap* (Jive B000000509, 1993).
23. Arrested Development, "Tennessee," *3 Years 5 Months & 2 Days in the Life of—* (Capitol B000003JBE, 1992).
24. bell hooks, "Speech: A Love Rap—Leader of Rap Group Arrested Development—Interview," *Essence* (November 1993).
25. Goodie Mob, "Soul Food," *Soul Food* (Arista B0000013GF, 1995).
26. On *Queen of the Blues* (Sony B000002AI4, 1997).
27. For more on the development and sub-regional deployment of southern hip-hop, see Roni Sarig, *Third Coast: Outkast, Timbaland, and How Hip-Hop Became a Southern Thing* (Cambridge, MA: Da Capo, 2007).
28. The name of Banner's group, Crooked Lettaz, refers to the "s's" in the name of his state.
29. David Banner, "Ridin," *Certified* (Umvd B000A2H3CQ, 2005).
30. Roberts, *From Trickster to Badman*, 176.
31. Robin D. G. Kelley, *Race Rebels: Culture, Politics, and the Black Working Class* (New York: Free Press, 1996), 190.
32. Greil Marcus, *Mystery Train: Images of America in Rock and Roll* (New York: E. P. Dutton, 1975) d.
33. Donna Ladd, "Tough Questions for David Banner," Jackson *Free Press*, May 15, 2003.
34. Billy Watkins, "Provine Grad Scores Big! $10M Record Deal, No. 1 Album," Jackson (MS) *Clarion-Ledger*, June 16, 2003.
35. David Banner, "Mississippi," *Mississippi: The Album* (Umvd B000095J4F, 1993).
36. TopNotch, interview, May 13th, 2008,
37. U.S. House Subcommittee on Commerce, Trade and Consumer Protection Hearings on Hip-Hop, "From Imus to Industry: The Business of Stereotypes and Degradation," in response to Imus controversy (Dyson/Banner/Masta P). Available at youtube.com/watch?v=2RFy192Xj7g.

38. Although the verbal texts of crunk can themselves reveal a wealth of cultural understandings, the music also provides a space for other kinds of signifying. Voice, rhythm, dance, visual aesthetics, and the incorporation of traditional cultural elements complicate and negotiate the music's surface meanings. By introducing the concept of signifying practices into media and cultural studies via the complexities of crunk, we come to better understand the slippages in encoding/decoding described by Stuart Hall at the outset of the Birmingham school project: "The meaning of a cultural form and its place or position in the cultural field is not inscribed inside its form. Nor is its position fixed once and forever. . . . The meaning of a cultural symbol is given in part by the social field into which it is incorporated, the practices with which it articulates and is made to resonate."
39. U.S. House Subcommittee, "From Imus to Industry."
40. New York rapper Nas, whose father, Olu Dara, is from Natchez, Mississippi, recalls this imagery on the cover of his 2008 album.
41. Watkins, "Provine Grad."
42. David Banner, "Cadillac on 22's," *Mississippi: The Album.*
43. Phone conversation with author, May 17th, 2008.
44. "Outro," *Mississippi: The Album.*
45. Jerome "TopNotch the Villain" Williams, interview, Clarksdale, Mississippi, October 8, 2005.
46. Ibid.
47. The group began to refer to themselves as Three Six Mafia upon gaining national popularity in 1995, but local fans continue to call the group by their original, burlesquely sinister name.
48. Money Mission Entertainment, "Crank Dat Clarksdale." Live performance available at youtube.com/watch?v=aXCDO1Uhyio.
49. Neal, *What the Music Said,* 14–15.
50. James Peacock, *Grounded Globalism: How the U.S. South Embraces the World* (Athens: University of Georgia Press, 2007), 182–83.

Chapter 6

1. Ali Neff, "Young 'voters' are worried about war," *Clarksdale Press-Register*, November 01, 2004. Available at zwire.com/site/news.cfm?newsid=13265126&BRD=2038&PAG=461&dept_id=230617&rfi=8.
2. Bubba Burnham, "Oh! For those days of illegal alcohol," *Clarksdale Press-Register*, March 09, 2007 zwire.com/site/news.cfm?newsid=18054761&BRD=2038&PAG=461&dept_id=230617&rfi=8.
3. The rental situation had changed drastically since 2004 with the increase in local blues tourism.
4. Deacon Fred and Dorothy Lenard and their family were especially generous in offering their hospitality at Pleasant Grove.
5. Kurt Carr Singers, "Jesus Can Work It Out," *Awesome Wonder* (Gospocentric B00005TSOV, 2000).
6. Robin D. G. Kelley, "Looking for the Real Nigga," in Forman and Neal, *That's the Joint!* 120.
7. See ibid., 127, for a discussion of the implications of poor ethnographic work on the pathologization of dozens players: "For example, white ethnographers seemed oblivious to the fact that their very presence shaped what they observed. Asking their subjects to 'play the dozens' while an interloper records the 'session' with a tape recorder and notepad has the effect of creating a ritual performance for the sake of an audience, of turning spontaneous, improvised verbal exchanges into a formal practice."
8. Soyini Madison, *Critical Ethnography: Methods, Ethics, and Performance* (Thousand Oaks, CA: Sage, 2005), 5.
9. James Clifford and George Marcus, *Writing Culture: The Poetics and Politics of Ethnography.* (Berkeley: University of California Press, 1986), 15–17.
10. Elaine J. Lawless, "'I Was Afraid Someone Like You . . . an Outsider . . . Would Misunderstand': Negotiating Interpretive Differences between Ethnographers and Subjects," *Journal of American Folklore* 105, no. 417 (Summer 1992): 302–14.

11. Phone conversation with the author, August 8, 2007.
12. DJ Dr. Pepper, transcribed from performance, July 20, 2007.

Conclusion

1. Jerome "TopNotch the Villain" Williams, interview, Clarksdale, Mississippi, July 17, 2006.
2. Recorded by the author, Crowder, Mississippi, July 16, 2006.
3. Miss Martha Raybon, interview, Crowder, Mississippi, July 19, 2006.
4. Kimyata Dear, interview, Clarksdale, Mississippi, July 15, 2006.
5. Jerome "TopNotch the Villain" Williams, video recording, Clarksdale, Mississippi, July 25, 2006.

References

Bibliography

Abrahams, Roger D. "Playing the Dozens." In *Mother Wit from the Laughing Barrel: Readings in the Interpretation of Afro-American Folklore* edited by Alan Dundes, 295–309. Jackson: University Press of Mississippi, 1990.

———. *Singing the Master: The Emergence of African American Culture in the Plantation South.* New York: Pantheon, 1992.

———. *The Man-of-Words in the West Indies: Performance and the Emergence of Creole Culture.* Baltimore: Johns Hopkins, 1983.

Asante, Molefi Kete. *The Afrocentric Idea*. Philadelphia: Temple University Press, 1987.

Babcock, Barbara. "The Story in the Story: Metanarration in Folk Narrative." In *Verbal Art as Performance*, edited by Richard Bauman. Prospect Heights, IL: Waveland Press, 1977.

Baker, Houston A., Jr. "Critical Change and Blues Continuity: An Essay on the Criticism of Larry Neal." *Callaloo* 23 (Winter 1985): 70–84.

Baldwin, Davarian. "Black Empires, White Desires: The Spatial Politics of Identity in the Age of Hip-Hop." In *That's the Joint! A Hip-Hop Studies Reader*, edited by Murray Forman and Mark Anthony Neal. 159–76. New York: Routledge, 1999.

Baraka, Imamu Amiri. *The LeRoi Jones/Amiri Baraka Reader*. New York: Thunder's Mouth Press, 1991.

———, and Amina Baraka. *The Music: Reflections on Jazz and Blues.* New York: William Morrow, 1987.

Bauman, Richard. "The Field Study of Folklore in Context." In *Handbook of American Folklore*, edited by R. Dorson and I. G. Carpenter. 362–68. Bloomington: Indiana University Press, 1983.Brown, H. Rap. "Die, Nigger, Die." In *Mother Wit from the Laughing Barrel: Readings in the Interpretation of Afro-American Folklore*, edited by Alan Dundes. 353–56. Jackson: University Press of Mississippi, 1990.

Burnham, Bubba. 2007. "Oh! For Those Days of Illegal Alcohol." *Clarksdale Press-Register*, March 9, 2007.

Carby, Hazel. "It Jus Be's Dat Way Sometime: The Sexual Politics of Women's Blues." *Radical American* 20, no. 4 (1987): 8–22.

Chang, Jeff, ed. *Total Chaos: the Art and Aesthetics of Hip-Hop.* New York: Basic Civitas Books, 2006.

Charters, Samuel. *The Poetry of the Blues.* New York: Oak, 1963.

Chernoff, John Miller. *African Rhythm and African Sensibility: Aesthetics and Social Action in African Musical Idioms.* Chicago: University of Chicago Press, 1979.

Clifford, James. *The Predicament of Culture: Twentieth Century Ethnography, Literature and Art.* Boston: Harvard University Press, 1988.

———, and George Marcus. *Writing Culture: The Poetics and Politics of Ethnography*. Berkeley: University of California Press, 1986.

Cobb, James. *The Most Southern Place on Earth: The Mississippi Delta and the Roots of Regional Identity.* New York: Oxford University Press, 1992.

Dance, Daryl Cumber. *400 years of African American Folklore from My People: An Anthology*. New York: W. W. Norton, 2000.

Davis, Angela Y. *Blues Legacies and Black Feminism.* New York: Vintage, 1999.

Du Bois, W. E. B. 1903. *The Souls of Black Folk*. Boulder, CO: Paradigm, 2004.
Dundes, Alan, ed. *Mother Wit from the Laughing Barrel: Readings in the Interpretation of Afro-American Folklore*. Jackson: University Press of Mississippi, 1990.
Dyson, Michael Eric. *Between God and Gangsta Rap: Bearing Witness to Black Culture*. New York: Oxford University Press, 1996.
———. *Is Bill Cosby Right? Or Has the Black Middle Class Lost its Mind?* New York: Basic Civitas Books, 2005.
Evans, David. "Techniques of Composition among Black Folksingers." *Journal of American Folklore* 87, no. 345 (1974): 240–49.
Evans, David. *Tommy Johnson*. London: Studio Vista, 1971.
Ferris, William. *Blues from the Delta*. Garden City, NY: Anchor Press, 1979.
Fish, Stanley. *Is There a Text in This Class? The Authority of Interpretive Communities*. Boston: Harvard University Press, 1982.
Forman, Murray, and Mark Anthony Neal, eds. *That's the Joint! A Hip-Hop Studies Reader*. New York: Routledge, 2004.
Franklin, John Hope. *From Slavery to Freedom: A History of Negro Americans*. New York: McGraw Hill, 1994.
Gaunt, Kyra D. "Translating Double Dutch to Hip-Hop: The Musical Vernacular of Black Girls' Play." In *That's the Joint! A Hip-Hop Studies Reader*, edited by Murray Forman and Mark Anthony Neal. 251–64. New York: Routledge, 2004.
Genovese, Eugene. *Roll, Jordan, Roll: The World the Slaves Made*. New York: Pantheon, 1974.
Gordon, Robert, and Bruce Nemerov. 2005. *Lost Delta Found: Rediscovering the Fisk University–Library of Congress Coahoma County Study, 1941–1942 / John W. Work, Lewis Wade Jones, Samuel C. Adams, Jr.* Nashville: Vanderbilt University Press, 2005.
Gwaltney, John Langston. *Drylongso: A Self-Portrait of Black America*. New York: New Press, 1993.
Hadley, Frank-John. "Hip-Hop Meets the Juke Joint: Adventurous Artists Attempt to Resurrect Blues from Its Death Bed." *Down Beat—Jazz, Blues & Beyond* 72, no. 2 (February 2005): 48–51.
Handy, W. C. 1941. *Father of the Blues*. New York: Da Capo Press, 1991.
Harris, Trudier. "Genre." In *Eight Words for the Study of Expressive Culture*, edited by Burt Feintuch. Champaign: University of Illinois Press, 2003.
hooks, bell. *Yearning: Race, Gender, and Cultural Politics*. Boston: South End Press, 1990.
———. "Speech: A Love Rap—Leader of Rap Group Arrested Development—Interview." *Essence* (November 1993).
Hurston, Zora Neale. 1935. *Mules and Men*. New York: Harper Perennial, 1990.
Hymes, Dell. *In Vain I Tried to Tell You: Essays in Native American Poetics*. Philadelphia: University of Pennsylvania Press, 2004.
Jones, LeRoi (Amiri Baraka). *Blues People: Negro Music in White America*. New York: Morrow, 1963.
Jones, S. L. A. *Addresses for Special Occasions* (self-published, n.d.).
Keil, Charles. *Urban Blues*. Chicago: University of Chicago Press, 1992.
Kelley, Robin D. G. "Looking for the Real Nigga." In *That's the Joint! A Hip-Hop Studies Reader*, edited by Murray Forman and Mark Anthony Neal. 119–36. New York: Routledge, 2004.
———. *Race Rebels: Culture, Politics, and the Black Working Class*. New York: Free Press, 1996.
Keyes, Cheryl L. "At the Crossroads: Rap Music and its African Nexus." *Ethnomusicology* 40, no. 2 (1996): 223–48.
———. "Empowering Self, Making Choices, Creating Spaces." In *That's the Joint! A Hip-Hop Studies Reader*, edited by Murray Forman and Mark Anthony Neal. 265–76. New York: Routledge, 2004.
———.*Rap Music and Street Consciousness*. Urbana: University of Illinois Press, 2002.
Ladd, Donna. "Tough Questions for David Banner." *Jackson Free Press*. May 15, 2003.
Lawless, Elaine J. "'I Was Afraid Someone Like You . . . an Outsider . . . Would Misunderstand': Negotiating Interpretive Differences between Ethnographers and Subjects." *Journal of American Folklore* 105, no. 417 (Summer 1992): 302–14.
Lemann, Nicholas. *The Promised Land: The Great Black Migration and How it Changed America*. New York: Vintage, 1992.

Levine, Lawrence W. *Black Culture and Black Consciousness: Afro- American Folk Thought from Slavery to Freedom.* New York: Oxford University Press, 1974.

Lomax, Alan. *The Land Where the Blues Began.* New York: Pantheon, 1993.

Madison, Soyini. *Critical Ethnography: Methods, Ethics, and Performance.* Thousand Oaks, CA: Sage, 2005.

Malone, Jacqui. *Stepping the Blues: The Visible Rhythms of African American Dance.* Urbana: University of Illinois Press, 1996.

Marable, Manning. *How Capitalism Underdeveloped Black America.* Boston: South End Press, 1983.

Marcus, Greil. *Mystery Train: Images of America in Rock and Roll.* New York: E. P. Dutton, 1975.

Maultsby, Portia K. "Africanisms in African American Music." In *Africanisms in American Culture*, edited by J. Holloway. Bloomington: University of Indiana Press, 1990.

McCarthy, Timothy Patrick, and John McMillian. *The Radical Reader.* New York: New Press, 2003.

Meintjes, Louise. *Sound of Africa! Making Music Zulu in a South African Studio.* Durham, NC: Duke University Press, 2003.

Melnick, Mimi Carr. "I Can Peep through Muddy Water and Spy Dry Land: Boasts in the Blues." In *Mother Wit from the Laughing Barrel: Readings in the Interpretation of Afro-American Folklore*, edited by Alan Dundes. 267–76. Jackson: University Press of Mississippi, 1990.

Mitchell-Kernan, Claudia. "Signifying." In *Mother Wit from the Laughing Barrel: Readings in the Interpretation of Afro-American Folklore*, edited by Alan Dundes. 310–28. Jackson: University Press of Mississippi, 1990.

Morgan, Marcyliena. *Language, Power and Discourse in African American Culture.* New York: Cambridge University Press, 2002.

Morrison, Toni. *Beloved.* New York: Plume, 1988.

Murray, Albert. *Stomping the Blues.* New York: McGraw-Hill, 1976.

Neal, Mark Anthony. *New Black Man: Rethinking Black Masculinity.* New York: Routledge, 2005.

———. "Postindustrial Soul: Black Popular Music at the Crossroads." In *That's the Joint! A Hip-Hop Studies Reader*, edited by Murray Forman and Mark Anthony Neal. 363–88. New York: Routledge, 2004.

———. *Songs in the Key of Black Life: A Rhythm and Blues Nation.* New York: Routledge, 2003.

———. *What the Music Said: Black Popular Music and Black Public Culture.* New York: Routledge, 1998.

Neff, Ali. "Young 'voters' are worried about war." *Clarksdale Press-Register.* November 1, 2004.

Oliver, Paul. *Yonder Come the Blues: The Evolution of a Genre.* Cambridge, UK: Cambridge University Press, 2001.

Palmer, Robert. *Deep Blues.* New York: Viking, 1981.

Peacock, James. *Grounded Globalism: How the U.S. South Embraces the World.* Athens: University of Georgia Press, 2007.

———. "The South in a Global World." *Virginia Quarterly Review* 78, no. 4 (2002).

Roberts, John W. *From Trickster to Badman: The Black Folk Hero in Slavery and Freedom.* Philadelphia: University of Pennsylvania Press, 1989.

Rose, Tricia. *Black Noise: Rap Music and Black Culture in Contemporary America.* Middletown, CT: Wesleyan University Press, 1994.

Sarig, Roni. *Third Coast: Outkast, Timbaland, & How Hip-Hop Became a Southern Thing.* Cambridge, MA: Da Capo, 2007.

Scott, James C. *Domination and the Arts of Resistance: Hidden Transcripts.* New Haven: Yale University Press, 1990.

Southern, Eileen, ed. *Readings in Black American Music.* New York: W. W. Norton, 1971.

Stuckey, Sterling. *Slave Culture: Nationalist Theory and the Foundations of Black America.* New York: Oxford University Press, 1987.

Tate, Greg, ed. *Everything But the Burden: What White People Are Taking from Black Culture.* New York: Harlem Moon/Broadway Books, 2003.

———. "Love and Crunk: Rowdy Big Boi and Fly Andre 3000 Divide and Conquer the Dirty South Book of Hiphop Rules." *Village Voice.* September 30, 2003.

———. "What is Hip-Hop?" In *Rap on Rap: Straight-up Talk on Hip-Hop Culture*, edited by A. Sexton. 17–21. New York: Delta Books, 1995.

Thompson, Robert Farris. *Flash of the Spirit: African and Afro-American Art and Philosophy.* New York: Vintage, 1984.

Titon, Jeff Todd. *Downhome Blues Lyrics: An Anthology from the Post–World War II Era.* Champaign: University of Illinois Press, 1995.

Toop, David. *Rap Attack 2: African Rap to Global Hip Hop.* New York: Serpent's Tail, 1991.

Tosches, Nick. *Unsung Heroes of Rock 'n' Roll: The Birth of Rock in the Wild Years before Elvis.* [CITY:] Secker & Warburg, 1984.

Turner, Nat. 1831. *Confessions.* Transcribed by Thomas R. Gray. gutenberg.org/etext/15333.

Wald, Elijah. *Escaping the Delta: Standing at the Crossroads: Robert Johnson and the Invention of the Blues.* New York: Amistad Harper Collins, 2004.

Watkins, Billy. "Provine Grad Scores Big! $10M Record Deal, No. 1 Album." *Jackson Clarion-Ledger.* June 16, 2003.

West, Cornel. *The Cornel West Reader.* New York: Basic Civitas Books, 1999.

White, Shane, and Graham White. *The Sounds of Slavery: Discovering African American History through Songs, Sermons, and Speech.* Boston: Beacon Press, 2005.

Media

Adventures in Hollyhood (MTV show) (DVD, Sony B000Y7WGM4).

DJ Dr. Pepper recorded live performance, July 20, 2007.

Ferris, William R. Transcripts of the dozens recorded in Lyon, Mississippi. Available through the UNC-Chapel Hill Southern Folklife Collection.

———. 1975. *Give My Poor Heart Ease* (film, 29 min.). folkstreams.net.

———. 1975. *I Ain't Lying: Folktales from Mississippi.* (film, 22 min.). folkstreams.net.

"From Imus to Industry: The Business of Stereotypes and Degradation." U.S. House Subcommittee on Commerce, Trade and Consumer Protection Hearings on Hip-Hop in response to Imus Controversy. youtube.com/watch?v=2RFy192Xj7g.

Lomax, Alan. 1979. *The Land Where the Blues Began* (film, 58 min.). folkstreams.net.

Madd and Marilyn in the Morning (radio show), interview with Jerome "TopNotch the Villain" Williams. WROX, Clarksdale, Mississippi, July 19, 2007.

Money Mission Entertainment. "Crank Dat Clarksdale" (live performance). youtube.com/watch?v=aXCDO1Uhyio.

Nelson, Valeria (personal website) southernfriedreflections.blogspot.com/.

Neff, Ali Colleen, Brian Graves, and Jerome Williams. 2006. *Let the World Listen Right: Freestyle Hip-Hop in the Mississippi Delta* (film, 29 min.). folkstreams.net.

Papachasa Showcase Party (Clarksdale V.F.W. Hall), February 24, 2006 (DVD, Papachasa Entertainment).

Scorsese, Martin. *Martin Scorsese Presents the Blues: A Musical Journey* (DVD, Sony B0000CBHOI, 2003).

Williams, Jerome "TopNotch the Villain," video recording of cotton field freestyle, Clarksdale, Mississippi, July 25, 2006.

Wright, Early, recorded on-air performances, WROX, early 1980s.

Interview Materials

Barnes, Obbie Lee (Puttin' Hatchett), January 4, 2008.

Buggs, Anthony DeWayne "Buggs Diego," Clarksdale, Mississippi, July 15, 2006.

Dear, Keithan "K-Deezy," Clarksdale, Mississippi, July 15, 2006.

Dear, Kimyata "Yata," Clarksdale, Mississippi, July 15, 2006.

———. From interview with author for an article in *Deep* magazine. August 16, 2007.
DJ Dr. Pepper, August 4, 2008.
Johnson, Linda (Lady Cherry), phone interview, September 18, 2005.
Jones, Andrew, Lambert, Mississippi, October 8, 2005.
Metcalf, Taurus, Clarksdale, Mississippi, July 6, 2006.
Nelson, Valeria, September 14, 2007.
Raybon, Miss Martha, Crowder, Mississippi, July 19, 2006.
Williams, Jerome "TopNotch the Villain," Clarksdale, Mississippi, September 3, 2005.
———, Clarksdale, Mississippi, October 9, 2005.
———, Clarksdale, Mississippi, July 12, 2006.
———, phone conversation, August 8, 2007.
———, dictation by author, September 20, 2007.
———, phone conversation with author) April 7, 2008.
———, phone conversation, May 17, 2008.
Williams, Jeweline, Lambert, Mississippi, July 14, 2006.
Williams, Terry "Big T," Clarksdale, Mississippi, July 13, 2006.
Williams, Timothy "Small Tyme," Clarksdale, Mississippi, July 15, 2006.

Discography

Arrested Development. "Tennessee." *3 Years 5 Months & 2 Days in the Life of—* (Capitol B000003JBE, 1992).
Banner, David. "Cadillac on 22's." *Mississippi: The Album* (Umvd Labels B000095J4F, 2003).
———. "Mississippi." *Mississippi: The Album* (Umvd Labels B000095J4F, 2003).
———. "Outro." *Mississippi: The Album* (Umvd Labels B000095J4F, 2003).
———. "Ridin." *Certified* (Umvd Labels B000A2H3CQ, 2005).
Big Tymers. "Hood Rich." *Hood Rich* (Cash Money B000065UJJ, 2002).
Blues Brothers. "You Can't Play the Blues in an Air-Conditioned Room." *Red, White and Blues* (Turnstyle B00000E959, 1992).
Brown, James. 1971. "Soul Power." *20th Century Masters: The Best of James Brown* (Polydor/Umgd B00000JMKD, 1999).
Ealey, Theodis. "Stand Up in It." *Stand Up in It* (Ifgam B0001XAKLA, 2004).
Kurt Carr Singers. "Jesus Can Work It Out." *Awesome Wonder* (Gospocentric B00005TSOV, 2000).
Goodie Mob. "Soul Food." *Soul Food* (Arista B0000013GF, 1995).
Grandmaster Flash and the Furious Five. 1979. "Superrappin'." *The Best of Enjoy Records* (Hot Productions B000001QIX, 1990).
Hayes, Isaac. "Hyperbolicsyllabicsesquedalymistic." *Hot Buttered Soul* (Stax B000000ZGO, 1969).
Hopkins, Lightnin. "Never Miss Your Water." *Lightning Special, Vol. 2 [Original Recording Remastered]* (Js B000OV123O).
———. "Smokes Like Lightnin'." On *Smokes Like Lightnin'* (Obc B000000XYR, 1995).
House, Son. "Death Letter Blues." *The Original Delta Blues* (Sony B000007T4P, 1998).
Johnson, Robert. 1937. "Me and the Devil Blues." *Robert Johnson: The Complete Recordings* (Columbia/Legacy C2K 64916, 1990).
———. 1936. "They're Red Hot." *The Complete Recordings* (Columbia/Legacy C2K 64916, 1990).
KRS-One. "Sound of da Police." *Return of the Boom Bap* (Jive B000000509).
Last Poets. "True Blues." *This is Madness* (Celluloid B00000JWSB, 1995).
Markham, Pigmeat. 1968. "Here Comes the Judge." *Here Comes the Judge* (Blues Journey B00026K8YK, 1991).
Nas. 2004. "Bridging the Gap." *Street's Disciple* (Sony B0006B2AFQ, 2004).
Taylor, Koko. "I'm a Woman." *Deluxe Edition* (Alligator B00005UF1W, 2002).
Thomas, Rufus. 1963. "Walking the Dog." *The Very Best of Rufus Thomas* (Stax B000RIWAQC, 1996).

Index